N
W — E
S

DAGENHAM

Power Station

Pylon

Dagenham Docks

Ford Motor Co.

○ Chimneys

Rainham Creek

○ Chimney

RAINHAM

BARKING REACH

Crossness

HALFWAY REACH

THAMESMEAD

Chimney ○

Jenningtree Point

Chimneys

ERITH REACH

○ Chimney

○ Chimney

Coldharbour Point

Spire

ERITH

Chimneys

ERITH RANDS

Hotel

PURFLEET

LONG REACH

Erith Y. Club

Crayford Ness

Dartford Creek

Dartford Marshes

Chimney ○

Barking

Margaret

AMES

ONG REACH

3

Les

The Tuesday Boys

THE TUESDAY BOYS

by Rozelle Raynes

Thomas Lyster

British Library Cataloguing in Publication Data
Raynes, Rozelle *1925–*
  The Tuesday boys
  1. London (England), Children, Care
  I. Title
  362.73209421

ISBN 1-871482-06-2

Published by Thomas Lyster Ltd
GRN Buildings, 48 Southport Road
Ormskirk, Lancs L39 1QR

Typesetting by Chapterhouse,
Formby, Merseyside.

Printed in England by The Alden Press, Oxford

Contents

★ ★ ★

Acknowledgements

All photographs are taken by the author or Emily Murphy apart from that on page 194 which is reproduced by kind permission of the East London Advertiser.

TO DICK

without whose encouragement
the Tuesday boys might have
remained the everyday boys.
And to John, Peter,
Philip, David, Victor,
Stephen, Mark and Jeff —
the heroes of this story.

Endpapers — maps–illustrations by the author
Front: River Thames — Lower Pool to Long Reach
Back: Felixstowe to Walton-on-Naze

★ ★ ★

Prologue

'Suppose you were crossing the Atlantic Ocean in a small sailing-boat,' said Captain McLaren, fixing Victor with a steadfast gaze; 'and there was a big sea running with a strong wind on the starboard quarter. One of your crew had shinned up the mast to free the mainsail halliard which was caught round the cross-trees, when the boat took a sudden lurch to port causing him to lose his grip; he was flung out of the rigging, head over heels, and plunged straight down into the sea! What would you do if you were in charge of the boat?'

Captain Ian McLaren, the Deputy Head of the School of Navigation near the Tower of London, had come to the Royal Albert Dock Basin on a raw November morning to give the Tuesday boys their annual examination. This was their second year and he had already praised Peter and Victor's skill at handling a boat during the first hour of practical seamanship; and he was now wedged in a corner of the cabin conducting the tests on chartwork, buoyage, tidal problems, Rule of the Road at sea and some general knowledge questions.

Victor's face was the colour of a boiled lobster, what with the bitter wind and the silence of those dreadful moments while everyone awaited his reply.

'I'd grab hold of the lifebelt on the backstay and chuck it over the rail first,' he panted nervously; ''case the geyser hadn't got his life-jacket on. Then I'd check the compass course and dive into the cabin to fetch the bread...'

'Why the bread?' the Captain interrupted, his eyebrows rising a few millimetres above his spectacles.

'Well, if you'd got a cut loaf, see, you drop a slice over the side every few seconds till you've got the boat turned round and sailing back where she's come from, then you foller the slices and they'll lead you to the spot where this bloke fell overboard, see what I mean?'

'What a brilliant idea!' exclaimed Captain McLaren, roaring with laughter as he made an entry in his secret notebook. 'I doubt whether any of my Second Mates would come up with such a good answer as that.'

PART I
THE FIRST YEAR

Chapter 1

'What's up, Miss? Spot of bovver wiv the old motor? Won't we be going out on the river after all, then?' He was small, dark and elfin-faced, with fierce grey eyes that probed mine like a searchlight. He sat on the edge of the pontoon plunging his new plimsolls up and down in the scummy water of the Royal Albert Dock Basin.

Behind him crouched three more children — pink and white cherubs with neatly trimmed hair and round expectant eyes, each wearing a T-shirt announcing the theme that was dearest to his heart: glancing from left to right I read 'Up the Hammers!', 'Bay City Rollers' and 'Elvis for Ever'. And beyond this group, looming emphatically in the background, were three grown-ups: two very large men and a young woman who looked sturdy enough to grapple with a rampant tiger. Her eyes sparkled with amusement as she surveyed the scene, but the men wore dead pan expressions that revealed nothing; they carried the world on their shoulders and, clearly, were reserving judgement till later.

I had been grovelling in the bilges for the past few minutes, my face, arms and new white blouse smeared with oil and grease, and a premonition of despair seeping through my veins. Emerging from the depths I assumed a shrewd air calculated to fool anyone who doubted my expertise as a mechanic, and stared straight back into Peter's eyes.

''Course we're going out in the boat. It's just a question of fixing the clutch cable, see. Why don't you and your friends go and look at the old paddle-steamer over there, on the far side of the dock?'

The boys exchanged glances which told me, as plain as apple pie, that the old paddle-steamer was the last suggestion that I should have made — an unplumbed haven of wicked possibilities away from the strict surveillance of tiresome grown-ups. Emily, the tiger-grappler, stepped forward to extinguish any plots the boys were about to hatch; and, simultaneously, a bearded saint wearing a grubby boiler-suit and carrying a couple of large spanners stepped aboard the Folkboat and said; 'Can I help? You were looking a bit harassed, I thought!'

By a stroke of good fortune he was a qualified engineer who lived aboard his own motor-cruiser in the dock, and was quite used to the aura of helplessness that hung about me when faced with the mysteries of the internal combustion engine.

'What seems to be the trouble?' he demanded, in the manner of a doctor addressing his latest patient. He peered at the loose metal stalk that I was holding up for his inspection, muttered 'Aha!' then, 'Back in a jiffy;' and made off at full speed towards his own boat.

There was a rustle of excitement on the pontoon. Four pairs of rounder-than-ever eyes were fixed on me unswervingly, and suddenly I knew that it was immensely important to get the engine running at all costs and never, never to disappoint those four little boys whom I had only met once before in my life.

★   ★   ★

The seed was first sown a few months after Dick and I decided to build a larger boat. We had sailed for many hundreds of miles around the coastline of northern Europe in our brave little Folkboat, *Martha McGilda*, but the time had finally arrived when we began to dream of greater comfort on our voyages — standing headroom inside the cabin, a chart table, a hanging cupboard for our shore-going clothes and the chance to cook a proper meal and sleep belowdecks when the boat was under way in a rough sea.

We had arranged to sell *Martha* back to her original owner, Noel Jordan, while McGruers were building our ten-ton cutter up in Scotland. Despite two heart attacks he was delighted at the prospect of sailing again in his first and best-loved boat, built for him by Chippendales at Warsash in 1953; and, already, he had insisted on buying a third share in *Martha*, the remainder to be paid for when our new boat was launched and we were ready to part with the old one.

But *Martha*, who was well aware of these negotiations, began to display some unusually aggressive aspects of her character about that time: first she split her mainsail from top to bottom, then she ran aground although there were three experienced navigators aboard (Noel was with us that day); and the following morning her boom hit Dick a resounding blow on the head, whereupon he fell backwards on to a sharp stake and required eight stitches in his leg to repair the damage. It seemed as if the old boat was trying to tell us something — something I already knew as, secretly, I had hated the idea of parting with her after so many happy voyages together.

A month before *Roskilde*, the new boat, was due to be launched Noel died of his third coronary. Later that spring his widow, Ursula, asked us to sail her out to sea in *Martha* to scatter his ashes over the waters on which he had spent so many happy hours in his boat.

Folkboat

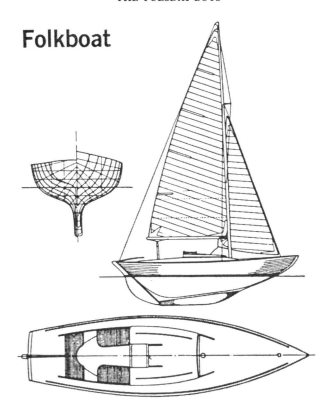

It was inconceivable to sell the Folkboat to a complete stranger after we had left Noel behind on that shining summer sea: also there was an unforeseen problem in that we now owned only two-thirds of *Martha* and Ursula declared that she had no desire to part with her share. We seemed to have reached a complete deadlock when, quite unexpectedly, everything began to work out like a dream come true.

The first question to tackle was how to keep two clinker-built wooden sailing-boats in good shape and usefully employed? The new boat, *Roskilde*, was intended to be our weekend and holiday boat, but what should we do with little *Martha*? Ursula admitted that she had no seafaring plans of her own to put forward.

Dick was Deputy Medical Officer of Health in the Borough of Newham at that time, and he had made friends with the three top men in the Social Services Department: Mr R. H. Mathews, the Director, Ken Boyce, his Deputy, and Peter Cobb, his Principal Assistant. I cannot remember when the idea was first mooted, nor who said what to whom; but suddenly there was this marvellous plan for using *Martha* to teach children in long-term Care how to handle a boat, and everyone was smiling and saying, 'What a splendid idea!' And it was not until many months later that I realized how courageous the leaders of Newham Social Services had been to give their blessing to something that might so easily have ended in disaster.

Sailing into the River Swale with Ursula aboard one evening in May, we discussed the *big plan* with her and she told us that she would like to join in and help with the boys when she returned from a visit to her brother in Australia; and, furthermore, she insisted on sharing the annual expenses of *Martha*'s upkeep. We were stealing down a glittering pathway towards the setting sun, the chords of a Beethoven symphony drifting out of the cabin and the flood tide chuckling as it hurried along beside us when I had a sudden foreglimpse of enormous happiness: everything was going to be all right, a small voice whispered to me, and little *Martha* would have a special role to play in the future.

The practical side of the big idea was the next important phase to work at. We secured a berth in the London Marina, North Woolwich, and sailed

Martha McGilda *on her way round to London.*

Martha round there from Walton-on-Naze during the spring of 1975. We had arranged — rather reluctantly on my part — to have a 7 H.P. Vire petrol engine installed the previous winter. The boat had managed perfectly well with a Seagull outboard motor for the past nineteen years, I contended. But Dick, and everyone else whose opinions we consulted, argued that the strong tides on the Thames and the necessity to use the lock in and out of the Royal Albert Dock Basin where the marina was situated, would make an inboard engine essential for the safety of her crew.

Peter Cobb, meanwhile, had found a small Children's Home in Forest Gate where eight boys were living in long-term Care. He and Ken Boyce agreed that it would be better to include all the children in the venture, whether or not they had any special leanings towards a boat; otherwise some might feel deprived if they were not allowed to take part in this new and possibly exciting experience. I refused to take more than four of them on the boat at any one time, so each boy would have the chance to sail once a fortnight. And Tuesday was the day selected for our project because it was Ursula's only free afternoon.

The next crucial step was to meet the boys' house-mother. Without her approval and co-operation the whole enterprise was doomed to failure, so I found myself rather dreading that first encounter. I visualized her as a type of

Emily Murphy, the house-mother of the Edith Moorey Home, playing her guitar.

female dragon who wore severe tweed suits and had sharp features, rabbit teeth and sparse hair pulled tightly into a bun at the back of her head.

Peter Cobb invited us to a dance at the Greenhill Centre for the Disabled one Saturday evening that spring, and he introduced us to a young woman wearing jeans and a striking T-shirt whom I had already picked out as being the best jiver on the dance floor. She had longish brown hair, expressive blue eyes and a big smile, coupled with a lilting Irish accent that made everything she said sound more amusing than the commonplace remarks of people around her.

'Meet Emily Murphy,' Peter said, 'She's the house-mother of the Edith Moorey Home in Norwich Road, and she's very keen to hear more about this boating lark of yours!'

I took one look at Emily and felt sure that we should have no problems in getting along together. She invited us to the home a few days later to meet the boys. We brought some slides of *Martha*'s voyage to Norway to show them, and there was certainly plenty of interest shown and questions fired at us from all sides. One of the boys, however, told me ten years later that his

Seven of the Tuesday Boys in the back garden at 26 Norwich Road.
Left to right — back row: Victor, Philip, Stephen,
front row: Peter, Mark, Jeff and David.

main concern had been the joy of being able to miss school for one precious afternoon a fortnight!

Their ages ranged from eight to thirteen years: John, Peter and Philip were the oldest and Philip, being the tallest and strongest of all the boys, seemed a natural choice as First Mate of his group. Little Peter, on the other hand, boasted that he already knew more about boats than any of his mates because he had sailed in a Sea Cadet's dinghy up at Maldon on one or two occasions.

Jeff, who was one of the youngest boys in the home, was a thin child with wispy blonde hair who wore dark-rimmed spectacles about which he was very sensitive. He looked a pathetic little fellow, and he had a way of clinging to people and demanding more attention than was his due.

Emily, I surmised, was a fine house-mother to her brood. She combined strict discipline with a warm and generous nature, and she and the boys treated each other with a cheerful camaradarie. It must have been a daunting job, one had to admit, for each child wanted someone to love him exclusively and whisper in his ear that he was the one and only, the most favourite child above all others.

The last big hurdle and, as it proved, the hardest one of all, was the interview with Miss O'Brien, the Deputy Headmistress of Rokeby School where six of the boys were pupils. I needed her consent for them to be allowed a half day out of school once a fortnight. Peter Cobb had made the appointment, and he and I sat on a child's bench outside her office waiting to be called in. I am convinced that she was not excessively busy that morning, but decided to keep us waiting as a matter of principle!

'What shall we do if she refuses to let them go?' I asked Peter anxiously. 'And how about the two boys who go to different schools?'

'Don't you worry; we'll get round the old cow somehow,' he whispered. 'And the others are no problem as they go to special schools where the Heads are only too glad to get them interested in outside activities — anything to keep them out of mischief!'

Peter, who is huge and forceful and thinks nothing of getting to grips with a bunch of hooligans on Stratford Broadway, seemed strangely subdued by the time we were invited to enter and sit on low chairs in front of the Head Mistress's desk. He began by giving her a brief outline of our plans, and mentioned that the Director of Social Services considered it would be a great benefit to these children, who were deprived in so many ways, to learn a skill that might lead to jobs at sea for them when they left school.

Miss O'Brien beat a steady tattoo on her desk with a pencil and, without appearing to pay much attention to Peter's remarks, she swivelled in her chair and fixed me with a searching stare: 'And may one inquire what your intentions are towards these unfortunate boys?' she asked, with more than a hint of child abuse implied in her tone.

Suddenly I knew why this abrasive little Welsh woman was considered such a fine schoolmistress in one of the toughest East End schools for boys. No frills nor polite conversation for her — straight to the point, and make no mistake. I foraged nervously in my handbag for my Merchant Navy Lifeboatman's Certificate and newly acquired Yachtmaster's Offshore Certificate and, offering them to her diffidently, I mumbled a few incoherent words about hoping to teach the boys some seamanship and coastal navigation while giving them an enjoyable afternoon on the river — something to increase their self-confidence and broaden their horizons for the future.

Peter and I exchanged furtive glances, but it was clear to both of us that we were on to a sticky wicket. Then, with a rare flash of intuition, I decided to drop Ian McLaren's name into the stew-pot.

'Do you mean Captain McLaren, the Deputy Head of the Sir John Cass School of Navigation?' demanded Miss O'Brien, her head tilted to one side like a thrush that has just encountered a worm.

'Yes!' I bared my teeth enthusiastically, clutching at this heaven-sent straw. 'He was our instructor for a year when my husband and I were working for our Master's Tickets, and he has promised to give the boys an annual examination so that they will have a definite goal to work towards; and he might arrange for the ones who do well to get some form of unofficial certificates as well.'

Miss O'Brien beamed — yes, actually beamed. It was like a glimpse of the first evening star on a murky night at sea.

'I wish your venture good luck!' she declared, rising to indicate that our audience was over. 'And I would very much like to join you and the boys aboard your boat one afternoon next term, to see how they are getting along?'

'Bitch!' Peter muttered under his breath as we retreated from the court-room, after bandying a few insincere pleasantries with our interrogator.

A faulty engine was an irresistible challenge to the saint in a boiler-suit, and he gazed at my unresponsive heap of metal with the same eyes that a mother might regard her first-born when it has just displayed a strong urge towards original sin. After a few deft pulls with a spanner he removed the offending clutch cable, probed the darkest recesses of the engine compartment with fingers like prawn's antennae and announced: 'She'll be O.K. now if you use the gear lever from inside the cabin. Have to order a new clutch cable to connect up with the outside position in your cockpit.'

I could have hugged the man I felt so relieved. The afternoon would not be a total disaster after all and, although I dared not take *Martha* out on the river yet with the problem of having to go inside the cabin each time we needed to change gear, at least we could motor round and round the dock. This proved a happy alternative to the patient group waiting on the pontoon. I think Ken Boyce and Peter Cobb's worst fears were allayed when they knew that the children would not have to face the perils of the river that afternoon. And the boys were so excited with the business of putting on their new life-jackets and safety-harnesses that they had no time to brood on what they were missing.

Besides little Peter, the one who claimed he knew all about boats, there was John, a tall boy who was two or three months older than Peter, and two younger boys, Victor and Mark, the latter with wicked blue eyes set in a round butter-wouldn't-melt-in-his-mouth type of face.

At last we were ready to go. Emily took the helm, Peter was in charge of the bow line, John the stern line, Victor pushing off with the boat-hook and Mark hauling the fenders aboard. I performed acrobatic feats, meanwhile, flitting between the gear lever inside the cabin and the throttle control in the cockpit, where I could keep a sharp eye on what was going on in the outside world.

The Deputy Director and his Assistant had returned to work, thank goodness; but I soon realized that Emily was enjoying the responsibility of being helmswoman so much that it was not going to be easy to dislodge her without causing pain! My plan was to let each boy steer in turn so that he could have a brief but magic taste of being in charge of a boat for the first time in his life. I explained this to their house-mother who saw the point, but released the helm to John with marked reluctance.

Round and round the dock we circled with John getting the feel of the helm, asking if he could bring his fishing-rod next time and sometimes pushing the tiller the wrong way so that I had to leap forward and grab it from him before we hit a tug or fishing-boat.

Little Peter's turn came next and he soon proved that his boasts had not been idle. He had a light touch on the tiller and knew exactly what he was doing. After a few turns around the basin he asked if he might try bringing *Martha* alongside the old paddle-steamer, an exercise that provided a stimulating few minutes all round. I was hanging upside-down like a bat over the engine, attempting to put the gear lever into neutral, when Mark dropped a fender into the dock in a burst of zeal to do the right thing; Victor, meanwhile, had grabbed the ship's gunwale with the boat-hook and was having a sharp tussle to disengage it before he was dragged overboard; and a gruff voice projected through a megaphone demanded to know what the hell we thought we were up to? Once I had resumed a perpendicular posture I was able to trace it to an upper window of the dockmaster's office.

It was Mark's turn next, the cherub-faced one with gaps between his front teeth and a huge grin that never left his face.

'D'you think I'll make a good Sea Captain one day?' he asked me, weaving the tiller to and fro with joyful abandon.

'I don't see why not if you work really hard and pass all your exams,' I told him. '*and* look where you're going when you're in charge of the boat!' giving the tiller a sudden heave to starboard with my right buttock.

The others began to mull over this exquisite prospect, and it was not hard to interpret their enraptured smiles as they pictured themselves pacing to and fro on the bridge of some vast liner issuing orders to lesser mortals who were waiting around for the express purpose of doing the Captain's bidding!

The spring sunshine transformed the basin into a gleaming pool shot with emerald and sapphire lights, and I had a warm contented feeling that all was well. *Martha* seemed to like her new crew — at any rate there had been no repetition of her tricks of the past year, when her fate still hung in the balance.

Victor was now in charge, and I had just hoisted the jib to give the boys a first taste of the beauty of wind-power; we would run before the breeze with the engine in neutral, and motor back upwind. I glanced over one shoulder at the helmsman who was steering a very straight course across the dock. He had glowing eyes and a rapt expression on his face, and I knew that the magic had already entered his soul and transported him far away into another world. Suddenly I was seventeen again and clutching a tiller for the first time in my life: and I had this amazing sensation of power as I wove a course among the big ships, manipulating that simple piece of wood that was quivering so rapturously in my right hand. I was equal, in my own estimation, to any of those grand gold-braided Captains standing on their bridges high up among the clouds.

After Victor had brought *Martha* gently alongside the pontoon, I showed the boys how to moor the boat and they practised tying one or two useful knots. Then Emily unpacked a picnic basket and I fetched a cake and some cans of Coca Cola from the cabin, and we sat around in the cockpit and on the cabin-top having a noisy cheerful tea-party. I had often wondered what it would feel like to have the boat full of children spilling coke and crumbs all over the decks and swinging like monkeys from the boom; and now I knew...It felt wonderful and, surprisingly, it only took a few minutes to clear up the mess and make her look spick and span with Auntie Em, as the boys called her, in charge of the cleaning brigade.

Martha has a Visitor's Book which dates back to 1956, the year that Noel sold her to me. When the work was finished I asked each of the boys if they would like to write something in it and sign their names, and this is what they wrote:

Peter	—	28th May 1975	— 'I look forward to next time aboard *Martha McGilda.*'
John	—	28th May 1975	— 'It couldn't have been a nicer day today.'
Victor	—	28th May 1975	— 'It has been a wonderful day.'
Mark	—	28th May 1975	— 'I had a very beautiful time today.'

A short while afterwards two cars left the London Marina and, when they reached the A13, drove abreast towards the setting sun. One car had four tousled heads hanging out of the windows and I could distinctly hear a shrill voice urging the driver: 'Burn it up, Auntie, burn it up! Don't let 'er get in front of us!'

Chapter 2

I knew virtually nothing about children in Care, or Care Orders or Council Homes for children in long-term Care before that first summer of the Tuesday Boys. I had always imagined they were horrid vicious young hooligans who set fire to their own homes, strangled their baby sisters or attempted to murder their parents, and that was why they had landed where they were — and richly deserved it.

It was quite an eye-opener, therefore, when I gradually began to piece together the tragic histories of some of the children who were put in Care through no fault of their own. In many cases the mother had simply abandoned her family and gone off with another man, and the father was unable to cope with bringing up the children on his own; or, alternatively, the man had left home and, owing to ill health or psychiatric problems, the mother just could not manage. Then there were the totally callous ones; when one parent died suddenly, or went to prison, the remaining one did not care what became of their children.

Little Jeff was, perhaps, one of the worst cases in our group as his mother could not stand the sight of him, although she was quite attached to some of his brothers and sisters who had remained with her at home. She had parted from her second husband after giving birth to seven children, and one of the older boys had committed suicide by hanging himself with a necktie from a hook behind the bedroom door. Young Jeff knew about this horrifying incident — I'm not sure that he had not found his half-brother hanging there — and it often preyed on his tortured mind. A year or two later his mother arranged to have him put in Care, where she herself had grown up. She could not trust herself to keep her hands off him, especially during the school holidays when he was around all the time, she told the lady from Social Services. It appeared that he reminded her too much of the negative parts in her own character, the black spots that had turned her into a tragic failure.

Jeff suffered from eneuresis and some kind of brain damage that seemed to make him incapable of learning or exerting himself in any small ways like putting on his own clothes or doing up his shoes. He attended a school for maladjusted children and Emily had to do everything for him at home. The other boys resented all the attention he demanded and some of them were very cruel to him, apart from Philip, who was the only one who tried to bring some sunshine into the poor child's existence. He lived in a strange fantasy world in which he would often make remarks like: 'My Mum's buying me a Scale-Lectrix set for my birthday,' or 'I'm going to Southend with my Mum for a week's holiday tomorrow.'

Jeff, one of the youngest boys in the home.

We all knew that these statements were figments of his imagination and, later on when he had moved to a Foster Home, he often ran away and trudged for miles across London to see the family whom he adored; and next morning, without fail, there would be a hard metallic voice on the telephone to Newham Social Services Department announcing; 'He's here again! Come and fetch him back as soon as possible, will you?'

There seemed no answer to the problem of little Jeff, but when he started coming aboard *Martha* with the second group, it soon became apparent that there was one thing he could do well when he had decided to concentrate, a skill of which he became very proud in the years to follow.

A week later it was Tuesday, 3rd June, with a north-westerly gale blowing and the sun shining fitfully through angry layers of scudding clouds. They reminded me of moorland sheep on the run as I gazed disconsolately out of the window. I had a pinched white face and puffy eyelids, the results of a sleepless night spent tossing and turning in a fever of anxiety.

'It's full spring tides just now, and supposing I lose one of them overboard?' I appealed to Dick. 'They'd get sucked under the swim of a barge and might never be seen again.'

Refusing to rise to the drama of my speculations, he murmured: 'Don't forget the dog's meat and those canvas trousers of mine you left at the cleaners, will you?'

'Who thought up this crazy idea in the first place?' I called down the stairs after his retreating backview.

'You did!' I heard a faint giggle from two floors down; and I felt like a trapped rabbit about to suffer from acute diarrhoea.

An hour or so later I was kneeling on *Martha*'s cabin-top doing a sail-maker's whipping round the end of the main halliard. The angry clouds had given way to fluffy white cauliflowers and the water danced and chuckled around the clinker-built hull. Out beyond the lock gates there were white horses galloping by as the flood tide rushed headlong into the arms of the westerly gale; but inside the basin it was a beautiful sunshiny prospect and I felt better already. Doing a few jobs on the boat always made the day seem brighter and the land affairs less urgent.

Tony Cohen, whose family owned the London Marina, sat in his glass-fronted hut at the inner end of the pontoon making jokes with a large brunette and keeping a sharp eye on his domain. Very little escaped his notice and he had already warned me that the children must be kept under strict surveillance at all times.

Presently Emily drove up in her blue Corsair Estate and four boys burst out of the doors like corks released from bottles of champagne. Philip came first — he was Victor's big brother and I had planned that he should be First Mate of the second group. Next there was David, two years younger with brown hair and a pink smiling face. The third boy, Stephen, was Mark's elder brother — Emily had divided the two pairs of brothers on purpose as they did not always get along well together. He had tufts of thick blond hair sprouting from the top of his head like corn stubble, and he wore a quizzical expression but his eyes were as bright and mischievous as a monkey's. Last of all came little Jeff, well wrapped up in a blue anorak decorated with red circles and a navy-blue woollen pirate's cap pulled so far down over his forehead and ears that his face consisted of little else but a large pair of spectacles glinting up at you.

'Here we are once again!' announced Emily in her lilting Irish voice. 'Sure, you've been waiting on us a long while?'

Philip and David had already found *Martha* and were gazing with awe at the top of her mast. Jeff was clinging tightly to Emily's left hand and Stephen was twanging the backstay of a fibreglass yacht moored along our pontoon.

'You see that man sitting in the hut with his eyes fixed on you?' I said to the boy. 'Well, he'll never let you come here again if you touch anyone else's boat.' Better start tough, I thought, till I know what I'm up against.

'He must be a turd!' Stephen snorted, making a rude gesture at the hut; but he stopped twanging the rigging.

'We're going to motor and sail round the dock today,' I told the boys

First time aboard Martha McGilda — *Jeff, Stephen, Auntie Em and Philip, David sitting down in front.*

firmly, hoping no one would express a compulsive desire to go out on the river.

No one did. Some of them, in fact, looked rather relieved as we set about the task of fitting them into their life-jackets. Philip already knew how to put on his own, so he was able to help me with David and Stephen while Emily looked after Jeff. Safety-harnesses were worn beneath the life-jackets, and the rule was that any boy leaving the cockpit to do some work on the foredeck or to sit on the cabin-top must clip on to the guard-rail or to one of the pair of check-wires extending along either side of the cabin-top. This was not a popular rule but, at least, I knew they would still be attached to the boat if one of them fell overboard.

Great gusts of wind ruffled the water in the dock as we set off on our circumnavigations with each boy steering in turn. It was blowing much harder than the previous Tuesday and the boys were delighted to learn that they were coping very well with much tougher conditions than those to which the first group had been exposed.

There was one big surprise for all of us that afternoon; and that was Jeff, the helmsman. He steered quite as well as the other three boys, and for a few precious minutes he lost the bewildered expression that so often haunted his wan little face and it was replaced by a triumphant grin — as if he had been granted a fleeting glimpse of the stuff that dreams are made of.

Philip, our first mate, and his younger brother, Victor, were, I soon grew to realize, two of the luckiest boys in the Edith Moorey Home as they had a mother who was devoted to them, although she was not well enough to make a home of her own and bring them up herself. Her husband had gone away to the north of England to live with another woman some years ago, and poor Margaret had been in and out of hospital ever since. But, each time she emerged, her first thought was for her boys; and she never wasted a moment in coming round to Norwich Road to reassure herself that they were well and happy.

Stephen and Mark's story was exactly the reverse. Their mother had run off with another man when Stephen was three or four and his brother a mere baby. They were put in Care, then taken out by their grandmother for a short period before they returned to settle in a long-term home. Their father, although he came to visit them from time to time, admitted that he could hardly bear to set eyes on them as it upset him so terribly when he had to go home and leave them behind.

We hoisted the storm jib, a tiny pocket-handkerchief of a sail, on account of the strong wind. It was Emily's turn to steer the boat, and she spun us round the basin with a certain bold confidence that signified she was already master of the situation. When I inquired, many months later, how the boys had progressed with a seamanship book full of useful diagrams that I had bought for them after the first Tuesday, it transpired that they had never seen the book as Auntie Em had been too busy studying it herself! And a few weeks later she enrolled for the autumn Coastal Navigation and Seamanship Course at the School of Navigation on Tower Hill.

'What's the great boat that's just turned in from the river?' David asked me, pointing to a vessel with a black hull that seemed to fill the entire lock.

'That's a Thames sailing-barge,' I told him. 'Hundreds of them used to sail up and down the London River carrying cargo not so many years ago. D'you want to run round there and watch it come into the basin when they swing the bridge?'

We had just finished tea and Emily stayed behind to help me clear up while the four boys leapt ashore.

'I bet that was deliberate, pointing out that boat to you so they needn't help with the washing-up!' she told me. 'Mustn't let them get away with too many tricks of that sort.'

The barge moved majestically through the inner lock gates, and when she came alongside her berth in the marina there were four small boys waiting to receive her lines. As soon as she was secured the skipper invited them

aboard, and a few minutes later Emily and I were astonished to see them heaving on the end of huge iron bars that turned the anchor winch, thereby helping to raise the gigantic mast.

'Wish they'd work like that at home,' she laughed, as we strolled along the quay to retrieve our crew.

'Where's the toilet, Auntie?' Jeff bellowed as we drew nearer; and it was clear that he was about to pee in his pants with excitement if we didn't get him ashore very soon.

The Visitor's Book was produced as soon as Jeff was comfortable; it had already been mentioned by two of the boys who did not wish to miss out on anything that last Tuesday's boys had done. We soon realized that there was going to be intense rivalry between the two groups.

In order of ages, each boy signed the book and wrote as follows:

Philip — 3rd June 1975 — 'I had a very good day.'
David — 3rd June 1975 — 'I had a very very good day.'
Stephen — 3rd June 1975 — 'I hope you enjoy your time with us.'
Jeff — 3rd June 1975 — 'Very good day. Enjoyed most of all steering the boat.' (He dictated what he wished to say to Emily as he could only just sign his name.)

I stayed on for a few minutes after Emily and the boys had left, as I wanted to do some work on the engine and read what they had written in my book.

'Funny that entry of Stephen's,' I mused. 'I wonder what he has in mind!'

'Well, how many boys did you lose over the side today?' Dick inquired cheerfully as I ran upstairs to start cooking the dinner.

'Four fewer than you were expecting,' I told him. Now that the second Tuesday afternoon was over and the nightmares of fearful disasters had receded, I felt a wave of growing confidence. But, at the same time, a small warning voice whispered to me, 'Beware! There are plenty of ghastly things that might yet happen, so don't become too cocksure!'

★   ★   ★

Chapter 3

Tuesday, June 10th, was a day created specially for our first outing on the London River. The east wind blew fresh and gusty bringing magic whiffs of the North Sea right up Gallion's Reach, and big cotton wool clouds sailed majestically across the jade-green sky. The river was intensely alive, a seething torrent of windswept water flashing gold and silver darts out of its swirling tide-rips; and the boys came tumbling out of Ken Boyce's car like newly hatched seagull chicks borne on the wings of the wind.

Emily could not get away that afternoon but Ursula Jordan, just back from Australia, was there to help me and Ken said he would join us for tea when he returned to fetch the boys later on. Mark had not been allowed to come as he had played truant from school the previous day, so our crew consisted of John, Peter and Victor.

Ursula was a small neat person with immaculately coiffured grey hair and a rather fragile apperance that belied her resolute and independent character. She was an expert china-mender and I sometimes pictured her as a Dresden shepherdess — a live figurine who resembled one of the treasures that she mended with such loving care. She was always stylishly turned out, and when she came with the children aboard *Martha* on that first occasion I expected her to be purely decorative and of little practical use on a boat. But we soon noticed that she would invariably be the first person to lend a helping hand whenever there was any dirty work to be done.

Ursula had what the boys described as 'a posh voice' and, on account of this, they surmised among themselves that she must have come from a very aristocratic background — quite different from mine, which they thought was probably more on a par with their own. The introductory phase passed off reasonably well, despite the somewhat unlikely conversational gambits on either side.

'What d'you reckon West 'Am's chances are, after what they done last Saturday?' Peter asked her while she was tying a fancy knot with the strings hanging down from the back of his life-jacket.

'I really couldn't say; you see I was at the Royal Festival Theatre watching

Ursula at the helm of one of Noel's racing boats.

that superb new production of Chekhov's "Uncle Vanya". Have any of you boys been to see it yet?' Her eyes swept the row of quizzical faces, searching for a glint of comprehension.

'How about us getting the boat ready to sail?' I suggested, to break the impasse. 'I think the lock-keeper's started tinkering about with the bridge already.'

Peter and Victor remembered everything they had learnt two weeks ago, but John was more concerned with his fishing-rod and what time we should be back from the river so that he could start casting.

'This is a weekday when you should really be at school,' I reminded him; 'so you've got to try and learn something on the boat. It's not just a free afternoon for your enjoyment, see.'

Peter and Victor, who had already donned their life-jackets and safety-harnesses, jumped aboard to help me put the battens in the mainsail and hank the jib on to the forestay.

'My turn to put the birdie up today,' Peter declared in a forceful tone.

'What on earth's a birdie?' I was completely baffled.

'The red and white flag that flies from the top of the mast.' He gave me a withering glance and grabbed the burgee stick from Victor's hands.

'Oh, you mean the burGEE!' exclaimed Ursula, who knew about those sort of things.

Peter was too busy making a pair of clove hitches on the stick to pay much attention. When he began to tug on the halliard, however, the burgee became trapped in the shrouds half way up the mast. Victor and John roared with laughter as they pointed skywards and called him 'an effing know-all!' This caused a few of the more sensitive boat-owners to prick up their ears, while Ursula dived into the cabin 'in search of a handkerchief'.

'Look, this is how you do it.' I used what I hoped was a loud school-mistressy type of voice as a cover-up measure. And I grabbed the halliard from the angry little boy and stood on the pontoon hauling the burgee down again, then slowly upwards, carrying on a running commentary about holding up a wet finger to find out from which direction the wind was blowing, then selecting the halliard on the opposite side of the mast to the wind, etcetera, etcetera.

At last we were ready to go. The engine was ticking over, the mooring-lines singled up and each boy standing proudly at his post. At that precise moment the lock-keeper's telephone rang and he hurried back to his office where we could see him laughing and gesticulating into the receiver for the next twenty minutes, while we circled round and round and round the dock. Just as I had given up all hope and mentally written off the afternoon as a tragic and utter flop, the man strode back to his bridge and started turning a small iron wheel; and, miraculously, the bridge began to open, inch by inch, and *Martha* edged cautiously into the lock.

It was not long after high water which made it an easy introduction for the boys working their first lock. The lock-keeper lowered the water level very gently and we had dropped less than a metre down the wall when we reached the same level as the river. Ursula helped John, who was in charge of letting out the stern line, while I knelt behind Victor, carefully releasing the bow line on the foredeck. Peter was responsible for holding the boat away from the dock wall with the boat-hook, but his eyes had become riveted upon the bugs and shrimps jumping about in the oily seaweed in front of him.

'They're beginning to open the gates!' I shouted as *Martha* rose to the swell of a passing tug. 'Push off with the boat-hook, Peter; stand by to haul in the lines, boys.' I took a flying leap into the cockpit, engaged the clutch in ahead and pushed up the throttle to counteract the swirl of the tide around the lock gates.

A moment later we were out on the broad sparkling river with the lighthouse at Margaret Ness beckoning to us from the south bank and the lock-keeper shouting 'Goodbye!' from the pierhead behind us. It was a

moment of supreme significance and I wondered if any of the boys would
remember it in the years to come. Peter and Victor had clipped their
harnesses on to the forestay and their feet hung over the bows while they
clung to the pulpit and shrieked with delight each time a wave broke over
their legs. John was talking to Ursula in the cockpit and I asked her to steer
into the wind for a few minutes while I hoisted the mainsail.

'She must be able to steer pretty well,' I reasoned with myself while
wriggling across the heaving cabin-top. 'After all, she went racing with Noel
in the old days and she does own a third of the boat . . . '

A siren blew thunderously on our port bow and the boys on the
foredeck roared something at me that I failed to catch; but it was
immediately clear to all of us that we were on a collision course with a big
freighter steaming upriver against the ebb tide. Back to the cockpit, tiller
hard over, engine full astern; then we swung round into the wind again and I
just had time to hoist the mainsail and jib before the harbour-master's launch
appeared round a bend in the river.

The boys soon perceived that Ursula knew even less about boat handling
and seamanship than they did themselves. But this proved a bonus in the
long run as they were invariably enchanted when she pushed the tiller the
wrong way, or let go the jib sheet too soon, or forgot which side to pass an
oncoming vessel. It made them feel like supermen who knew the seaman's

way of handling a boat — even if they did make a very occasional mistake themselves. And she provided so much else in her quiet way towards the success of our outings that they soon grew very fond of her, and hated her to miss a Tuesday.

Each boy steered in turn as we tacked down Gallion's Reach towards Barking Power Station, and they managed remarkably well considering it was their first voyage in *Martha* under full sail. Whenever a big ship passed us our helmsman would wave to the officer of the watch high up on the wing of his bridge; and when he received an answering wave his happiness was complete — one Captain saluting another on the high seas! I remembered so vividly how it felt.

The others spent most of their time on the foredeck with either their heads or feet overhanging the stemhead and arms clasped tightly round the pulpit, anticipating the swell caused by each vessel that passed us with joyful shouts of 'Washers!' (A 'wash' became a 'washer' right from the beginning, just as a 'fender' became a 'defender').

Peter was the only boy, however, who exhibited a real flair for steering the boat close to the wind. He had a sensitive touch on the tiller and could 'feel' the wind on his face or neck so that he always knew how to steer in order to get the best out of *Martha*. This was very encouraging as so many people grip the tiller like a vice to begin with, and weave it to and fro with powerful movements until the boat's natural progress is partially arrested by the froth of water churning around her rudder.

Peter was a tough little boy, very much of a loner, who would work like a delirious ant on any project that really interested him. His mother was Jewish, but she had broken down under the stress of living with Peter's father and retreated to hospital, no longer able to cope with her home and children. And his father appeared as hard and unemotional as a granite boulder. He made a point of coming round to the home to visit his son on alternate Sundays, and he held stern views about the boy's behaviour; but there was little warmth or love, or hints that he longed, as Peter hoped he did, to share his home with his children again. After the visit, always as regular as clockwork, the man felt that he had done his duty and nothing more was required of him.

Victor, not to be outdone by his mate, had looked up the time of high water at London Bridge in Reed's Almanac, remembered to add an hour for British summertime, and was now trying to find the right page for the River Thames tidal constants so that the could predict the time of high water outside the London Marina. On the leeward side of the cockpit John was having a serious discussion with Ursula about bait — which type of worms were best for still-water fishing and which appealed most to the fish that lived in running water. Ursula, I was glad to hear, was well able to hold her end up for she countered with a story about some ten-inch long Australian worms that were luminous at night.

We turned back towards the London Marina an hour or so later. The ferryboat from Thunderer Jetty altered course to allow her passengers a closer look at us, and the Ford Works at Dagenham rose like a monstrous grey cliff along the north shore, depriving us of all wind during our final tack. The tide was ebbing fast and the fresh north-easter had dropped to a gentle breeze, so I switched on the engine and hauled down the sails; then Ursula steered a meandering course back to Gallion's Reach while the boys helped me to furl the mainsail and unhank the jib.

Our return through the lock proved quite a hazardous business as the tide had dropped a long way and the lock-keeper let the water in with a whoosh, so we had a hard struggle to haul in our long lines at great speed when *Martha* began to rise. First her bows swung dangerously towards the angry whirlpool in the centre of the lock, then her stern; and it took all our strength to prevent one end of the boat or the other from being crushed against the slimy walls. A glimpse of Ken Boyce's anxious face appearing above the bridge was a welcome distraction; also the lock-keeper's cheery grin as he opened the inner gate and set the bridge in motion.

'Thought I'd give you a few thrills seein' that it's the kids' first outing on the river!' he beamed at me. At that moment I wished that I was one of the kids themselves, and could make a rude gesture back!

Peter and Victor vied with one another for speed of action and the professional touch when we reached our pontoon and began to moor the boat and make everything shipshape on deck. No doubt Ken's critical eye added zest to their efforts, but John seemed quite oblivious of all the activity going on around him as he perched on the stern and began to cast. Much to everyone's excitement he had two bites in quick succession, but did not manage to land a fish.

'I'll make some special sandwiches for you next week,' Ursula declared after she had examined our tea-time spread. 'What are your favourites, boys?'

'Salmon-jam-corned-beef-honey-tomato-shrimp!' they shouted in one big breath.

'Sounds like a dog's dinner to me,' laughed Ken.

'Never mind. I shall make a surprise sandwich that no one has ever tasted before,' she promised. And that was what she did. Ursula's sandwiches were to become famous among the Tuesday boys in the months to follow.

Three days later a car travelling at 60 mph roared through a halt sign at the end of a small street leading into The Highway, E.1., and hit mine a knock-out blow on the side of the bonnet causing it to swerve across the main road and end up as a mangled heap of metal on the opposite pavement. The following Tuesday, as a result of this, I had no car and one arm in a sling; so Ursula and I did some quick thinking to devise a new type of outing for the boys.

We both agreed that there were two important factors to bear in mind: firstly, it must be a 'nautical' afternoon; and, secondly, it should have some educational value even if the boys decided to treat it as no more than a welcome escape from school.

I caught a bus to Forest Gate that morning, as we had arranged to meet at the Edith Moorey Home in Norwich Road. It was a two-storey Edwardian house with a brick façade embellished with thick white window surrounds and white columns guarding the red front door. Passing through a wicket gate you walked along a short path of fancy paving-stones that led you to the door where, as likely as not, the silhouettes of a number of small heads could be seen through the frosted glass of the upper panels.

Once inside, the house-mother's private-sitting room — seldom as sacred as the title suggested — opened off the right-hand side of the hall; next came the kitchen, a warm and friendly place that I pictured as being the heart of the house. Apart from the serious business of eating and drinking, and learning that everyone had to take a turn at the dull chores like peeling potatoes and washing the dishes, it was a place for laughter and tears, exciting revelations and dark discussions about the problems of this world. The last room on the ground floor was the children's sitting-room where they could play mini-snooker, watch television or sit in large armchairs arguing vociferously. A hatch connected one wall with the kitchen so that anyone working at the cooker or sink could chatter to whoever was in the next-door room.

A staircase led from the hall to the bedrooms and bathrooms on the two floors above; and, finally, a long narrow garden with a playshed in one corner lay at the back of the house and could be reached through a door at the far end of the boys' sitting-room. This was the domain of the two tortoises and the dogs, Judy and Sam.

Number 26 Norwich Road looked a cheerful sort of home to me — not at all my idea of a Council run institution. And when you struck a good day with nobody stirring up trouble nor acting the fool, and no complaining parents come to shout about this or that to relieve their own uneasy consciences, it was rather a happy home where the children were never repressed, although the discipline was fairly strict and they were taught the importance of good manners.

Ursula had already arrived for our Tuesday outing, and she and Philip had gone into the garden where he was introducing her to the tortoises and showing her a model boat that he and Peter were trying to build. Veronica, the under house-mother, was in charge that day, a big girl from Barbados with a rich voice and warm smile.

The boys and I piled into Ursula's car and she drove us to Tower Pier where we embarked on a launch running downriver to Greenwich. I soon realized that our pupils had no intention of spoiling their afternoon out by too much brainwork, and my carefully selected questions about various parts of a boat met with little enthusiasm.

'Tell me the name of the red and white striped object in the middle of the ship just passing us?' I asked David, who coloured up and gave me a vacant stare.

'It has smoke pouring out of the top of it,' I prompted; then I noticed his eyes swivel furtively to the left, and was just in time to intercept Philip's mouth contorted into a curious shape that could only mean one word.

'Funnel!' shouted David two seconds later, beaming radiantly at me — as if he had invented the word himself.

David shared my birth-sign — we were both Scorpions — and it also seemed that we shared some foreknowledge of how the other person was liable to react to certain situations, which was quite disconcerting at times; I could, in fact, clearly perceive some of my own worst traits being enthusiastically enacted in front of my nose!

He had two brothers, and when his mother ran off with a West Indian his father arranged to have the three boys taken into Care. Then the worst possible thing happened: David's mum, to whom he was devoted, came to live in a house close to the Edith Moorey Home in Norwich Road with her new man and, quite soon, a clutch of new babies; and she hardly acknowledged her son's existence when she met him in the street. His predicament had become almost as tragic as Jeff's, and those frequent disturbing encounters all added to the bleakness of his existence at that period.

Stephen, meanwhile, was studying Ursula with rapt attention while she talked to him about an amazing new production of 'Macbeth' at the Old Vic. This was a habit of hers that I found particularly infuriating when I was trying to teach the boys something — with sombre memories of my interview with Miss O'Brien lurking in my subconscious. But Ursula's eyes twinkled merrily, as she knew exactly what I was thinking; and the children listened avidly to her in case I should fire another question at them.

The launch began to turn preparatory to its run in to Greenwich Pier when Jeff, who was swinging from side to side like a pendulum, announced in a loud voice that he wanted to go to the toilet.

'Little scum-bag always carries on like that when we take him out somewhere with us,' Stephen explained to Ursula in a confidential whisper.

Poor Jeff's face was turning white and blotchy with desperation, but I noticed that Philip took charge of him as soon as we stepped ashore and led him quickly across the pier to the lavatories. As soon as they returned we made straight for the *Cutty Sark* which was to be the meat in our sandwich, so to speak, the place where the boys would be able to absorb the breathtaking beauty of a square-rigged sailing-ship together with its enthralling history, as portrayed in the museum on the lower deck. It was one of those days, however, when nothing went quite according to plan. No sooner had we bought the tickets for our group and stepped aboard than all four boys disappeared.

'Where on earth d'you think they've gone?' I asked Ursula anxiously. 'I've got a whole list of new words connected with the masts and rigging to teach them on the upper deck.'

'I daresay they suspected you might have something like that in mind,' she replied, preserving a dead pan expression as best she could.

We turned a corner and noticed a wedge of blue anorak peeping out from behind a life-jacket locker, and suddenly a small figure on all fours scuttled out and disappeared down the for'ard hatch which had a rope across the entrance and a notice attached to it stating '*No Entry*'. An urgent whistle rent the air on our left side and I swung round in time to see a head of rough blond hair appear briefly in the neck of a cowl ventilator; then disappear.

'I'm beginning to wonder if I'm seeing things!' Ursula observed drily. 'We'll have to find a focal point on this crowded ship where we can round them up and keep an eye on them.'

We both saw our focal point at the same moment. A tall boy was standing behind the great steering-wheel on the poop, gripping two of its spokes while he gazed up at the masts and rigging with a far-away look and steered an imaginary course towards some distant shore.

Philip at sea.

'Which way's the wind blowing today, Phil?' I asked him.

''Bout north-north-east I'd say.' He held a wet finger aloft and peered at the ship's compass.

Philip had a very nice smile that encouraged people to make friends with him. He looked, and was, strong, handsome and good-natured, but he could easily be led by people with more dominant characters than his who wished to use him as a scapegoat for their own questionable intentions. He had, at the age of thirteen, already developed a certain sense of responsibility for the younger boys in his group, and he soon managed to round them up and escort them to the museum on the lower deck.

We wandered around the old photographs of sailing-ships battling against mountainous seas off Cape Horn, the stands devoted to intricate ropework which greatly appealed to David, and the exhibition of old ships' figureheads which drew ill-concealed yawns from several of the boys. We were not exactly riding on the crest of a wave when Ursula suggested that we should return to Tower Pier by the hydrofoil, instead of the ordinary river launch.

The hydrofoil proved a jewel of an idea. No sooner had we crossed her gangplank than the boys made instinctively for the tiny stern deck outside the glass-encased cabin where all the other passengers were huddled.

'Get a bit of the old spray in our eyes out here!' Stephen predicted, firmly blocking the entrance so that no one else could share our chosen place.

A deckhand did, in fact, manage to squeeze past him to let go the stern mooring-rope and was clearly considering how best to get rid of us, as passengers were not usually allowed outside the cabin. But when he opened his mouth to speak he came face to face with the four boys grouped together *en bloc*, fixing him with a single penetrating stare that must have originated somewhere near the North Pole, so cold and uninviting did it seem; thus, being a sensible type of lad, he quickly closed his mouth again without emitting a sound and retreated to the for'ard end of the vessel.

The engines roared dramatically beneath us as we drew away from Greenwich Pier, gaining speed by the second. The hydrofoil rose on its spindly legs and a thundering turmoil of yellowish water surged around us; it was not long before the stern deck was completely enveloped in spray. Ursula and I wedged ourselves against the guard-rail and attempted to secure our headscarves round our galeswept hair. Jeff was bellowing with excitement as we hung on to his arms and pinioned him between us; and shrieks of 'Brilliant!', 'Wicked!', 'Evil!' came from all sides while the shoreline of the Isle of Dogs flashed by in a liquid haze.

By the time the hydrofoil had begun to slow down near Wapping River Police Station the boys admitted that the afternoon had turned out better than they expected it would.

'I've been practising two of the knots, what you showed us last time.

Would you like to see them?' David asked me, by way of a nice return gesture. And he pulled a grubby length of string out of his trouser pocket and tied a perfect clove hitch, followed by a fisherman's bend.

'Why, that's wicked!' I exclaimed (I was quickly learning a whole new vocabulary).

Stephen, who was looking rather put out, elbowed David out of the way and said: 'Would you like to see a picture of me and Mark that our nan took when we was little? I'll fetch it next time if you like?'

'What a splendid idea,' Ursula replied; whereupon Philip announced that he was going to do a project in school all about *Martha McGilda* which he would bring to show us as soon as it was finished. And Jeff asked: 'When can I steer the boat again? I did orright last time, didunt I?'

We told him he would be a Sea Captain when he grew up if he steered as well as that every Tuesday. All our pupils were grinning happily as we crossed the gangplank on to Tower Pier, and I thought it felt like reaching the top of a sunlit mountain after a hard slog up the grey stony flanks.

Chapter 4

The land approaches to the London Marina were new territory for me, a harsh dilapidated region that never failed to intrigue me. The traditional East End with its slums and street markets, jellied-eel parlours and mission halls seemed a thousand miles away from that sparsely covered marshland with the Beckton Alps — a series of hills created from the giant clinker tips of the Beckton Gas Works — forming its eastern frontier, and the outline of tall cranes, ship's masts and funnels away to the south.

The moment I turned off the A.13 into Tollgate Road I noticed the difference. First there was Ziff Meats, a long-established slaughter-house that lurked offensively on the outskirts of a small housing estate. Depending on the wind that day, Ziff might linger in your memory a long while after it had disappeared from sight.

The road swung south-east, meandering towards the Royal Docks and the river. Savage Gardens soon appeared on the right-hand side, a row of red-brick houses with gabled roofs, small gardens behind and a communal plot of land sown with grass in front. It looked quite ordinary to me, but Peter Cobb assured me that every house contained a problem family or a nest of villains.

The road soon swung east again leading straight to Cyprus, a forgotten corner of North Woolwich composed of grubby small-holdings harbouring a few tethered animals, an old school, rows of semi-derelict pre-fabs and a handful of streets of little terraced houses with unexpected names such as Plevna Street, Livingstone Street, Stanley Street and Cameron Street. One morning I discovered the neighbourhood shop in that moon district — so remote did it seem from the great city of London. It was a small grocery store kept by a pair of aging sisters whose eyes were as bright and innocent as baby's. The conversation was often sharp and spicy among the tins of baked beans, bottles of H.P. Sauce and jam Swiss rolls, and once I had passed the stern appraisal of their initial scrutiny I would often find some excuse to stop there and make a few purchases, just to hear the latest Cyprus gossip...

''Ello, 'ello, 'ello! And 'ow's young Madge this mornin'?' A burly docker had just entered and was playfully prodding the senior sister in the ribs.

'Musn't grumble, Squire, 'cept fer me rhoomatics. And 'ow's yerself?'

'Or'right, darlin'; it's me kid bruvver what's the trouble today. Best lad as ever drew breff is our Albert, as you well know, Madge.'

Madge brushed aside this comment with a brisk motion of her left hand and leant forward to whisper anxiously: ''E ain't gawn and got Brahms again and done somefink 'e didn't aughta, 'as 'e?'

''Ow did you guess, doll? 'E'd bin playin' 'is squeeze-box in the beer-shop, see, 'avin' a right good time on a Saturday night. 'E goes ahtside ter git a breff o' fresh air an' relieve 'isself, when along comes a copper an' puts an 'eavy 'and on 'is shoulder, like, so our Albert swings rahnd an' kicks 'im in the orchestras!'

Albert playing his squeeze-box in the beer-shop on a Saturday night.

The docker waved his tattooed arms around expressively and we all clucked with excitement as the drama gradually unfolded itself.

Back aboard *Martha* I consulted my booklet of Cockney rhyming slang, as I was not yet familiar with all the words I picked up in the Cyprus store.

'Brahms = Brahms and Liszt = pissed,' it told me; and 'Orchestras = orchestra stalls = balls.'

An angry voice reverberated through the big shed where the marina shop was located; 'You there! I told you before not to come nosing round inside this building. Get out *at once*, and never let me see you in here again, d'you understand?'

Tony Cohen's purple face appeared in the doorway of the shed, and I could see Ursula hurrying along the quay with four cherub-faced children trotting beside her.

'What happened?' I inquired anxiously, as the party drew closer.

'Mark ran on ahead while we were unloading the car, saying that he wanted to have a look at the bo'sun's whistles in the shop,' Ursula explained, wearing an expression that told me everything.

The boys stepped demurely aboard and the afternoon of nautical training began with a serious lecture about the fate of those who tampered with other people's property. I painted Tony Cohen as a type of ogre to the boys, an uncompromising company director who would not tolerate children disobeying his orders and creeping surreptitiously around inside his sheds, touching this and that. And I have seldom seen an expression of such injured innocence on a child's face, as Mark fixed me with one of his round blue stares while he assured me of the utter purity of his motives when he decided to visit the shop!

It was a perfect June day with an anti-cyclone firmly established over the British Isles and a stiff easterly breeze blowing up Gallion's Reach. After such an unfortunate start, Peter, John and Victor, as well as Mark, realized that their river outings might come to a sudden end if any of them overstepped the mark; so each boy worked with unaccustomed vigour to reef the mainsail and prepare *Martha* for sailing.

The lock-keeper who was to become our special friend — he told us later on that he himself had grown up in Care — was on duty that afternoon. As soon as we were ready he passed us gently through the lock, and twenty minutes later we motored out into Gallion's Reach and hoisted the sails. The fresh wind was strongly spiced with down-river smells: the smoke from Barking Power Station, a whiff of Dagenham Dock, the belching funnel of an old tramp steamer chugging round Margaret Ness and the flotsam and jetsam that had paused to rest in a bight of the river near Barking Creek.

A copper-red sun blazed down on the old boat and her crew, and the spray flew over her bows as she beat swiftly downstream on the ebb. We were carried along on the wings of the wind, or was it a magic carpet that day, each one of us gloriously alive and supremely contented. There were no thoughts of the past nor future — only the beautiful never-to-be-forgotten present.

Peter was our star helmsman once again, and it was proving increasingly difficult to prise the tiller out of his hands so that the other boys could have their turns. It was not in his nature to share things with other people — I suppose no one in his childhood had thought of sharing anything worth having with him — so he saw no reason to waste time on such soft gestures himself.

Some while later Mark was at the helm and steering surprisingly well in the strong wind. John had just given one long blast on the fog-horn as we approached a bend in the river to announce our presence to any ship converging with us on the far side when, suddenly, a warship and four landing-craft swept round the corner amid a welter of foam. Victor leapt on to the stern deck to dip our ensign as we came abeam of the leading ship, and Peter and John hung on to the forestay, oblivious of the giant 'washers' as they waved to the sailors high above them. It was a proud moment when the warship gave us a blast on her siren and dipped her own ensign as we passed each other.

'I've just decided what I'm goin' to do when I grow up: I'm goin' to be a sailor!' Peter announced decisively, as the wash died down and the Navy ships sped west towards the Woolwich Barrier.

'I 'spect I will be too,' murmured Victor from the stern, not to be outdone by his mate.

Ursula and I exchanged optimistic glances. Wasn't this the answer to our dearest hopes and schemes? But coming so soon, it seemed almost too good to be true. The grey-green river sparkled and danced in the sunlight and white-crested waves romped along beside us when *Martha* turned for home. She surged triumphantly through the water, a thousand little voices hissing and gurgling around her straining hull as it rose and fell to the rhythm of the waves.

We came back through the lock gates in the late afternoon. Despite the strong gusts of wind there were no disasters as the lock-keeper was there to receive our lines and protect us from the buffetings of the waves until the gates were closed behind us. It was surprising how easy the whole business of locking in and out could be, I reflected, given a good man in charge of it and crew who were anxious to pull their weight.

John began to fish as soon as *Martha* was moored alongside the pontoon, while Peter and Victor produced some thin lengths of rope from their anorak pockets and started work on a couple of eye splices. There was great competition between the two of them as to who should make the best splice in the fastest possible time. Meanwhile Mark, who gave every appearance of watching the ropework with great interest, was scanning the marina minutely through rapidly swivelling eyes whenever he thought I was too busy to notice.

'What do you think his next move will be?' I whispered to Ursula, who was polishing the varnished wood in the cabin with some chamois-leather.

'The paddle-steamer, I shouldn't be surprised,' she murmured, giving the bulkhead an extra hard rub.

We had Ursula's big surprise for tea that day — banana and apricot jam sandwiches, which were greeted with as much suspicion as toadstool sandwiches might have been — till Victor announced that they were evil; whereupon everyone bared their teeth and munched away with great enjoyment.

Ursula was to drop the boys back at Norwich Road on her way home, so we put the boat to bed and carried our gear along the pontoon to the car-park. On these occasions I noticed that John was usually the gallant one of the party, offering to carry all the heaviest bags when he saw that we were overburdened.

Whenever I looked at him I was reminded of a book I read as a child called *Japeth in Search of a Father* — for that was the story of his life. The other boys called him Buck-Tooth because of his protruding front teeth, and he often seemed to live in a fantasy world of his own far removed from the everyday life of Forest Gate; dreaming, perhaps, of his missing father.

When John was a small boy his mother had run off with another man and his father put him into Care before disappearing to some distant part of the country. A foster home was soon found for the poor child; and then another and another. It was not until he had reached his seventh foster home that the woman became devoted to him and did her best to make his childhood happy. But her husband, who was a very jealous man, soon grew to hate John; and, after his wife was suddenly taken ill and died, he wasted no time in arranging for the boy to go back into Care. Newham Social Services Department then placed him in the Edith Moorey Home.

His real father had reappeared on one occasion and John, I believe, had caught a brief glimpse of him which was really worse than nothing at all, as the man soon vanished again without leaving his address. Some years later we heard that he had made a new home for himself in New Zealand; but never a word to his yearning son.

Driving home towards the sunset that evening, I was struck by Ursula's profile in the car running alongside me. I had been thinking about *Martha*'s clutch cable when I noticed that my speedometer was nearing its maximum reading; and, simultaneously, I became aware that we were racing neck and neck along the A.13. I glanced at her again and perceived the light of battle in her eyes: that fierce expression, determined chin and whitening of the knuckles as she gripped the steering-wheel told their story... and her passengers, who had bulging eyeballs, tousled hair and hoarse voices, were urging her to greater and greater excesses of speed!

Chapter 5

It was a brilliant sunshiny afternoon in late August 1975 when Emily brought seven of the boys to our house to watch the Thames Sailing Barge Race from the balcony. It was also the week of the Festival of Sail and the river was alive with square-rigged sailing ships, schooners, brigantines and barges, all moving majestically upstream on the last of the flood; and, like candle-flames attracting moths, each vessel had its attendant escort of small motor-boats and dinghies filled with dream-sailors.

The summer months had fled by with long gaps between our Tuesday outings, as Dick and I had spent several weeks aboard *Roskilde* sailing to Belgium and Holland; then the school holidays had split up the two groups,

Victor, Stephen and Mark on our balcony during the Festival of Sail.

Jeff eating a bun while the Thames Sailing Barge Race approaches along Limehouse Reach.

with some of the boys away camping and others at Council homes by the sea. But at last we were nearly all together again with the barge race from the Medway to Tower Bridge taking place before our eyes.

Victor and Mark, both wearing smart new T-shirts, one green and the other mauve, were perched on the wall at one side of our balcony whispering urgently to one another, so I moved closer to listen to their conversation.

'Did you take a look into the barf-room as we climbed up all those stairs?' Mark was asking his mate. 'Cor! The room's big enough to throw a party in, and the toilet's all boxed in wiv wood so you got to watch it or you'll pee all over the seat!'

Victor's mouth hung open with astonishment at these revelations and, a few minutes later when I was talking to Philip who was kneeling on the

balcony floor stroking our old Airedale, Texel, he came over to me and said: 'Please can I go to the toilet, Auntie?'

I had some difficulty preserving a neutral expression as I told him where to find it (as if he didn't know already!). And, shortly afterwards, Emily observed that she thought the boys seemed far more interested in the interior of our house than the pageant of sail out on the river.

Chris Cortauld, who was a Chaplain at the London Hospital and the owner of a very beautiful yacht, *Duet*, which was on loan to the Ocean Youth Club for much of the year, had joined us on the balcony and was clearly having an inspiring conversation with little Peter. After listening to some tales of the adventurous voyages made by the OYC boats, Peter asked hopefully if they might take him one day if he worked really hard at his seamanship and navigation.

'I'm sure they would,' Chris told him. 'You're just the sort of lad they're looking for.'

A glittering band of silver lozenges came dancing across the river from the Rotherhithe shore and every few minutes a stately Thames barge crossed that shining pathway, its tanned sails casting a dark shadow that moved silently upriver beside the parent vessel. It was a stirring scene, but when I asked Stephen what he thought of it he said he liked watching the reflection of the ripples from the water dancing on our ceiling — had I noticed it? Also he wouldn't mind trying out the pink armchair in our sitting-room.

'We don't have any chairs like that at Norwich Road,' he confided. 'They're all big and strong as elephants there, so if anyone throws a wobbler he can't break 'em up!'

The last barge passed, Chris Cortauld went back to work and Emily and I began to collect the boys together to go on a hydrofoil from Tower Pier to Greenwich and back, to see the tall ships at their moorings. Two boys were missing, but we soon found them sampling our big armchairs in the library.

'Have you really read all those books?' Mark wanted to know. 'Me and Dave was sitting here trying to count 'em but they go right up to the ceiling on bofe sides and it takes hours. I've never read one book, as it 'appens.'

We crowded into Emily's mini-bus and set off for Tower Pier. While she and I discussed this and that in the front, there was a steady buzz of muted whispers coming from behind us: 'Did you see that model of a racing-car downstairs?...the chimbley going right up frew the ceiling in the bedroom?...the dolphin soap-dish in the barfroom?...the glass bear swimming in ice in the kitchen?...etcetera, etcetera.'

Picking our way among the great gathering of sailing-ships...

It occurred to me that the Festival of Sail — the main point of the outing — had, so far, left only a luke-warm impression compared with the exciting discoveries the boys had made in every room in our house!

The hydrofoil trip was sheer perfection. Encouraged by the four who had been before, we all crowded on to the stern deck; and the deckhand took one look at the boys then found some urgent work that required his attention on the foredeck. By the time the hydrofoil had risen on to its spindly legs we were already through Tower Bridge and picking our way among the great gathering of sailing-ships. All round us their tall masts pierced the scudding clouds, and famous names like *Sagres, Tovarisch, Georg Stage* and *Danmark* flashed past our eyes in a thin veil of spray.

Victor was learning out over the quarter, his face and hair streaming and an expression of total happiness in his half-closed eyes. He and David had just told each other that the hydrofoil was wicked. Peter and Philip, as befitted the two eldest members of the group, had taken up a firm stance on the stern sheets ('to stop any of the little kids acting the fool,' they told us) and were discussing the respective merits of the various types of sailing-ships in a knowledgeable manner. Stephen was sitting by himself humming a tuneless dirge and looking rather miserable; later on, I came to understand that this behaviour sometimes signified that he was thinking of his mum and wondering why she had abandoned him. And Mark, who seemed to have green sparks flashing out of his eyes, was staring furiously at Jeff who was occupying the prime position just then — on Auntie Em's lap!

No one wanted to go ashore in Greenwich, so we remained glued to our seats in case any new-comers should take a fancy to them. And a few minutes later we were on our way upriver again, creaming past the harbourmaster's launch, a Roman galley, the schooner *Sir Winston Churchill*, and a few other late arrivals at the Festival of Sail.

The boys said it had been a brilliant day as we came ashore at Tower Pier: plenty of action, everything buzzing the way they liked it, and they wouldn't mind coming to tea in our house one day soon...?

Three days later Dick and I and our dog, Texel, left the London Marina at dawn and sailed *Martha* downriver among all the great sailing-ships that were setting off on a race from the Thames Estuary to Lisbon. A silvery-grey mist hung over the river while phantom-ships glided by on both sides of us, many with their yards dotted with small figures who were struggling to release the huge square sails while others hauled them taut way below. A note in our log-book off Erith says, 'River stuffed with shipping — barques, schooners, naval ships, tugs, tourist launches and yachts. The Romanian barque, *Mircea II*, coming up fast astern...she dipped her ensign as she passed us...fancy that!'

We turned for home soon after Tilbury and Gravesend, as the ebb tide had

Emily and Victor aboard the hydrofoil.

Leaving Tower Bridge — Jeff and Stephen on the hydrofoil.

run its course and the flood would soon be surging into the river. Looking back, I noticed that the mist still clung to the low hills on either side of Sea Reach but the broad grey river was like a dream of long ago. Scores of ships under billowing clouds of canvas were running before a fresh breeze towards the open sea.

September 1st was to be our last day out on the river for some weeks owing to engine trouble. Ursula was still away on holiday so Emily brought the boys — Philip, David, Stephen and Jeff — and we set off into the hazy sunshine with a gentle northerly breeze sending intermittent catspaws to ruffle the calm grey water outside the dock. The tide was ebbing fast and there was hardly enough wind to sail, but the engine petered out five minutes later so Philip sprang on to the cabin-top to help me hoist the mainsail while Emily steered. As soon as it was set I went below and changed the sparking-plug, then the engine started again much to our relief.

A few minutes later it stopped once more, so we sailed rather precariously up to a big-ship mooring-buoy off the Ford Works at Dagenham. Philip managed to pass a mooring-rope through the ring despite the pull of the tide that was sweeping us away from it. At that point, urged on by a few biting comments from Auntie Em about the flabbiness of their muscles, all four

Philip steering Martha *down the river on a calm day.*

boys hung on to the rope until we had subdued the flapping mainsail and secured the end of the rope to our samson-post.

A period of calmness ensued, broken only by Jeff's plaintive bleat, 'How can I go to the toilet, Auntie?' and Stephen telling David that, in his opinion, it was time we had something to eat. So we unpacked our sandwiches and poured out the soup, and David whispered to me: 'How come your soup always tastes better than ours? Thicker and more meatylike?'

Stephen turned his head away and began to giggle while Emily told the boys they were a spoilt and useless bunch of creeps, and if they thought they were going to have Campbell's best chicken soup at every meal, they had another thing coming to them!

The tide began to turn while the sandwiches were being noisily devoured; and a sudden ominous booming noise up for'ard told me that *Martha* was riding up on the mooring-buoy. Philip and David volunteered to sit on the foredeck fending off with their feet, while Stephen and Jeff helped Emily clear away our lunch and I bled the petrol system. Presently I managed to start the engine again, but hastily switched off to preserve it for a more important moment; and as soon as the cockpit was shipshape David hoisted the sails and we tacked slowly back to the London Marina.

A final burst of power brought us inside the lock. It was dead low water and the outer sluice-gates were not working, but we reached an iron ladder just in time for some of the boys to scramble ashore and give the lock-keeper our bow-line to tow us through to the inner lock. Perhaps because he himself had grown up in Care, he always made time to talk to the boys and show an interest in what they had to tell him — quite unlike some of the other lock-keepers who would let the water in with a great woosh, knowing how hard it was for us to keep *Martha* under control.

Jeff had broken his glasses and could hardly see beyond the end of his nose, but we allowed him to steer while the lock-keeper led us out of the lock and into the basin. 'All yours, Captain!' he shouted, as he pushed us away with his long boat-hook and Stephen hoisted the jib.

Jeff was grinning so broadly that I feared his face would never revert to its normal shape again. 'Did you hear what the man said, Auntie?' he whispered as I took the tiller from him to manoeuvre the boat alongside our pontoon.

A large American lady from a neighbouring pontoon took our lines and helped the boys to moor the boat. 'Gee, you've gotten together a swell crew there,' she commented. 'You must bring all those guys to tea aboard our trimaran some day soon.'

Chapter 6

There is no doubt that the Victoria and Albert Docks were the dream-children of someone who thought *big* — a Victorian giant who conceived those 175 acres of water flanked by 7 miles of quays; some of the finest docks in the world during the latter half of the nineteenth century. Even our particular haven, the Royal Albert Dock Basin, had a depth of 36 feet at the entrance and could receive the largest ships afloat at that period.

I liked to stand on the bridge between us and the Royal Albert Dock, facing west, and close my eyes; and suddenly a vision of full-rigged ships, barques and schooners would appear — a beautiful vision with the smell of tarred rope and the shouts from sailors aloft on the yards...

The Great Eastern Railway built an extension from the City to Gallion's, a terminus close to the dock entrance; also the Gallion's Hotel, a spectacular building where passengers were encouraged to await the arrival of their vessels in comfort. It had a gabled roof, numerous tall chimneys and a domed turret surmounted by a weathercock. Below the roof and a broad band of ragstone tiling appeared a white frieze of plump ladies and children in the nude. Ornate windows set in white plaster adorned the lower half of the building, and the interior was said to have contained many solid mahogany fittings — built to defy the passage of time. There used also to be ample stabling for horses, as well as a railway platform, incorporated in the back yard.

During the 1930s the Gallion's was often used by the families of officers whose ships were berthed in the Royal Albert Dock, and two subways gave direct access from the hotel to the quay so that passengers or crew members could reach their ships without emerging into the open. It was, however, a forlorn and empty shell of a place when the boys and I first began to prowl around there in 1975. But there it stood, just outside the London Marina gates, with hints of its former glory still visible and that amazing aura of the great British Empire still oozing from every moss-filled cranny in the solid brick façade.

No one had stayed, officially, at the Gallion's Hotel since the end of the

Second World War; but there were countless rumours of illicit political meetings, criminals in hiding, murders and even ghosts prowling through the rooms on the night of the full moon. The boys were, I suspect, rather scared of penetrating the Council's robust window hoardings and governessy warnings about the prosecution of trespassers; but they were, at the same time, drawn towards it as if by some powerful magnet that whispered enticingly in their ears, 'You can get inside through a broken window covered with brambles round the back. Why not try, just to see what it's really like inside?'

The month of September was an ideal period for daring exploits as *Martha*'s engine had resisted the expert probings of several engineers, including a pair of Vire specialists from the B. and M. Power Plant at Ipswich where the engine was purchased the previous year. They spent a whole day grovelling in the bilges to no avail, and left at dusk completely baffled by the fact that you could start the engine without difficulty but it refused to run for longer than two minutes, once engaged in gear.

In the meantime Ursula and I devised various means of keeping the boys occupied on a Tuesday, some more successful than others. Dick and I had a nine-foot dinghy at home, and one evening we launched her and dropped downriver on the ebb to North Woolwich. *Water-Rat*, as she was called, had a small mast and lugsail, and a strong tendency to leak through the centreboard casing; she often became rather unstable in strong puffs of wind, but we decided that it was safe enough to sail her inside the dock in gentle winds, provided the boys always wore their life-jackets and knew how to swim.

The first group, Peter, John, Victor and Mark, were delighted with *Water-Rat* – a boat that they would soon be able to sail on their own without any interfering grown-ups to tell them what to do. Both Emily and Ursula had come to the marina that first afternoon of the dinghy, and each brought a special contribution to our lunch; so all seven of us were feeling relaxed and well-fed by the time the afternoon's work began.

I had decided to establish a fairly strict schedule: 2–3 p.m. for coastal navigation and ropework; 3–4 for dinghy rowing and sailing tuition; 4–4.30 for free time in which the boys could do whatever they liked, as long as they kept clear of Tony Cohen and the dockmaster's office and did not get into any trouble; and at 4.30, a big tea aboard *Martha* which gave me an excuse to visit the neighbourhood shop most Tuesdays.

'Cor! You ain't 'arf gotta good happetite!' Madge would remark as she rang up my purchases on her till. 'Unless it's fer all them nippers what I sees you wiv last week?'

We started by laying off courses on the chart of the Dover Strait, allowing for variation and leeway, and predicting the time of high water at Dover on

Laying off a course on the chart

various dates during the year. Victor excelled at these problems and Peter was almost as good, for he had no intention of being outdone by a younger boy. Emily also showed great interest as she had just started attending her course at the School of Navigation. John tried to become involved, but I often caught him peering hopefully at the surface of the water out through the cabin door. And Mark fixed me with eyes that seemed rounder and bluer than ever — a look of pure innocence that deceived no one. Presently he began to stifle a few sniggers and, following his gaze, I noticed that Ursula had closed her eyes and was snoring gently!

During those September Tuesdays the boys who were interested learned very fast, and all of them except Jeff enjoyed doing ropework and easily mastered the seven or eight most useful knots. Peter and Victor were even learning to splice by the end of the month.

The free half hour was, I suspect, the magic period in the boys' schedule. John would nearly always fish, with a rapt expression on his serious face and a glint of excitement in his eyes when he felt a jerk on the end of his line. The other boys liked to take *Water-Rat* out on their own and row to the far corner of the dock where they had established a secret harbour. It was round the back of a group of tugs, the driftwood boat and a motor fishing-vessel — a place where they could disappear from sight and climb about on the boats without being observed.

'What do you *do* round the back there?' I would sometimes ask them.

And Peter, their spokesman, would tell me; 'We scramble about on one of the big boats and pretend we're out at sea. I'm the Skipper, Vic's First Mate and has to see to the cargo and ropes, and Mark's the Chief Engineer 'cos he likes being alone down the engine-room.'

It was not until some while later that I figured out why he liked being alone: in case there were any small loose items to filch! I suppose most of the boys were like that at times when they craved for plenty of money to spend, and could only get it by selling what they had picked up to richer children at school.

'Steve's a real conman!' Emily would tell me with a laugh; 'but not always as quick as our Mark. Let me tell you what happened the other evening: Mark's social worker came round to visit him, and while she was having a cup of tea with me he nicked a £1 note out of her handbag and buried it in the garden. Knowing our Mark, she counted her money before she left and, finding £1 missing, she told him to cough it up pretty quickly. Well, he put on his injured innocence look and said he never, but he'd help her look for it if she liked. She did like, so a few minutes later he called from the far end of the garden: 'Look, Auntie, what I've found! The wind must've blown it out of 'er 'andbag and into this corner where the tortoise sleeps!'

After listening to a number of such tales, Dick, Ursula and I often expected to find a few things missing after the boys had been to visit one or other of our homes; but we never did. Perhaps they took things that we would not notice till long afterwards... or perhaps they didn't. Whatever the answer, we built up a kind of mutual trust that gave us a nice warm feeling, even if we were taken for a ride now and then.

The second group in September came to the London Marina with Emily, but she had a meeting to attend that afternoon so Ursula and I agreed to bring them back to Norwich Road later on. The log-book tersely records: 'Hellish Tuesday; the boys behaved like devils all afternoon!'

It was pouring with rain when they arrived, and Philip was sulking because he felt he had not been placed in the Number 1 group. Emily had arranged the groups when we first started, and it had not been easy for her as she knew that the two pairs of brothers were better kept apart and poor little Jeff would be the weak link in whichever group he was placed. Because Philip was usually kinder to him than the other boys, it had seemed a good idea to put them together while separating Philip from Victor of whom he was rather jealous. None of the boys were renowned for their modesty, and Victor's boastful remarks about his dramatic exploits on his Tuesday afternoons afloat did nothing to soothe Philip's injured pride.

It was all very foolish, for although Peter was the best helmsman, Philip was as good a seaman as any of the others and by far the strongest. He was not as keen on chartwork and tidal problems as his brother, but the lessons I attempted to teach the boys on his Tuesdays were probably more to his taste. I had a set of miniature buoys painted in their correct colouring, and a few tiny metal tugs and liners; and with these 'toys' we would move in and out of an imaginary harbour laid out on the floor of the cabin or cockpit, avoiding sandbanks and wrecks and making sure that we obeyed the Rule of the Road at sea. It was like playing a game but, later on, when the children were confronted with real ships and buoys out on the river and sea, some of them found it very exciting to relate those fast-moving vessels and huge bouncing shapes to their early lessons aboard *Martha*.

That particular Tuesday, the American lady who lived on the trimaran came round to see us just after Emily had delivered her cargo and said she would like to invite all those darling boys to tea later on, and would let us know when it was ready.

'Sure and that's something nice for you all to look forward to!' Emily beamed at the boys. She was always very keen on them meeting other people socially — people from the outside world who would help to break down the barriers for them and make some of them less withdrawn.

I was glad when four o'clock came as it had been a difficult afternoon with the boys erupting into violent squabbles, glaring at one another, pushing Jeff (whom they called 'Skunk') around unmercifully and laughing at him when he tried to tie a clove hitch. The rain had stopped by then so Stephen and David said they wanted to go for a row in *Water-Rat*, while Philip declared that he would rather take a stroll by himself; and Jeff made it clear that he preferred to stay with us.

'Don't be away long,' I shouted at the departing dinghy and the sulky figure trudging along the pontoon; 'because the American lady might call for us to come over to tea very soon.'

By standing on our cabin-top I could see that she was bustling around in her cockpit, putting out extra cushions for us to sit on; so Ursula and I took Jeff ashore to the toilet block where we all washed our hands and combed our hair in preparation for the tea-party.

Returning to *Martha* a short while later, I climbed on to the cabin-top again to see if *Water-Rat* was in sight — and promptly wished that I had stayed put in the cockpit! She was, in fact, half way back to the pontoon by then, very clearly within earshot, and Stephen was standing up in the dinghy shaking a dripping oar over David's head and calling him an 'effing cunt.' David responded in like fashion, only he had a choicer vocabulary and more carrying power to his voice.

Ursula and I sat down rapidly and pretended that we were deeply engrossed in teaching Jeff how to tie a reef knot; but we were only too well aware that *everyone* could hear what was going on in the middle of the dock

— even Tony Cohen in his little office and the dockmaster, way across the far side, who had opened his window wide so as not to miss a word!

In due course the boys came back to *Martha* — Philip from his walk, and Stephen and David in the dinghy. They moored her with meticulous care, then went ashore to wash their hands and comb their hair before tea. They soon returned to the boat and we waited and waited...Ursula and I exchanged a few desultory remarks, but the call to tea never came.

Finally we opened some cans of coke inside the cabin and shared out the few cakes we had brought with us.

'Let that be a lesson to you,' I told the strangely silent and deflated children. 'All the same, I do think she's a bit mean!'

Chapter 7

'Me an' Stitchum was talking things over after we went to bed last night, an' we was wonderin' when we'll get to sea again as it's already October an' the winter's nearly on us?'

Peter fixed me with a frosty stare which made me forget the purpose of my visit to Norwich Road that gloomy Tuesday afternoon – to give the boys a lesson in chartwork and how to calculate the depth of water at any given state of the tide by means of the Rule of Twelfths.

'I'm sorry that *Martha* has been out of commission for all these weeks,' I told him and Victor; 'but it's not very safe to use her on the river without an engine and you *have* been learning new things all the time, haven't you?' I put on my fiercest expression and glared back at the boys, although I was secretly rather pleased that the boat had grown to matter to them in such a short space of time.

Perhaps our guardian angel was listening in at No. 26 that afternoon, for it was only a few days later that things took a decided turn for the better. John Halls, a partner in the well-known East Anglian boatbuilding firm who had installed our Vire engine the previous winter, said he would come to London especially to try and find out what had gone wrong. So *Martha* was hoisted out of the water on October 7th, and it took John less than half an hour to discover that the tufnell block had swollen, causing the propeller shaft to stick whenever the gear was engaged. He quickly dealt with this problem, while Emily and two other friends helped me to slap some anti-fouling paint on the bottom.

Later that afternoon *Martha* was lowered back into the water, and a few brisk turns round the basin proved that all was well. At last we could go out on the river again.

Grey storm clouds and sharp pellets of rain greeted us the following Tuesday but nothing, absolutely nothing, could cast a blight over the children that afternoon.

There were seven of us aboard *Martha* — Emily, Ursula and I, and Peter, John, Victor and Mark whose nicknames I was gradually beginning to learn; also that most of them were not intended to flatter the recipient. John, for instance, was known as Bucktooth, Peter as Flatnose, Victor as Stitchum and Mark as Chums. Auntie Em was Wirelegs, but it was never revealed what Ursula and I were called!

Because the weather was so bad, we circled the dock under engine with each boy in charge for ten minutes or so. We started with 'Man Overboard' drill, using an old fender as the body; everyone in their turn had to bring the boat close to it and give the correct orders to the engineer and bowman for recovering it, judging the wind and leeway just right. It was not as easy as it sounds, but each little Captain revelled in his task and the chance to shout orders at everyone else.

Afterwards we practised bringing *Martha* slowly and gently alongside an old fishing-boat on the far side of the dock to land some of our crew, then circling round to retrieve them a few minutes later. This was a very popular manoeuvre that everyone loved, and the children who had trans-shipped on to the fishing-boat did a little 'exploring' while the rest of us were circling. Approaching the climax of our fourth circumnavigation, a window was thrown brusquely open in the dockmaster's office to frame an angry red face: 'What the 'ell d'you lot think you're up to, clambering abaht like monkeys all over P.L.A. property, I'd like ter know? An' makin' enough noise ter waken the dead, inter the bargain.'

'Piss off, you silly old turd!' hissed Mark, who was Captain just then.

I raised my voice to blanket any further remarks from my crew and shouted back that we had almost finished our training session for the afternoon and were just about to return to our berth. John, Peter and Mark then took *Water-Rat* for a sail, being careful to keep well away from the far side of the dock; Victor, meanwhile, said he'd like to work at another tidal problem.

It had been a good day, I decided, and everyone had tried hard — even little Chums who was not renowned for the depth of his concentration. The rain had stopped by then and we had a very cheerful tea-party in the cockpit when the dinghy crew returned. Ursula's banana and apricot jam sandwiches were devoured with even greater relish than usual while she told the boys about the pantomime she was planning to take them to in the Christmas holidays.

'How do you find out when there would be enough water to enter Sandwich harbour on October 21st?' I asked Peter, just to make sure that he was not dropping behind Victor in his tidal calculations.

His face went pink and blotchy and he opened and shut his mouth once or twice, but not a sound escaped from it. A profound hush had settled over *Martha* while everyone waited for his reply; especially Victor, who had begun to titter inside the cabin.

'I wonder what you'd look like if you was to take off your 'eadscarf,' Peter observed at last, fixing me with a quizzical gaze. 'Ever since we first come 'ere I never seen you wivout one!'

Everyone began to laugh and forgot about the tides at Sandwich, and I thought to myself: 'You win that round, Flatnose; but never mind, I'll get even with you next time!'

We followed a similar routine the following Tuesday when Emily brought Philip (nicknamed Drurner), David (Gums), Stephen (Weapon) and Jeff (Skunk). Once again, all the children worked very hard and manoeuvred the boat with great skill; and the dockmaster was otherwise engaged that afternoon and never appeared at his window at all.

It was a cold autumn day and almost dark by five o'clock, so we lit the old Beatrice paraffin stove as well as the cabin-lamp and the primus for the first time that year, and all crowded inside *Martha*'s cabin for tea. Stephen, who was humming a little tune and grinning broadly, remarked: 'I reckon this is the best part of sailing, lighting up the ole stoves an' getting all warm an' cosy inside.'

David said they should have a competition after tea, to see who could polish the brass portholes best — one porthole each and Auntie Em and me as the judges. And Jeff, whose glasses and teeth were gleaming in the lamplight, said it was brilliant inside the cabin and he did wish his mum could see what it was like. Philip said he was going to bring his school project for us to read very soon, and Jeff said he was going to make me a little boat at 'wood-work' in school. There we all sat, huddled together in a warm cocoon, our faces pink from the chill autumn air and the glow of the stoves, and the water lapping gently against *Martha*'s hull in harmony with the munching of six pairs of jaws.

It was about this time that I began to realize that 'going sailing' meant different things to different children. For some it was the glory of beating hard to windward with spray flying over the bows; for others a chance to sit peacefully on the stern, hoping to catch a fish; and for others again, the warmth and security of the cabin in winter to make up for some of the frightening times out on the river and sea. It was no use expecting that each boy would become a future seafarer; but I hoped that *Martha*, in her wisdom, would find some way of sharing her own special magic with all the children from the Edith Moorey Home.

We spent two more days out on the river before the winter really closed in. It was half term on the first Tuesday, so Peter and his group had the whole day free.

We sailed *Martha* downriver to Erith, past Barking Power Station and the tall red and white pylons on either side of the river above Dagenham Dock, past the monster Ford Works and the little red lighthouse on Jenningtree Point, then Frog Island at the mouth of Rainham Creek and, over by the south shore, all the tall chimneys and church spires and big-ship mooring buoys that announced the beginning of Erith Reach. The river was grey and wintry-looking, and there was no one to wave to on the coasters and container-ships chugging downstream on the last of the ebb. All the sailors were tucked away inside their warm glassed-in bridges while *Martha*'s gallant crew, clad in a strange assortment of much-too-big jerseys, clung to the deck-rails and pulpit shouting with joy each time we altered course to breast some gigantic 'washers'.

The jersey-bag on *Martha* contained a variety of ancient gloves, scarves, Balaclava helmets, submarine socks and jumpers — some of them knitted for Dick by his Auntie Molly when he was a medical student, and others issued to me by the Navy when I was a boat's crew Wren. Each boy soon developed distinct preferences about which garments he would select from the bag, but when two wanted the same jersey the sparks began to fly.

We ran aground off Erith at dead low water that day, but no one quite believed my assurances that we would soon be afloat again on the flood tide — until it happened some ten minutes later and we were able to secure *Martha* to a mooring-buoy while we ate our lunch.

'If you knew how to do your tidal problems, Flatnose, you'd 'ave worked that out for yourself!' Victor told Peter with a smug look on his face.

'And if you'd remembered to turn on the petrol, you might've been able to start the engine, Stitchum!' Peter, who had quite a flair with engines, stuck out his tongue at his mate.

The wind had dropped by the time we were ready to cast off, so we started the engine and motored upstream to Gallion's Point with the flood tide gurgling merrily beneath us. Back inside the London Marina with the lamp and stove alight, we felt like Viking sailors at the end of a tough assignment out at sea.

Our last river-Tuesday was on November 4th, a beautiful golden autumn day with hardly a breath of wind. Philip could not come that afternoon so our crew consisted of David, Stephen and Jeff, and I had invited a neighbour of ours, Sally Morris, to come along too.

Ursula and I had experienced enough Tuesdays by then to distinguish the signs, early on, of what was likely to be a 'good' or 'bad' day; and this one quite clearly came into the first category, despite the exhibitionist tendencies of our crew!

We turned right outside the lock gates, immediately feeling the push of the strong flood tide as we motored upriver with Stephen at the helm. He was wearing Auntie Molly's brown woollen pullover, an enormous pair of trawlerman's gloves and a Balaclava helmet with a bobble on top that reminded you of a tea-cosy. All that was revealed of Weapon to the outside world were a few horizontal tufts of hair projecting like barbed wire defences above a pair of very bright eyes and a pink mushroom of a nose.

No sooner had we turned into Woolwich Reach than *Sir John Cass*, the smart vessel used by the School of Navigation, made towards us in a froth of foam. She often brought her students to Gallion's Reach for compass-swinging tuition, but that afternoon they had not yet started work and seemed intent on circling *Martha* with several pairs of binoculars trained upon us, while we plunged up and down in a welter of 'washers'.

Stephen rose proudly to the occasion. Remembering which way to push the tiller to stem the waves head-on, he stood bolt upright on *Martha*'s stern-deck and gave a naval-type salute when the two vessels were abeam of one another, making it quite clear who was Captain of the smaller one. A door slid open on the bridge of *Sir John Cass*, and a bearded mariner in uniform with gold braid on his sleeves stepped out and returned his salute.

'Well, that was quite something!' Sally exclaimed. 'I hadn't realized that you boys were on those sort of terms with other captains on the river.'

Stephen smirked with self-satisfaction while David and Jeff looked as if they were about to be sick.

'I think it's Jeff's turn to steer now,' I announced, to preserve a peaceful atmosphere in the cockpit.

Jeff loved steering when *Martha* was motoring. He had been unable to grasp the concept of sailing, but the growl of the engine under the deck-boards gave him a feeling of confidence. The woollen garment covering his head and face was soon thrust aside, and wearing an enormous grin he steered a straight course along the river to the point where the Woolwich

ferries crossed in midstream; and the skipper of the one called *Ernest Bevin* came out of his cabin specially to wave to our Jeff.

David, being a true Scorpion, loved to be noticed and to galvanize people's attention, whenever possible. It was his turn to steer coming back along Woolwich Reach and he began by waving the winch handle around to engage Sally's attention.

'See those black'n'white cows on the bank up there?' he asked her. 'Well, they're movin' at 70° to our course just now, but if I push the tiller right over, like this, we'd hit one of 'em in a few minutes' time!'

Sally had just begun to observe how unusual it was to meet cows when you were out in a boat, when I noticed that we were heading straight for the shallow water close to Woolwich Arsenal Pier. I leapt across the cockpit like a startled bullfrog, releasing a warning bellow as I rammed the tiller hard over to starboard. 'D'you realize that we'd have stuck in the mud there for ten hours or more, with the tide only just beginning to ebb?'

The children's reaction was not at all what I had expected. They bared their teeth at me then turned their faces away to giggle in pairs, while Stephen, voicing all their thoughts, said: 'I'd like to see Auntie Em's face if we never got home tonight an' she thought we'd all got drownded!'

Even inside the dock, our day ended on a note of drama. The evening had turned cold and frosty, so everyone was anxious to moor the boat as quickly as possible and crowd into the cabin for warmth. Perhaps because of this, I did not pour enough methylated spirits into the saucer round the burner on the primus to warm it properly before lighting up — so the stove promptly caught fire!

This inspired David to great heights of heroism as he seized the kettle and wet floor-cloth with which to douse the flames. In a few seconds he had brought the fire under control while the rest of us clutched the deck-rails in speechless horror.

After this ordeal the log-book records: 'Jungle heat inside the cabin with the Beatrice turned right up. We had a splendid tea-party!'

Ursula and I met at the wash-basins in the toilet block before leaving the London Marina that night, and after discussing the events of the afternoon I remarked: 'Well, that's our last river outing over till next spring so we can sit back and have a quiet time for the next few months.'

To which she replied with a throaty laugh: 'I wouldn't be too sure!'

Martha McGilda *in a fresh breeze, from a painting by Montague Dawson.*

Peter steering, with John and Victor out sailing for the first time in Gallion's Reach.

Our dog Texel, from a pastel by Paul Christian.

Mark and Philip were the first pair to occupy the steering position . . .

Chapter 8

'I have some *news* for you!' Peter Cobb announced on the other end of the line, his voice pregnant with the sensational tidings he was about to divulge: 'Our friend, Miss O'Brien, has expressed a desire to come down to the London Marina next Tuesday, to see how the boys are getting along!'

'I don't believe it!' I gasped. 'It's far too late in the season and she'll freeze to death.' Any excuse to stop her coming, for I still had nightmares about that interview in her office and suspected that she would be watching the boys very closely to see if they had really learned anything useful during the past six months.

'I told her that,' Peter chuckled; 'but she said she loved boating and would wear her thickest trousers and Shetland sweater. So there you are; I'm to bring her down with the boys at one o'clock, and I'll stay for lunch then leave you to get on with it!'

November 11th was a cold sunny day with a hint of frost in the air. I had worked myself into a state of nervous exhaustion by one o'clock, what with the decks to scrub, the brass to polish, the engine to check over in great detail and the soup and sandwiches to prepare. I kept on telling myself that they would not come: the car would refuse to start, there would be an accident on the way ... anything to put off the horror that hung over me like a black cloud.

But they did come. On the dot of one o'clock all six of them scrambled out of Peter's car; the boys did not seem at all nervous nor subdued, and Peter was actually sharing a joke with the dragon herself — I could hear his abominable laughter as they advanced rapidly along the pontoon. I was the only one, it appeared, who was sweating like a stoker on a steamship in the Red Sea.

Miss O'Brien in beige tweed trousers and a hairy Shetland sweater looked larger than I recalled — a stalwart brown-clad lady with a glint of humour lurking behind those severe spectacles that were focused on me like naval guns seeking the range of an enemy ship. Pretending not to notice, I placed cushions at suitable intervals around the cockpit and John helped me lay out the food and pour the soup into bowls. The boys were transformed into angel-children, offering the choicest morsels to our guest, behaving most demurely themselves and being careful not to use any foul language in her presence. Mark, who was wearing his butter-couldn't-melt-in-his-mouth expression, suggested that she might care to sample a slice of chocolate gateau — no, he did not want the cake cutting for himself; only for the pleasure of watching her eat a slice. I began to feel quite sick!

All too soon Peter Cobb stood up, hit his head on the boom and just refrained from saying what had sprung to mind. 'Time to get back to work,' he simpered instead. 'Enjoy yourselves, boys and girls, and I'll be back for you later on.'

I need not have worried for the boys knew how important it was to impress Miss O'Brien if they wished to retain their free Tuesdays, so they had worked everything out in detail beforehand. I was left gasping with astonishment by the end of the afternoon.

'We're going to start by circling the dock under engine to do various manoeuvres such as rescuing a man who has fallen overboard,' I explained to our guest, but before I had a chance to develop my theme little Peter announced, 'My turn to start the engine;' and jumped into the cabin to turn on the water and advance the choke on the carburettor.

Mark, who was having trouble doing up his life-jacket, sprang on to the stern deck and reported, 'Plenty of water comin' out,' as he peered over the edge at the exhaust outlet. I caught him on the way back and made a big show of checking his safety-harness and helping with the life-jacket for Miss O'Brien's benefit. As soon as he was securely fastened up I glanced around and saw Victor standing on the bows and John on the stern, each holding a mooring-line ready to cast off; and Peter whispered urgently: 'Can I be Captain first, please Rozelle?'

'O.K.,' I whispered back; 'but I'll work the engine if you shout out the orders.'

Well, we put on quite a performance that afternoon — even the dockmaster threw open his window and peered at us with mouth hung open and binoculars glued to his face. Four 'men' were thrown overboard and retrieved with great skill by each boy in turn. When Mark was Captain, a cheer escaped from Miss O'Brien's throat as he brought the boat head-to-wind right up to the 'body' and gave the command for it to be hoisted aboard. During our dropping and picking up of crew members from the fishing-vessel, no one went exploring while *Martha* circled the dock; and the level of fender and boat-hook work and coming-alongsides was of a very high standard indeed.

While all these manoeuvres were taking place, Victor ruffled the glassy surface of the pool from time to time by throwing a pebble in such as: 'I just looked up the time of high water, Auntie, and it's 1854 at London Bridge this arternoon, so the tide'll start running back downstream outside this dock about twenty minutes before then.'

Or — 'When we was on our way down to Erith two weeks ago, I heard a fog'orn just before we come to that bend wiv the light'ouse on it. It gave one perlonged blast, and that was the special warning for any ships coming towards it round the uvver side of the bend, wasn't it?'

'Perlonged blast?' Miss O'Brien queried, her eyebrows arching above the frame of her spectacles. I was perched slightly behind her just then, facing Victor whose face resembled a lobster being immersed in boiling water.

'Prrr...' I silently mouthed at him and, being a child who was quick off the mark, he swivelled his eyes towards a tall chimney belching smoke on the far side of the river for a moment's contemplation, then back to look his headmistress straight in the eyeballs.

'I said "prolonged", did'unt I, Miss?'

'Perhaps you did, Victor,' she grinned. 'Anyway I am most impressed with your nautical knowledge.'

Peter's eyes had begun to flash like hard emerald chippings so I asked how his splicing was coming along; whereupon he pulled an old bit of rope out of one of the cockpit lockers and rapidly made a perfect eye-splice, which was much admired by our guest. Not to be outdone by these two show-offs, John and Mark then demanded more rope and tied every sort of knot they could think of along the guard-rails and Mark suddenly announced, out of the blue, that a Turkish ship at anchor in a fog would have some geezer beating on a drum (instead of ringing a bell, like on English ships), to make sure no one ran into them!

'Well, well, well!' laughed Miss O'Brien; 'I wish I could say that you boys absorbed as much knowledge from your lessons in school, as you seem to on a boat.'

I sat on the gunwale, flushed with pride, and told their teacher that I hoped to get Captain McLaren to give them their first nautical exam in a few months time. Everything had gone well — far better than I had dared to hope for — and I felt relaxed and pleased with myself when the time came to return to our pontoon, as Miss O'Brien said she must get back to school before closing time.

'I'll take the tiller to bring her in,' I said, pushing John out of the way as I feared he might spoil the whole effect of such a brilliantly successful afternoon by making a clumsy come-alongside at the last moment.

I steered towards our berth, having placed Victor on the foredeck and John on the stern to grab hold of the mooring-lines; and just as we came gently alongside the finger pontoon I put the gear lever into astern and revved up for a moment to take the way off the boat. At least, that is what I had

intended to do, but because Miss O'Brien was aboard and I was still in a state
of nerves, I rammed the gear lever into ahead by mistake and, as I revved up,
Martha hit the end jetty with a resounding crash and rose into the air as if
she were planning to climb ashore!

She still bears the scar (I call it the O'Brien scar) on her stem to this very
day.

★　　★　　★

Dick and I had been invited to a rather grand dinner-party on November
18th, so I went to the hairdresser's on Monday afternoon and had a special
wash and set. And all day Tuesday I kept my beautiful new coiffure encased
in a thick hair-net surmounted by a woollen headscarf.

It was a fine sunny day, but bitterly cold. The mooring-ropes were stiff
with hoar-frost when I reached the London Marina that morning, and Tony
called out of his cosy little office to ask if I would like to borrow a pair of his
longjohns! Ursula was away visiting her brother — a card had arrived two
days ago describing the beauties of the Australian summer and the golden
beaches near his home where they went swimming every day.

Emily brought Philip, David, Stephen and Jeff, and we decided to have
lunch inside the cabin for a change as there was still a sharp nip in the air,
even at midday. After lunch and a short session of tying knots and moving
the toy ships around on the cabin floor, I gave the boys a lesson in reefing the
mainsail which was not a great success. Philip grasped the principles of what
we were trying to do after a few minutes, but David continually tied the
wrong reef points together, attaching one from the first line to another from
the second; and Stephen grumbled incessantly about his cold fingers while
he tied some of the reef points right round the boom and secured them with
granny knots. Jeff just stood there beating his hands together and bleating:
'When am I goin' to be Captain again, Auntie?'

After twenty minutes of this I could have cheerfully wrung all their necks;
and, to make matters worse, my head was beginning to feel hot and itchy
under all its protective wrappings.

'How about a dinghy race?' I suggested. 'We've got the rubber dinghy here
as well as *Water-Rat* now, and if you boys would like to pump it up with the
bellows you can have a race, and Auntie Em and I will run round the dock to
see who comes in first.'

This proved a very popular idea and no one complained of the cold during
the next hour. Emily and I panted round and round the marina, cheered on
by a group of mechanics at one end and the lock-master and his assistant at
the other. The boys, meanwhile, fought and shrieked and splashed their way
across the basin, Philip and Jeff in *Water-Rat* and David and Stephen in the
rubber dinghy on the first lap; then they changed boats and Philip

discovered that it was much harder to row the inflatable dinghy than the wooden one.

I had bought a few bars of chocolate in the Cyprus neighbourhood shop that morning, so we had some prizes ready to present to the winners; and it was already dusk by the time the last race had been rowed.

'Can me and Gums go for one last round in *Water-Rat*?' Philip asked, when they returned to the pontoon.

'Just for five minutes,' I told him; 'as long as you both help us to squeeze the air out of the inflatable when you get back.'

Emily and Jeff were inside *Martha*'s cabin lighting the stove, and Stephen was fiddling about in the rubber dinghy on his own. He climbed out just then, leaving one oar in its rowlock with the blade in the water, and he rocked the boat violently as he heaved himself on to the pontoon.

'You must always stand in the middle of a dinghy when you first step in or are about to leave it,' I lectured him. 'And *never* let me see an oar dangling from its rowlock again. That's how you lose them, and if you were out on the river when it happened you might be swept away by the tide.'

Stephen grunted and I jumped into the dinghy to recover the oar. I landed on the left-hand side because it was already slithering through the rowlock, took a grab at it and the little boat began to list ... Further and further over she went, and the next moment I was in the ice-cold water which murmured 'Glug, glug, glug,' as it closed over the top of my head!

After an interval that seemed like eternity, I surfaced and took in the situation at one watery glance. Philip and David were still away in the big dinghy and Emily and Jeff were inside the cabin, so that left just Stephen and I, partners in this gruesome nightmare; and how on earth was I going to

crawl out of the freezing dock without a ladder, with my sodden winter clothing becoming heavier by the second? Stephen, who is no fool, had also sized up the situation. He opened his mouth wide and released a bellow like an elephant in pain:

'Auntie Em, come quick!' he roared; 'she'll get drownded if you don't com'un help me!'

It is inexplicable how the most trivial details assume enormous importance in moments of stress; for instance, my ruined hair-do was all I could think of as Emily and Stephen got a rope under my arms and dragged me, inch by inch, out of that murky basin.

'Let that be a lesson to you!' I gasped ungratefully at the boy. '*Never* jump into a dinghy the way I did just then, or this is what will happen to you.'

I squelched along the pontoon, spitting out dock water to right and left and clutching a small hand-towel (all Emily could find in the cabin) and the jersey-bag, as I headed towards the toilet block. The other boys had returned by then and were clearly entranced by the drama of what had occurred — something, at last, to boast about to Number 1 group who had had all the glory of Miss O'Brien's visit and me ramming the jetty to crow over during the previous week.

They followed me right to the door of the lavatories, then kept up a running interrogation while I was attempting to dry myself and get changed inside.

'What did it feel like when the water closed over the top of your 'ead, Rozelle? Did you think you was goin' to die? Was there any big fish down there to bite your toes?'

'I've brought you two extra jerseys,' Emily's welcome voice came under the door; 'and there's some guy out here who's offering you a tumbler of neat whisky — says it'll warm the cockles of your heart!'

I certainly needed them warming at that moment, as my teeth were chattering like castanets and I had just made the chilling discovery that we had no spare trousers in the jersey-bag — only jerseys and scarves, etcetera. When I finally emerged I was wearing a red Balaclava helmet, my old blue and black striped school scarf, three jerseys, one on top of another, on my top half and two more, worn with my legs through the armholes, to act as trousers; a pair of thick striped skiing socks and Dick's old seaboots (five sizes too large) rounded off the picture.

The children fell about shrieking with laughter, clutching their ribs and gasping for breath as they told me how funny I looked. I made a note in the logbook before leaving *Martha* that evening: 'Be sure to keep a spare pair of trousers and big bath-towel on board in future!'

★   ★   ★

I was very late getting back home, so Dick and I were very late indeed arriving at our grand dinner-party in St John's Wood. I shuddered when I saw all those elegant ladies talking to immaculate penguins in black ties and dinner-jackets, who carefully avoided looking at me while we made our apologies to our host and hostess. And, after dinner, I overheard a whispered exchange: 'Michael tells me that woman with the hair like rat's tails has been swimming around in the Royal Albert Dock this evening; can you imagine it, my dear?'

'Well, there's no accounting for tastes, Lucinda, but our delightful host does get entangled with some very odd people at times.'

Chapter 9

'Whatever shall we do with them all through the winter months?' I asked Emily anxiously. 'There are only two or three who show any real interest in coastal navigation, but the others very soon get bored and start looking for trouble.'

'Well, most of them wouldn't want to give up their Tuesday afternoons and stay at school instead,' she laughed. 'So you can always hold that over them when they start messing you about!'

I need not have worried, looking back at that first winter of the Tuesday boys; for it turned out to be a happy and beautiful interlude — like the gentle prelude to a Wagnerian opera, before the bass drums begin to beat.

It was pelting with rain on the Tuesday after my plunge into the London Marina, so Emily and I with Number 1 group had lunch in *Martha*'s cabin then did an RYA assessment paper on the parts of a boat's hull — what they are called and their uses. This proved rather popular when worked into an 'I spy with my little eye' type of game, and it held Mark's attention for at least half an hour. After finding, naming and discussing the uses of a rudder, gunwale, knees, stem, samson-post, keel and a few other parts, the sun came out and we decided to drive across to Greenwich to visit the *Cutty Sark* and the old observatory.

Peter and Victor had, I suspected, long harboured a grudge about Number 2 group having spent an amusing afternoon on the old ship last summer while they had never been offered the chance to visit her. But when we arrived there they appeared to take the whole expedition much more seriously and Peter remained for some while in the bowels of the *Cutty Sark* examining the glass cases filled with intricate ropework, while John and Victor were riveted to the photographs of square-rigged sailing-ships battling against mountainous seas off Cape Horn.

'Where's Mark?' Emily suddenly asked Victor, glancing suspiciously around the lower deck.

'Don't know, Auntie,' he muttered, turning pink as he raised his eyes to stare at a mark on the bulkhead to one side of her head.

'Lead me to him,' she commanded, knowing full well that the boys often worked in pairs or groups, and this abnormally good behaviour in the museum was probably a cover-up for what was going on elsewhere.

Delaying for as long as possible and whistling noisily to warn Mark of our approach, Victor led us by a roundabout route to the gangway; and, following the direction of his eyes, we noticed the souvenir shop on the quay between the *Cutty Sark* and *Gipsy Moth IV*. But one glance in that direction told us that Mark had met his match.

A small ferretlike woman with sharp features and gimlet eyes had a firm grip on the scruff of his neck while she gave him a piece of her mind in a voice that reminded me of the squawking of an angry turkey: 'Listen ter me, Sonny, I seen you come creepin' round the back of my shop soon as you stepped ashore. An' if you thought you was goin' ter pull a fast one on me, you picked the wrong person, see? I'll call the Fuzz if I ever catch those thievin' fingers . . .' she gave them a sharp whack with a ruler, 'delvin' inter my stock again. Unnerstand, do you?'

She shook him hard, like a terrier might shake a rat. His round cherub's face no longer looked cherubic — puckered forehead, angry eyes, pouting lips and a pair of fingers stabbing the air under her chin as he wrenched himself out of her grasp and shouted something very rude over his shoulder as soon as he had reached the protection of his mates.

'I think it's time we drove up the hill to look at the old observatory,' I suggested; and no one put forward any objections.

Noel Jordan, *Martha*'s first owner, had left Dick and me a large handbearing compass in his will. I showed it to the boys when we were standing in front of General Wolfe's statue close to the observatory and told them that we were going to take some bearings, then plot them on the chart another day to introduce them to the secret of how to fix one's position on a ship out at sea. Peter and Victor each wished to be the first person to handle this strange instrument and take some magic bearings, a desire that almost caused to come to blows. This, in turn, inspired John to greater efforts, and even Mark — who wished to establish that he was no longer in disgrace. We left Greenwich Park some while later with four sets of bearings of various chimneys in Silvertown and North Woolwich, the spire of All Saint's, Poplar and a gigantic chimney known as Limehouse Lil, as well as a few distant landmarks in the City and beyond.

'We'll plot all these bearings on the chart next time we meet,' I promised the boys; 'and see who took the best cross bearings to mark our position in the park.'

'Dead easy!' sniffed Victor. 'After all, we *knew* zackly where we was standing, not like being on a ship out at sea.'

'Yes, but that doesn't mean that you know how to take an accurate bearing, does it, Mr Know-All? I'll give a prize to the one with the best set of bearings.'

December 2nd, when Emily brought Number 2 group to the London Marina, was to be our last working Tuesday before the end of the autumn term. After a lunch of chicken broth, egg, ham and tomato sandwiches, and tangerines and bananas, the children pointed at the weak winter sun and said it was an outside kind of day — meaning that they had no wish to use their brains too extensively — so could we take the boats out for a run?

We set off with Emily, Stephen, Jeff and me aboard *Martha*, and Philip and David with our dog, Texel, in *Water-Rat*. Texel was an elderly Airedale bitch who had never cared for children until she met the Tuesday boys. In the past she had often layed back her ears and exhibited yellowish fangs if a child approached her. But, quite suddenly, she underwent a change of character and seemed to enjoy spending a day at the London Marina, especially if Number 2 group was there as Philip was her favourite of all the boys.

We circled the dock a few times and did the usual manoeuvres with much noise and laughter, as the dinghy crew often reached the 'man' overboard a few seconds before *Martha* and seized him from under our noses, while the boy wielding the boat-hook nearly fell overboard with excitement.

After an hour or so we returned to the pontoon and spent some while studying buoys, the Rule of the Road and parts of a boat.

'Next time we'll try the RYA assessment paper like the others did last week, if you work really hard at those boat parts,' I told the boys. Then Philip sprang his big surprise:

'Me and Vic's finished our boating project,' he said; 'and Miss O'Brien give us top marks for it. I brought it today as a present for you and Dick!'

He held out a grubby yellow exercise book while Stephen, glaring fiercely, told me he had almost finished his project too, but his teacher had wanted to keep it in school cos it was so good; all the same, he'd try to bring it first Tuesday next term.

Sitting down in a corner of the cockpit I decided to start at the beginning, despite the four pairs of eyes boring into me like searchlights and the unearthly hush that prevailed as I turned page after page. There was a drawing of an Elizabethan galleon on the first page with a caption: 'Names of Boats and Ships', with a list of five names in the following order: *Martha McGilda, Cutty Sark, Q.E.2., Lifeboat, Blue Eagle*.

On the second page I found a picture of a caveman in his dug-out canoe, with a short history of how they were built and the uses to which they were put. Next came a page on mid-channel buoys with coloured sketches to illustrate the different types, followed by a treatise on anchoring a boat and how much chain to let out for safety.

After Page 5, the one I had seen when I first opened the book, followed other pages about handling a boat in a gale, different types of knots, a picture of the sailing-vessel *Blue Eagle*, Pyrene fire extinguishers and their uses, bending on, setting and taking in sails, mooring in a drying-out berth, tacking against a strong wind, the morse code and... lo and behold: an outline of a sailing-boat with thirteen different parts marked on it — some of them the same as in the RYA assessment paper.

Gradually the book became more and more colourful with pictures of port and starboard-hand buoys, a Suffolk Beach Yawl, a racing-yacht with a sky-blue hull (just like *Martha*'s), and the British Isles and France drawn in shocking pink, with fat pink arrows to mark the direction of the main stream of flood. Then there was a page which said 'Please open out, thank you.' And inside I found a home-made chart that included every sort of information: soundings, buoys galore, a separation zone, an oil rig, fishing stakes, a safety fairway, spoil ground, part of a compass rose, etcetera, etcetera. And on the last page of all, a beautiful picture — of a helmsman steering towards the setting sun.

'What a marvellous present! I'm not surprised Miss O'Brien gave you top marks. Why am I wasting my time trying to teach you all these things when you know more than me already!' I exclaimed.

'Well, it's not quite like that,' Philip replied; 'because it's easy to do a project about something you really like. But it's when you're out on the river and can't remember which way to push the tiller with a big ship about to run you down, or when the boom comes flying over, unexpectedlike, and gives you a crack on the nut that we need you there!'

Ursula came home two weeks before Christmas, and she invited us all to the Mermaid Theatre to see 'Gulliver's Travels' on December 16th.

The boys were wearing their new Christmas jerseys and trousers, and Emily had given each one a haircut the night before; a type of chop-around-the-pudding-bowl affair which made them all look very much alike — a neat, clean, highly-presentable family with only an occasional villainous gleam to tell you that they were not quite as perfect as their appearance led you to suppose.

Ursula loved the theatre dearly, and she carried us along on a wave of enthusiasm so that everyone felt they were having a whale of a time – something to boast about to the other kids at school who were always droning on about 'My Mum's taking me to...' or 'My Dad's buying me... for Christmas.'

Mind you, several of our children gave renderings of the same tune, trying to convince us and, perhaps, themselves that it was really true.

'What d'you think my Mum's buyin' me for Christmas, Rozelle?' Jeff clutched my arm.

'I don't know. You tell me?'

'A model Ferrari to run on the Scalelectrix what she promised me before!'

'SShhsH!' snarled a woman in the row behind us, which relieved me of the need to answer him.

During the interval Stephen and Mark told me that their Nan was going to have them to stay over in Dagenham during the holidays, which I thought was probably true; and Victor said his Dad was coming down from Carlisle specially to see him and Philip, and John murmured something about a brief sighting of his own father that had taken place the previous week.

After the matinée we drove back to Limehouse where Dick was already entertaining Peter Cobb and Ken Boyce. We had put some trestle tables along the length of our biggest room, and covered them with white table-cloths and red and gold crackers and Christmas food. The oak beams across the ceiling were festooned with holly and mistletoe and paper garlands, and the Christmas tree in the far corner glowed with shiny coloured baubles and little lanterns. Dick had already lit the candles and there was a pause when he opened the door...a sharp intake of breath followed by a gabble of

The Christmas tea-party at our house.

exclamations: 'Cor! Don't it look brilliant! Wait till I get my 'ands round those crackers! Look at the angel playin' a fiddle at the top o' the tree! I never seen a table wiv so many cakes on it before!'

Stephen, who had recently become very conscious of people who dropped their h's, as a special gesture, to show how hard he was trying, addressed Ursula as Hursula; a grand effort which, unfortunately, did not cause a flicker of a smile to touch her lips.

The boys were extremely subdued when we sat down to tea; even Emily, wearing a pretty white lace blouse for the occasion, was rendered almost speechless by the presence of the two big chieftains from Newham Social Services Department. The pulling of the crackers, however, livened up the party, especially when Mark and David nearly came to blows underneath the table over the contents of the last one. Although partially muffled by the table-cloth, words like 'turd' and 'cunt' pinged through the festive atmosphere like rifle bullets.

A freighter steamed majestically past the windows, and Victor scurried across the room to watch it and report on the navigation lights it was using. Somewhere downriver off the Isle of Dogs a ship's siren called plaintively out of the night; everyone, meanwhile, put on paper hats and read each other silly jokes. Ken suddenly rose to his full six and a half feet to lead the orchestra, as several crackers had yielded miniature musical instruments and strips of paper on which were printed a few bars of music.

The Deputy Head of Newham Social Services conducted with lusty brandishings of the bread knife which we had recently used to cut the Christmas cake, while the children blew out their cheeks and puffed mightily; and presently an alarming noise rent the air.

'God protect us!' Peter muttered, stuffing two paper napkins into his ears.

Texel lifted up her muzzle to the ceiling and howled in unison; then she gave a monumental heave before throwing up the contents of her stomach all over our new carpet. Balloons, like demented bumble-bees, flew past me right and left while I knelt on the floor to clear up the mess; children roared by, on their way to visit our famous lavatory, and Emily and Ursula, who had been out to their cars, returned bearing heavy baskets filled with parcels.

The candles were burning low and the presents were arranged in little piles around the base of the tree. A comparative silence had fallen, when you could hear the waves lapping gently against the back of the house — a brief interval during which the Christmas angel passed through the room. Suddenly the children exploded with excitement and parcels were tossed to and fro while shiny wrappings were torn apart. In the midst of all this hubbub, however, I noticed that some of the boys were keeping a sharp eye on us to see how we reacted to the presents which they, personally, had made for us in their pottery classes in school.

David had secured a prominent position in the front for his parcel so that we should open it first. A splendid lifeboat emerged, fashioned in a matt rust-coloured clay with a glazed blue base that he had shaped into snarling waves. The boat had a rudder and tiller, a pair of oars and some rope coiled down on the foredeck.

Next we unwrapped a yellowish-green monster with enormous ears and eyes, made by Victor; then a fat pig money-box, created by Stephen. I say 'created', because it was no common-or-garden pig; its head was tilted to one side, its tail was exceedingly curly and it exuded a strong personality of its own with its quizzical, rather smug expression.

Philip, Jeff and Mark had each made clay pots, two of them glazed, and Mark's had a serpent curled up inside it with its head appearing over the edge. Then there was a collective present from all the boys to *Martha* — a carefully-chosen box containing six sailing-boat coasters and a little wooden vessel whose metal mast and sail transformed themselves into a bottle-opener. Emily gave me a white oiled-wool Galway sweater and Ursula produced a beautifully illustrated book about the working sailing-craft on the River Thames.

Some while later Ken stood up and said he must go as he had to attend a Council meeting at eight o'clock; whereupon everyone began to put on their coats and say 'Goodbye' — everyone except Mark, who appeared to be missing. This gave the boys a good excuse to go exploring upstairs again and it was not long before we tracked him down to the library, curled up in one of the big armchairs like a mouse inside a dog's basket.

'I wouldn't mind livin' here, Rozelle,' he told me when I put my head round the door. 'Yes, I think this place would suit me orright, and I might even try readin' a book if I lived here!'

Our last meeting in 1975 was two days before Christmas. Emily brought seven boys to the London Marina: John, Peter, David, Stephen, Mark, Jeff and a sixteen-year-old boy called Gerald who used to be in Care at the Edith Moorey Home, and had come back to visit some of his old friends.

I told the children that they could choose what they wanted to do because it was holiday-time. The three eldest decided to go fishing and the younger ones asked if they could learn how to take compass bearings — just like Number 1 group had done in Greenwich Park a fortnight ago.

We climbed up on to a rickety iron bridge over a road that led to nowhere and peered across the misty river towards the Kentish shore. They selected a chimney on the edge of Plumstead Marshes and the lighthouse on Margaret Ness, then I showed the boys how to hold the handbearing compass and read off a bearing, and told them to shout the results to Emily and Ursula who would write them down for laying off on the chart. We even went a step further and took some transit bearings (two objects in line), and I explained how very useful they were when finding one's position at sea.

'You wait till old Stitchum gets to hear about this!' David gloated to Stephen (Philip and Victor had gone to visit their Mum that afternoon). 'We'll show 'im how to do somefink he never knew nuffink about before!'

Towards dusk all ten of us squeezed into *Martha*'s cabin to have a 4-course tea: soup, sandwiches, cake, mince-pies and fruit, washed down with a small glass of sherry each. Texel thumped around on the cabin-top while the old boat rocked and glowed in the lamplight; and we were all as warm and happy as a clutch of lemmings in their winter hole.

Chapter 10

A great explosion of fireworks from our neighbour's balcony and the magic call of ship's sirens up and down the river heralded the New Year, 1976. The weather maps were covered with tight little bunches of isobars hurrying eastwards from somewhere out in mid-Atlantic; and up above us the black storm clouds raced across the smoky pink sky.

I drove to Norwich Road later that morning to pick up four of the boys — Victor, David, Stephen and Mark — to take them to the Boatshow at Earl's Court. They were still wearing their smart Christmas clothes, had just finished lunch and were clearly intent on enjoying themselves. I noticed Stephen whispering in Victor's ear as I pulled up, and could picture him saying 'We'll soon make mincemeat of her wivout Auntie Em or Hursula to back her up!'

They greeted me with cherub's smiles, especially Mark; and there was a mini-scrum to get into the back of the car — I had borrowed Dick's four-seater for the outing — so that David, who was slower off the mark, was left to sit with me in front. Emily was very busy in the kitchen preparing for a party that night, but she ran out just as we were leaving to shout: 'Remember what I told you, boys? Any bad behaviour and this will be your *last* outing!'

A sound like piglets grunting came from behind my seat, followed by two words: 'Piss off!' hissed out like snake's spittle so that no one outside the car could hear them.

Managing difficult children and keeping law and order has never been my strong point. I have, in fact, been put to shame on more than one occasion by serious-minded co-helpers who have felt obliged to give me a bit of their minds: 'You really shouldn't set them a bad example like that! Throwing orange peel out of the window, climbing a fence to go exploring where there's a PRIVATE notice, teaching them how to swear in French ... etcetera, etcetera.'

Well, I set off that New Year's day deeply aware of these flaws in my own character; and, perhaps because of them, I had taken the precaution of inviting a very charming and intelligent young woman to join us at the

Boatshow. But the interval between leaving Norwich Road and arriving at Earl's Court proved a testing time, even for me.

Apart from a certain amount of subdued sniggering and a freezing draught round the back of my neck, I thought we were getting across London quite peacefully to begin with.

'Do we need to have all the windows open, boys?' I called over my shoulder. 'My ears are turning into icicles!'

'Sorry, Rozelle, but Chums feels sick in a car if 'e don't 'ave plenty of fresh air,' came Victor's reply, as crisp as a pistol-shot.

About that time I began to notice a curious phenomenon: each time I pulled up at a zebra crossing or red lights, with a pedestrian island in the middle of the road, if there were any Asians waiting to cross they behaved in a very strange way. Many of them appeared to have fierce expressions on their faces, one or two shook their fists at me and one spat at the car, only missing the open window by a fraction of an inch.

'I always thought the Asians were mostly gentle people,' I told the children; 'but we must have struck a bad patch where someone's been stirring up trouble.'

David farted noisily to cover up the gurgling sound that was rising in the back of his throat, and jammed his face against the passenger window so that I could no longer see his profile. I tilted the driving-mirror at a different angle to observe what was going on in the back of the car and drove on across Clerkenwell, feeling like a bird of prey with eyes trained all round it, ready to pounce. I did not have long to wait. At the next traffic lights there was a po-faced family of Bengalis — they may have been delightful people for all I knew — waiting on the central island to cross; rather nervous of being run over and not too sure when to set off. I slowed down, although the lights were still green, in case they should step out at the wrong moment; and, simultaneously, I glanced in the mirror and saw three heads hanging out of the windows with ugly mouths forming obscene words and three sets of fingers making very rude signs; then back to the Bengali family whose faces were contorted with rage as we swept past them.

I pulled up a short distance beyond the crossing, ordered the windows closed immediately and announced that anyone I saw making those racist gestures again could get straight out of the car and walk home. No Boatshow and no more outings.

'All the kids at school go Paki-bashing,' Victor began...

'I don't give a damn what they do at school, they don't while they're out with me.' End of conversation. We drove on to Earl's Court in a prickly silence.

By the time the car was parked and we were approaching the main entrance, I had forgotten about the Asians and we were beginning to enjoy ourselves again: then Joyce loomed ahead, large and smiling, her straight blonde hair swept upwards to form a beehive on top of her head. She surveyed the boys like someone trying to focus a microscope on a group of rare insects; and they, in turn, gazed steadily back at her. In that split second of awareness when an impression hits you with the force of a sledge-hammer, I knew that she despised them and they, realizing this, hated her with a pure unquestioning hatred.

I had chosen Joyce especially to meet my children, as I was beginning to think of them, because she had a very important job to do with making the world a better place to live in. She was forever talking about human rights and improving the conditions of the natives in Africa and of children all over the world; so I thought it would be a splendid chance for her to meet some real live children, even if they were not starving African ones, and to see how she set about helping them.

I prefer, on reflection, to draw a curtain over much of that afternoon. Joyce burbled relentlessly to me about some important conference at which she had delivered her famous speech ('Had I not read it in *The Times?*') on the plight of women and children in the Third World; and I attempted to utter polite noises while my eyeballs were swivelling right and left and my legs running up and down ladders, to keep track of all four boys at once. They wished to visit every boat on display, a desire that soon produced furrowed brows among the boat-salesmen, not to mention my own, as the bulges in their pockets grew larger and larger.

At five o'clock, with the nautical knick-knack shops as yet unexplored, I announced in a school-mistressy voice: 'Time to leave!'

We escaped without a major incident occurring, and what a relief it was to say goodbye to Joyce and drive back across the city. I even allowed a fraction of window to be opened, and put on a tape of the Big Ben Banjo Band to drown the noise going on in the back of the car.

Emily's party was already in full swing when Dick and I pulled up outside the Edith Moorey Home later that evening. The wind, which had begun to shriek in the branches of the bare winter trees, plucked dead leaves off the path and drove them into our faces as we forged our way through the wicket-gate. As soon as we pushed open the front door we were met by a powerful combination of intense excitement, rich cooking smells, distant music, the clinking of glasses and the sort of happy-party-atmosphere that children who grow up in their own homes would take for granted, but for the others it comes only once in a while, like a sparkling jewel pinned to a plain black dress. One of the reasons for this was the presence at the party of some of the boys' closest friends and relatives: Jeff, for instance, was sitting in the biggest armchair hemmed in by his brother and sister whom he adored; Philip and Victor had their mum, and David had his elder brother who lived in a different home in Care. Peter's dad looked in for a few minutes, Mark had his Social Worker and John, who had no one, was being cheered up by Florence, a very sweet nurse from the London Hospital and an old friend of Emily's.

Our hostess made sure that everyone had plenty to eat and drink before we descended into the cellar. She and the boys had been busy working down there since the beginning of the school holidays: first the walls were white-washed, then decorated with some favourite characters from the Comics. Close to where we were standing I could see the Bash Street Kids, Dennis the Menace and more than one Mickey Mouse. Clusters of Chianti bottles hung from nails hammered into the walls, other bottles stood on the tables acting as candle-holders, and the whole scene was lit by red fluorescent lights which gave a warm ruby glow to the cellar and its cheerful inmates.

Emily had been a dancer before she took up social work, and she had given the boys a good grounding in rhythm and how to hold their own on the dance floor. She and they gave a rousing demonstration of the dance of Zorba the Greek, but Ursula could not refrain from wincing when Stephen swept by and called brightly to her: 'Comin' to join us, Hursula?'

Those first encounters with the boys' relatives were something I shall never forget. Very guarded at first, like dogs snuffling round a lamp-post, then the faint flicker of a smile as confidence grew.

'My boys really enjoy going out in that boat of yours,' Margaret (Philip and Victor's mum) confided to me. 'Already they've started talking about joining the Navy!' She grinned broadly and screwed up her eyes at the corners in a friendly way.

Stephen and Mark.

Jeff and his sister.

'I like that woman,' I thought to myself; 'her children really seem to matter to her. Pity she can't make a home for them herself.'

Jeff's brother and sister were very like him — little pale-faced children who never spoke to anyone else nor showed any emotion, one way or the other. They just sat there squeezed tightly against him in the armchair, giving him immense pleasure and comfort by their presence. When the clock struck eleven and someone came to take them home, huge tears welled up in Jeff's eyes and he could no longer bear to watch the dancing and fun that some of the others were having.

The last waltz was danced just before midnight — nearly everyone on the floor, singing, laughing and doing their own special things.

'There's nothing really evil about these children when you look at their faces now, d'you think?' I whispered to Dick. Then I remembered the Asians crossing roads and the anxious salesmen at the Boatshow.

'No; they just get easily led at times, but they're no worse than many who come from so-called good homes.'

Outside in the dark night the wind had risen to hurricane force and the trees were alive with wildly flailing branches, while fierce clouds raced across the face of the moon. But the glow of Emily's party lingered on, untouched by all the harsh happenings in the world outside the Edith Moorey Home.

Some of the pontoons broke adrift at the London Marina that night. Dick and I hurried down there next morning to find that *Martha* was safe, but *Water-Rat* had disappeared. Eventually we found her wedged into a corner on the far side of the dock, so we fetched the oars and rowed her back to our pontoon.

I had received a number of strong hints at Emily's party, delivered to me personally by the boys who had not been part of the Boatshow expedition; so I drove across to Norwich Road a few days later, picked up Emily, Philip, John, Peter and Jeff, then over to Ursula's home in Highbury for lunch.

While we were doing the washing-up after our meal, Peter edged me to one side and whispered: 'How come your place is so different from this one, Rozelle? They might be on two different planets, see what I mean?'

'No, I don't,' I growled, beginning to feel rather bristly. 'I don't know what you find so different about them?'

'Well, Ursula's home, even though it's a lot smaller, is really neat and tidy, whichever way you look. See that mantelpiece? No ornaments and not a speck of dust — I just ran my fingers along it! And there's no ship models on the windowsills nor books all over the place nor bits of car engines lying about in the armchairs. And take the barfroom; it's like one of them show places you see on telly. I bet you'd never find sails and bits of ole rope 'anging up in there to dry!'

'Have you finished before I clout you round the ears!' I began . . .

'Don't get all worked up,' he put a soothing hand over my clenched fists; ''Cos I really like your place and I'd never get bored there!'

That afternoon our visit to the Boatshow was a very different affair to the previous one. Three demure young teenagers and a small boy with a big grin, accompanied by three grown-ups with a single purpose: to make sure the children behaved well and to enjoy being at the Boatshow themselves. I managed to find the stand where Mr Chippendale, who built *Martha* in 1953, was displaying some of his famous dinghies and introduced him to the boys, which gave pleasure all round.

Several hours later Emily, Ursula and I were tired of climbing about on boats and being jostled by the crowds, so we took the boys to have tea and said we were soon going home. The three eldest wanted to stay on till closing time and, much to my surprise, Emily agreed to this and gave them some money so that they could find their way home on the Underground.

'Must get them used to being responsible and finding their own way across London,' she explained, as we left Earl's Court with Jeff between us and walked to the street where Ursula's car was parked.

After the boys had gone back to school and Ursula to visit friends in the country, a quiet period ensued: a period of rubbing down *Martha*'s paintwork in preparation for the springtime; of teaching a rather subdued group of children about grease-caps, water-pumps and carburettors; and climbing on to the rickety iron bridge over the road that led to nowhere to take sights of far-away chimneys. Then there would follow the last half-hour when the boys set off in both dinghies to row to their secret harbour while Emily and I lit the stove, filled the kettle and chatted about this and that.

On January 20th it was Number 2 group's Tuesday, with a cold gusty wind and brilliant shafts of sunlight escaping through the close-packed clouds. I had just finished painting *Martha*'s cabin and was not anxious to have anyone inside it, let alone four little boys with sticky fingers firing off coke cans at each other; so I phoned Emily and said 'Why don't we go for an expedition today? I know a place called Purfleet where we can have our picnic on a little hill above the river, then do some Rule of the Road questions about all the ships that go by down there, and take lots of sights with the handbearing compass.'

Everyone enjoyed an expedition — somewhere new to explore, the uncertainty of what might happen to us, a whole range of exciting possibilities sprang to mind... I brought Texel along too, and we all crowded into Emily's station-wagon as soon as the boys came home from morning school.

'Is there a beach where we're going, Auntie?' Jeff nudged my arm. 'Will I be able to build a sand-castle?'

'No, it's not that sort of place at all,' I hastened to tell the boys. 'It's a nice spot on the river with a green hill on one side and a pub on the other. When we've had our lunch we're going to do some work, see? I chose it because there are lots of beacons and chimneys on the far side of the river, so you'll be able to get plenty of practice in taking transit bearings as well as ordinary ones.'

Jeff looked depressed, while Stephen and David told each other jokes in the back of the car and Philip put his arms round Texel and whispered something in one of her ears. Emily called over her shoulder: 'I hope you took in what Rozelle just said to you, boys? It's not a holiday today.'

Some while later we pulled into a parking space on one side of the Royal Hotel at Purfleet and David asked: 'Where's the hill where we was goin' to have our picnic?'

'Well, there used to be a little green hill just over there, last time we sailed by here in *Martha*,' I pointed miserably towards a mountain of sand and builders' rubble. 'But it looks as if they've started building a new housing estate there now!'

I could have burst into tears when I surveyed my shattered dream — the little green hill with the cosy pub beside it, and all the tugs and tramps and freighters steaming by. Even the pub had grown out of all recognition, with ugly modern limbs attached to its rickety old body.

Texel and the boys burst out of the Corsair and sniffed the air. It was blowing a gale from somewhere downriver, and there were patches of sapphire-blue sky with clouds like woolly lambs sprinting across it; first a dark gloomy patch, then a dazzle of sunbeams shining straight in your eyes out of a hole in the clouds. The tide was ebbing hard, transforming the river into a troop of white horses charging against the fierce wind from the sea. A tug with a tow of barges came chugging down Long Reach, its bows enveloped in spindrift and a man with a red rag tied round his head waving to us from the stern of the last barge.

'If it was night-time now, what lights would that tug be showing?' I asked Philip, as we spread out our lunch on the riverbank.

'Three white lights, one on top of the uvver, down its mast, and a red light on the left side and a green one on the right. And it might carry a small white light just behind its funnel for the geezer on the barge to steer by, but you're not allowed to see that light if you was ahead.'

'Very good indeed!' I grinned happily. 'And can you, Stephen, tell me why the tug carries three masthead lights?'

'To show it's a tug wiv a tow of more'ven . . . er' (he watched my lips which were forming the words subconsciously) 'six hundred feet long!'

We all cheered and Emily's eyes sparkled as she said: 'Sure, they've been doing their homework since you last saw them, Rozelle!'

We had almost finished our sandwiches when Jeff announced that he wanted to go to the toilet, so Emily and I told the other boys that we would take him into the pub and buy them some extra cokes for being so clever today. I asked Philip to look after Texel while we were inside.

A few minutes later we returned and were making for the Corsair to get the compass, when I noticed that the boys and dog had completely disappeared.

'That's funny, they were here two minutes ago,' Emily looked thoughtful. 'I bet they're up to some kind of mischief.'

I whistled loudly and Texel popped up on the summit of the builders' rubble, wagging her tail furiously and prancing about to show that she was having fun. Jeff had set off at full speed towards her so Emily and I followed, forgetting all about the compass and the chimneys on the far side of the river.

'Com'un join us,' Stephen called out from the bottom of a sand-pit. 'It's wicked down here!'

Then something extraordinary occurred. Emily and I sniffed the strong air which was spiced with salt, mud, seaweed and funnel-smoke; and we looked at the children who seemed as carefree and happy as a litter of puppies. And the next moment we had grabbed a couple of planks and were zooming down that mountain of rubble like tobogganists on the Cresta Run. Texel was barking her head off and leaping around on top of us while the boys shrieked with excitement.

'Let's 'ave a race, all six of us!' David bawled from the top of the mound. So we climbed up again, our clothes and hands coated with mud and sand;

and as soon as Philip gave the signal, off we went with Emily gaining speed on the rest of us, much to the boys' disgust.

'She hurtles down there, fast as a bleedin' oil-drum,' Stephen complained to the others as we scrambled out of the sand-pit.

Everyone wanted to be the winner so we slid down that slope over and over again. Then Jeff started building his sand-castle and Texel went paddling in the river with Philip, while David and Stephen dug a deep trench. Emily and I sat on top of the mound watching the clouds sailing across the blue heavens and the ships chugging up and down Long Reach.

'Let's hope Miss O'Brien never gets to hear about today,' I said.

'Nor Peter Cobb and Ken Boyce!' She clutched her sides and roared with laughter.

A deep-sea tug, the Avenger.

★　★　★

Chapter 11

February 1976 was full of ups and downs — steep hills and deep valleys — but the summit of the tallest hill was undoubtedly reached on the day we all went to France.

Before that, however, there were some sad and dark days caused by Texel's slipped disc. She had, by that time, become an important member of the gang — a dog who took part in our work and play, and whose presence lent a warm and familiar touch to our Tuesday afternoons.

We took her away to the country one weekend and she jumped over a fence in pursuit of a rabbit; and that was how the trouble first started. Some Tuesdays she would sit motionless at the end of our pontoon, shrunk into her fur with a tragic look in her eyes. And on one such day, when I was about to take some of the children for a sail round the dock in *Martha*, Philip asked if he could stay behind with Texel. Each time we came close to our berth, I could see him sitting there with his arms round her, holding her tight.

I stopped at the Cyprus store to buy some bread on the way home that evening.

'Where you bin, doll? We ain't seen nuffink of you since Christmas,' the sisters greeted me; then one of them adjusted her spectacles and peered into my face. 'Everyfink orright, is it, darlin'?' she asked sympathetically. 'I jus' thought you didn't look quite your ole self, know what I mean?'

So I told them about Texel who was sitting outside in the car. The younger sister got a meat pie out of the fridge, and she came outside with one or two customers to have a look at the dog and watch her eat the pie. It was a great treat and Texel's eyes brightened up for a moment as she leant forward to receive a morsel, but the stretching of her neck made her yelp with pain.

'Poor little sod!' remarked one of the customers, blowing his nose hard to cover up the moisture in his eyes. 'Dawgs is better'n 'umans in my opinion, fer what it's worf. You take 'er up the dawg's 'orspital, girl, an' see if they can't do nuffink to 'elp 'er.'

We already had; several times. But I drove her back to Whipps Cross next morning, and the vet said he would give her a cortisone injection and put her on a course of penicillin.

'If that doesn't work, the only thing left is to try an operation,' he told me. 'The trouble with a dog is that it can't tell you exactly where the pain lies, so you just have to hope you find the right disc.'

I came across an entry in the log-book soon after this which said: 'Bitterly cold, with an easterly gale blowing. Went to the London Marina to do some work on *Martha*. I could not start the engine and it was very rough (even in the dock). I felt sick!'

Another dismal Tuesday was the one on which the polar conditions made rowing round the dock a miserable pastime, and even the boys were quite pleased to go back to Norwich Road in mid-afternoon to do some chartwork. Peter and Victor both liked navigational problems, but John suddenly announced that he did not want to be part of the group any longer — he would sooner stay at school!

The following week a few watery sunbeams escaped through the clouds to shine down on the old boat. Stephen arrived wearing a thick red and white sweater, swaggering about like a young peacock.

'I've brought my project for you at last!' he shouted as he came running along the pontoon. 'What a pity Hursula's not here so she could see it too.'

It was bound inside a stiff blue cover entitled 'Rokeby School' and I opened it, by chance, at a page that seemed very advanced for an eleven-year-old, as it explained the theory of sailing by means of a sketch showing the counteraction between wind and water pressure on the sails and keel of a boat.

Deeply impressed with my first glimpse, I turned to Page 1 and saw a number of drawings of objects to be found on a chart with their names and uses written below them; this page was called 'A Little Navigation'. Other pages followed describing the different parts of a boat, with a diagram to show where to find them; some details about a sailing-yacht race from Australia to New Zealand; a list of thirteen types of boats, the second one being called *Martha Margildar*; and, 'A few Things needed for Sailing', which included an anchor, a life-jacket and some simple sales!

A charming sketch of a 3-masted schooner steering towards a distant conical buoy came next, then a page entitled 'A person', which began: 'There is a lady called Miss Rozelle who is a Famers lady, to me that is, who offered to take some people sailing. The headmistress is coming with a few boys. This person has been to France and Germany and to other places as well. The name of her boat is *Martha Margildar* and it has been hundreds of miles . . .' Then followed half a page of advice to those who had never been on a boat before.

There were a few boating photographs and short essays such as 'The First Gide for Sailing' and 'Rowing-boats with Several Oarsmen', and on the final page I came upon a remarkable drawing of a sailing-boat with a rather frightened-looking helmsman doing amazing things in a very rough sea.

'Well, I think that's a splendid book,' I told the boy; 'and I shall always keep it and show it to other people with great pride.'

Stephen had a glowing pink face as he turned to the others to see how they were taking it. But this proved a disappointing business as Philip was engaged in teaching Jeff how to tie a reef knot and David, who did not much care for these showy displays of penmanship, had gone missing.

'See if you can find him, will you?' Emily urged Stephen. 'You know the sort of places where he's likely to be.'

Stephen stomped off along the waterfront looking rather surly, but it was one of the men who worked in the mechanic's shop who brought David back.

'Nearly killed 'isself, 'e did!' exclaimed his rescuer, agitating his arms dramatically. ''E was up in the electric box above the bridge dickering around with the wires when I 'appens to look up — just in the nick of time!'

A touch of drama was something David never could resist, and what better moment to choose than a time when Weapon was lapping up all the glory!

Despite such excitements, things had taken a definite turn for the better by mid-February; also Texel was responding well to her latest treatment and had lost the terrible pain-racked expression in her eyes.

'Move over, Skunk!' Mark gave Jeff a sharp dig in the ribs with his right elbow. 'There's uvver people waiting to 'ave a squint in that box.'

It was February 23rd and we were, all fourteen of us — Ken Boyce, Peter Cobb, Emily and Veronica, the eight boys, Dick and I — up on the bridge of the Channel ferry *Free Enterprise V*, crossing the Dover Straits to France. I had worked as a purser on the first *Free Enterprise* and my old captain, Jack Dawson, who was by then Commodore of the Townsend Ferries, had arranged for our party to visit the bridge and engine-room during the voyage.

The boys, who had never been abroad before nor travelled on such a big ship, were thrilled to find themselves in the Captain's kingdom while all the ordinary passengers were huddled down below. When Mark had taken Jeff's place at the radar screen, I thought Jeff was about to pee in his pants with the excitement of his surroundings, so I rushed him down below to find the toilets. On our return I overheard Peter questioning the Chief Officer about his chances of being able to join the Merchant Navy now that he had to wear glasses; and Philip and Victor were pointing at various objects on the chart while they proudly showed off their navigational knowledge in front of the quartermaster.

The whole gang on the wing of the bridge aboard Free Enterprise V.
Jeff, me, Big Peter, Veronica, Philip, Dick, Emily, John, Little Peter.
Front row: Victor, David Stephen and Mark.

We went out on a wing of the bridge to catch our first glimpse of France. It was a magic moment for some of the party as they peered at the grey hump of Cap Gris Nez and took big gulps of the cold salty wind that plucked at their hair and clothes.

Veronica wore a headscarf patterned with brilliant autumn leaves and a big grin on her face as she seized the binoculars from John and stared at Calais Town Hall. 'It looks like a pink you-know-what from here,' she announced; 'and I can see some Frogs on the beach without any clothes on!'

'Get away with you, woman,' Peter Cobb grabbed the binoculars from her. 'I'll put you on the next boat back to Dover if you don't behave yourself!'

'Just you try, man!' she roared happily. 'Just you try.'

Jeff, meanwhile, had opened the lid of a life-jacket locker behind us and climbed inside. 'Look, Auntie!' he yelled. 'Come'n take a pitcher of me!'

Emily was talking to an officer on the other side of the bridge so I took Jeff's photograph. But a moment later she was beside me, white-faced with anger: 'Get out of that box at once, child,' she heaved him out by grabbing him under the armpits. 'Sure, you look just like a corpse inside its coffin!'

We all laughed at this, but we were to remember the incident seven years later and to wonder if Emily did not possess some uncanny power to look into the future.

We landed a few minutes later, and set off to walk from the car-ferry berth to the beach. The boys had noticed some ruined buildings in rough scrubby surroundings close to the harbour entrance, and they soon found their way back there to go exploring, play hide and seek and swing like monkeys from the crumbling rafters. This made Dick exceedingly anxious.

'Supposing one of them breaks his neck?' he appealed to Ken. 'We're responsible, and there'd be plenty of people ready to blame us for not looking after them properly.'

Ken made soothing noises and Big Peter said 'Calm yourself, Vicar; it might never happen! You can't keep the kids locked up in a safe little box till they're grown up. They don't have much of a life as it is, but they must spread their wings whenever there's a chance and find out about danger and excitement on their own. Why, think of all the risks we take when they go sailing, but look at the marvellous things it's doing for some of them; even old Jeff, who was boasting to me about what happens when he's allowed to be Captain!'

Slightly reassured, Dick tried not to worry; and soon after this the boys began to feel hungry and hint that it was time for lunch.

We had all brought sandwiches, fruit and thermoses of soup or coffee, and we found a good place to squat on the quayside above the small fishing-boat harbour, known as the Bassin du Petit Paradis. The boys had cans of coke to drink and the grown-ups were just opening a bottle of wine when a voice from below called up, '*A votre santé, mesdames messieurs!*'

'What's that geezer on about?' John nudged me and glared suspiciously down at the fisherman.

'He's just wishing us good health,' I told him. 'People are very polite over here.'

I looked at our party, by now comfortably established around the Little Paradise Basin, and noticed for the first time how colourful we were: Ken, who was clearly Monsieur le Commandant, wore a smart blazer over an emerald-green and pillarbox-red jersey, his curly black hair giving him the air of a Spanish matador. Big Peter, on the other hand, wore a blue and white striped pullover, above puce-pink trousers, and looked every inch a Londoner. Emily was encased in a Bugatti-blue anorak which made her eyes gleam like sapphires; and the boys had all chosen their own special brands of eye-catching feathers with which to dazzle the Frogs. Philip wore a sky-blue jersey, Peter and Jeff had both settled for purple, Victor's red T-shirt announced 'Up the Hammers!' while Emily's proclaimed 'Elvis I love you!'

John wore a yellow and brown sweater, and most of the boys sported smart new trousers — dark corduroys, brown and burgundy tweeds and the latest cut in jeans; all except Stephen, who stood out from the rest of the gang in a white polo-necked Galway sweater and a pair of elegant tartan pants!

David and Big Peter having lunch on the quayside above the Little Paradise Basin in Calais.

'I'm never going to be Mr Average. I'm going to be someone *big* one day very soon,' he was to tell me ten years later.

'Vous avez une grande famille, Monsieur; oh là là!' exclaimed our fisherman friend to Dick, while he drained the glass of wine that my husband had offered him in one gulp.

Dick laughed and asked about the fishing along the French coast, while the children formed themselves into a tight little bunch, wearing their 'Beware-of-all-Frogs' expressions.

'Come on, boys, clear up this mess — *not* into the harbour, but wait till you find a litter-bin.' Emily and Veronica soon had our picnic place looking clean and tidy, while the fisherman sucked his teeth noisily and called up, '*Vive l'Angleterre!*'

Dick had suggested a visit to the Port de Plaisance, the yacht harbour of Calais, as the man in charge was an old friend of ours. This proved a doubtful success, however, as Little Peter and Victor were the only ones who showed any interest in the boats, while the others glared angrily at Monsieur Bessodés who gabbled away to us in French, while he surveyed our big family without pleasure.

'There's only one hour left to go shopping, Dick!' David tugged at his sleeve impatiently; 'and me and Weapon want to buy some presents for me mum and his nan.'

Each boy had been given a small amount of extra pocket-money to spend on the outing, so we gathered the party together and strode off towards the main street in Frogtown. The boys had already made it clear to us that they wished to do their shopping on their own — all except Jeff who clung to Emily's hand. No more sightseeing nor tiresome grown-ups interfering with their private affairs; and if there was some spare time at the end, could we go back to the ruins near the harbour entrance which attracted them far more than a visit to the castle or the Town Hall.

'Well, it's their treat — their big day abroad,' Ken reasoned with Dick; 'so we must give them a bit of freedom to find their own feet in France.'

Dick nodded doubtfully, and at that moment a purple-faced woman appeared at the door of her shop, shaking a small boy like a terrier might a rat. '*Petit salaud Anglais!*' she spat; '*espèce de crapule!*' And a moment later Mark was discharged on to the pavement with considerable force.

His face was pink and blotchy with fury and he swung round to make rude signs at the woman just as Veronica caught his right shoulder with an iron grip and propelled him away from the shop. Strolling along the main street, we soon came upon further signs of deterioration in Anglo/French relations; nothing quite as dramatic as the first encounter but there were rumblings in the undergrowth, so to speak.

David cannoned into me round a corner, the whites of his eyes gleaming like double cream, and asked in a hoarse whisper, 'What's *'espess dee cochon'* mean, Rozelle?' And there was a noisy fracas taking place inside another shop where Little Peter was counting up his change and bellowing to Victor: 'The dirty cow's swindled me!'

'I think the Calais shop-keepers won't be sorry to see the last of us,' I remarked to Ken. 'How about us suggesting that they do the rest of their shopping in the souvenir shop on our ship going home?'

Everyone thought this was a brilliant idea, so we rounded off our visit to France with a carefree half-hour among the ruins, followed by a very successful few minutes in a waterside café near the lighthouse. The children sipped their glasses of watered-down *'vin rouge'* with faces wreathed in smiles of entrancing sweetness, and Big Peter nearly burst a blood-vessel when Madame came over to our table to declare: '*Vous avez une très charmante famille, mesdames messieurs!*'

'She should have seen the little buggers up the High Street,' he remarked to me, while Mark stretched himself luxuriously, inhaled the thick Gallic atmosphere of garlic, Pernod and Gaulloise tobacco, then purred like a contented tabby-cat.

'I like this caff,' he informed Dick. 'Bit o' the real ole France, the way me and Vic pitchered it 'fore we come here. Wait till I tell me mates at school about it!'

Dick promised to wait and, soon afterwards, we rounded up the gang, paid the bill and hurried back to the car-ferry terminal to board *Free Enterprise IV* for our return voyage to Dover.

Peace reigned at last. It was a dark roughish night and half the children were asleep in big chairs in the lounge, while the remaining ones finished their shopping or played with the fruit machines on the lower deck.

'Well, there's still fourteen of us in sight and no one got nicked by the French police after all!' Ken commented; 'so I'd say it's been a pretty successful outing, all things considered.'

We nodded our heads in agreement and Veronica pointed to a brilliant light flashing through a porthole and said: 'Looks like we'll soon be home again.'

A few minutes later the quartermaster announced 'Harbour Stations' over the Tannoy and, at the same time, the most magic things began to happen: Dick and I were busy collecting together our bits and pieces when a group of little boys surrounded us, each one still wearing his French-café-style expression and holding out a gift towards us!

I almost burst into tears for I had imagined all the shopping traumas were entirely for their own benefit, or for those who had a mother or brother who still kept in touch. But no; there we sat surrounded by miniature Townsend ferries, replicas of the Eiffel Tower, shell bracelets and tiny lighthouses inside snowstorms. And suddenly the ship's side bumped against the jetty and everyone began to scramble ashore.

Chapter 12

Martha motored out of the lock on March 2nd, her first escape to the river since the previous autumn. It was a silvery-grey afternoon with a fine mist softening the sharp edges along the Kentish shore, transforming the sailing-barge moored close to Margaret Ness Lighthouse into a type of dream-ship.

Emily had come with Philip, David and Stephen that day, and we turned sharp right beyond the lock gates and sailed swiftly upriver with a southerly breeze to fill the sails and the flood tide dancing along beside our straining hull. *Martha* had come to life again after all those months of creeping around inside the dank basin, and rubbing down, scraping, painting and varnishing with frozen fingers and icicles suspended from the tips of our noses.

We had a good sail that afternoon with everyone responding to the call of the river and the smell of freedom outside the lock gates. I switched off the motor after the narrow gully of the Woolwich Barrier through which the tide runs at an alarming speed; and each boy steered in turn for the next hour, showing off his skill and concentration in a way that I would not have thought possible a few months before.

'Who says Number 1 load of scumbags is the best group?' demanded David, waving a back-splice in front of my nose.

Stephen, who was helmsman at that moment and steering better than ever before, made a smart tack behind the Woolwich ferry, hauled in the jib-sheet on the starboard side and declared that Number 1 group were a pack of turds in his opinion.

Emily and I took turns at steering on the way back along Woolwich Reach. The wind had backed easterly and freshened suddenly, with ice-cold gusts that whipped up the river into a grey and white cauldron and drew gasps from those who were facing that way. A final note in the log-book that afternoon records: '1630 — Moored up alongside our pontoon and lit both stoves to thaw out. Had an enormous tea in the cabin. It's been a lovely day!'

★ ★ ★

Texel died the following week. The cortisone had only worked for a short while and the operation was not a success — the vet had warned us it would be a fifty-fifty chance.

People said that dogs of her size only had a ten-year life span anyway, so why didn't we get a young puppy to help us forget? But we did not want to forget Texel — ever; so we stayed as we were and carried on with life. I told myself that people lose their pets every day of the week; but, whichever way you looked at it, we still felt sad and diminished for a long while afterwards, and so did some of the children when she was no longer with us on a Tuesday afternoon.

Emily brought Peter and Victor the following Tuesday — a bitterly cold day with no wind at all. John had left the group and Mark had been playing truant from school, so he was forbidden to come as a punishment. This was a practice which often made me angry in the months ahead when the boys were working for their nautical exams.

The four of us had lunch in the cockpit, then did some tidal problems at which Victor excelled. The first one he solved was one that it had taken me some while to compose, hoping that he would not discover the hidden trap: 'What tidal allowances would you make for a boat sailing from Wick to an oil-rig twenty miles out in the North Sea due east of the harbour, leaving at 1000 on March 17th, 1976, with an average speed of 5 knots?'

Peter scratched his head furiously and gnawed his pencil while he wrestled with Reed's Almanac and the North Sea Tidal Atlas. Already he had developed a special 'feel' for engines — an instinctive knowledge of how to cure some of their ailments and gentle fingers when it came to probing inside intricate components like a carburettor or water-pump. But pure brainwork filled with numbers and tiny arrows darting to and fro across a series of miniature charts was not his favourite occupation, although his determination to do as well as Victor caused him to work as if his life depended upon solving each problem.

Peter and hard work were two things you could safely link together, whatever the task: making a model boat, polishing the brass barometer, working on the engine, rowing the dinghy...He never frittered away his time and, because he remained rather a loner, he was rarely diverted by his mates into bird-witted escapades.

Victor, on the other hand, had made up his mind to go to sea when he grew up and, although he seldom worked as hard as Peter, he was completely dedicated to this shining objective. Both boys knew that it was not easy to get into the Royal Navy or Merchant Navy without special qualifications, but already Peter was gripped by the awful fear that however hard he worked he might not be accepted because of his eyesight; and his talk with the Chief Officer on *Free Enterprise V* had done nothing to allay his fears.

After we had finished our tidal problems we drove to St Katharine's Dock to visit the *Great Britain II*, an enormous yacht which had just won the *Financial Times'* Clipper Race around the world. It was a strange experience to stand on that vast uncluttered deck and picture the arm-power required to haul in on those monster winches; or to conjure up the Spartan lives of the off-duty watch, existing belowdecks in the bare cabin; or to exchange a few words with some of the crew members who were clearly living on a different wave length to us puny mortals.

But the highlight of that Tuesday was our visit to the old Nore lightship, where we found a warm and cosy interior and an old seaman in charge who encouraged the boys to climb up into the light-tower, all over the engine-room and anywhere else they fancied.

'Bit of or'right, this ship!' Victor bellowed at me as he swung from a loose halliard above our heads — a happy monkey in its palm-tree.

The lightship guardian, the soul of tact and never one to spoil a beautiful moment, waved a length of plaited rope above his head and called up: 'I bet you two young sailors don't know how to tie half the knots we've got on display down here?'

A challenge was a sure way to get the monkeys out of the rigging — also a chance for them to show off their skills in front of an appreciative stranger. All of us were soon squatting on the wheel-house floor making sheepshanks, monkey's fists, bowlines-on-the-bight and various other devil-knots, with the old man as our referee.

'You lads really know a thing or two!' declared our new friend. 'I wouldn't mind bettin' you'll be sea captins one of these fine days!'

He went down to his cabin and returned with two table-mats — perfect examples of the patience and skill that the old sailors wove into their ropework. 'These are for you,' he said, giving one to each of the boys; 'two bits of ropework that I done when we was anchored on the edge of the sands — all them long winter nights with nothin' much goin' on out in the estuary.'

Nice old bloke, wasn't he?' Peter remarked in the car on the way home. 'I really enjoyed meself on that lightship.'

'Wait till I show this to the uvvers,' Victor grinned, ruffling the back of Emily's hair with his rope mat.

'We'll wait!' we grunted, knowing full well what the outcome would be.

Ursula returned to London at the end of the month, and she and I drove down to Lymington on a glorious spring day to collect *Martha*'s new mainsail. It had been made by the grandson of Richard Turrell McMullen, of 'Down Channel' fame, and it was a beautiful piece of workmanship that he spread out on the floor of his sail-loft for us to inspect. His was a small business compared with the great sailmakers of Cowes and Burnham, but you felt that each stitch had been completed with loving care and some special magic sewn into that huge triangle of rust-red Terylene which would soon transmit itself to the boat for which it was destined.

Before returning to London, Ursula and I had lunch at the Angel Inn with an old friend, Nyria Dawson, whose father, Montague, had painted us a picture of *Martha* as a surprise present the previous Christmas. She was portrayed on a close reach, sailing magnificently across a rough sea with a

Thames sailing-barge on her starboard bow beating to windward in a stately manner; this helped to accentuate the speed and glory of *Martha*'s passage across the dancing waves.

After lunch we went back to Nyria's home to gaze in wonder at some of her father's finest paintings: Cape-Horners weathering fantastic gales, tall clippers ghosting along in the moonlight, the night ferry approaching the Needles and a splendid picture of buccaneers landing their booty on some remote Pacific island.

★   ★   ★

The last Tuesday before the end of the Easter holidays was a bitterly cold day with intermittent snow showers, so we decided to take two cars and drive to Windsor Safari Park. There were ten of us that day: Emily, Veronica, Ursula and I, and six of the boys.

'We're not doin' any work today, O.K., Rozelle?' Mark wished to establish right at the beginning.

'That'll be a nice change for you, boy, after all that hard work you did last term!' Veronica fell about laughing.

'You got me all wrong, Auntie,' Mark looked offended. 'Miss O'Brien was really pleased wiv the way I handled the boat an' all the fings I'd learnt 'bout ship's lights an' fog signals an' uvver fings.'

'Go on, tell us more . . . ?' Veronica urged.

We ate our picnic lunch in Emily's station-wagon — it was far too cold outside; then we drove slowly round the park peering at sleepy lions and bashful leopards who glared at us without pleasure. We had booked seats in the dolphinarium for 'The Show That Will Make Your Hair Stand On End!' as it was billed outside the arena, so we returned there at three o'clock and sat on long wooden benches above the pool.

The first half-hour was taken up with some fine displays of dolphins leaping through hoops and performing extraordinary acrobatics with their trainer — clearly they loved to show off in front of an audience. The children, however, were just beginning to yawn and chatter to one another about West Ham's chances when a big shark swam into the pool. The trainer persuaded him to open his mouth, squeezed some toothpaste on to a giant brush and proceeded to clean the shark's teeth with his hand and one arm right inside the creature's mouth.

Victor let out a deep sigh and whispered, 'Cor! Doesn't he look like Mr Roberts!'

Mr Roberts was head of the fifth year pupils at Rokeby School, a man with sharp white teeth who knew how to handle teenage villians.

When the tooth-cleaning business was finished, the shark snapped his ivories together with a wicked glint in his tiny eyes and began to chase the dolphins round the pool. But the faster he swam the more the laughing dolphins swerved about and leapt in the air, while the audience cheered them on and roared with excitment.

After a sluggish start, the shark had certainly saved our day. Stephen summed up the general opinion when he declared: 'It's bin the sort of day you don't never forget, but I wouldn't want to risk my head inside a shark's mouf, would you, Hursula?'

★ ★ ★

Before the boys came to the London Marina again, I pumped the oil out of the gearbox — a vile messy task — and noticed that it was full of metal chippings. After this sobering discovery, I cleaned out the bilges with some strong detergent, then refilled the gearbox with fresh oil and took *Martha* for a run round the dock to make sure that all was well.

Tony Cohen was fluttering about like a startled pigeon when I returned, and there were several police-cars parked at the end of the pontoons.

'What's up? Someone nicked all the cash?' I asked him as we passed each other.

'No, nothing ordinary like that, worst luck. They've found a stiff in one of the yachts on B pontoon and he didn't die of natural causes neither — nothing respectable like a heart attack, see what I mean! Keep your mouth buttoned up, won't you, love?'

He was whisked away by one of the detectives, a worried man with the reputation of his marina at stake.

By the following Tuesday the news had leaked to the Newham press and the boys were full of morbid curiosity as they goggled at B pontoon.

'I wonder if he's still lurking inside one of the boats?' David gave a theatrical shudder.

'Who are you talking about?' Ursula asked sharply.

'The murderer of course! The man what done 'im in.'

'Don't be silly. I expect he's safely locked up in a police-cell by now.'

It appeared that the owner of the boat had been a business man from the Midlands, and he was pursued to London by someone who bore him a violent grudge. The murderer had lurked in the Gallion's Hotel until his quarry drove up to the marina, knowing that he might catch him unawares aboard his yacht.

'Puts you off exploring in places like the old Gallion's, don't it?' Stephen mused.

'And a good thing too.' Ursula pursed her lips and looked quite fierce.

'I saw my big bruvver dead,' Geoff informed us. 'There was a rope round 'is neck and 'e was 'anging from a...'

'Let's get on with putting on *Martha*'s new mainsail, shall we?' Ursula interrupted him, causing as much commotion as she could by pulling the sail out of its bag on top of everyone sitting in the cockpit.

Philip and David helped us feed the slides into the boom track and attach the shackle on the main halliard to the head of the sail. Emily, Stephen and Jeff, meanwhile, laid out our lunch in the cockpit. It was masticated very slowly that day, what with the murder to mull over and the scene of the crime only a stone's throw away. At last the boys finished and we cleared away the debris and hoisted the new sail. The breeze whipped it to and fro

The new mainsail fitted perfectly and the sun shone . . .

and each boy, in turn, sprinkled a few drops of rum over it to christen it and wish it luck!

It was a sparkling day out on the river, and Jeff was our star helmsman sailing on a broad reach downriver to Dagenham. The tide was just beginning to flood so we tacked back upstream to the Woolwich Barrier, then motored through the gap and on to Bugsby's Hole below East Greenwich where we dropped anchor. Stephen was the one who had the honour of dropping the anchor — for the first time ever — while Philip volunteered for the less glamorous task of hauling it up a few minutes later. He and David then cleaned the mud off the flukes and lashed it down on the foredeck.

The new mainsail fitted perfectly, the sun shone out of a flawless blue sky and a family of ducks quacked excitedly as *Martha* sped across their course. Philip, who was steering a compass course just then, looked up and said: 'That's three new things we done today, Auntie: christened the new sail, anchored the boat and steered a compass course for the first time. We're really goin' places today, aren't we?'

'You'll be going places in a minute if you don't watch out, boy!' Emily laughed, heaving the tiller hard over to port with her thigh. 'You didn't by any chance notice the Woolwich ferry bearing down on us, did you?'

Philip said he never, while Jeff climbed up on to the cabin-top to wave to the captain of the ferry which scraped past us with a few inches to spare.

The boys rowed *Water-Rat* over to their secret harbour after our return; and a few minutes later we heard frantic shrieks coming from the far corner of the dock. A window flew up in the dockmaster's office and I noticed a pair of binoculars being focused on to something down below. Ursula emerged from the cabin with our own binoculars at that moment, and levelled them at the corner where the action was taking place.

'Good God!' she exclaimed, her face white with horror; 'I do believe one of them's fallen in!'

We flew round that dock with wings on our feet and there was David, a dripping woebegone figure surrounded by the other children, the lockmaster and his assistant and a few men from the mechanic's shop — the centre of attention at last. As soon as we had joined the throng he relived his ducking for our benefit, almost walking backwards off the end of the pontoon for the second time in his desire to give us a realistic demonstration of what had happened!

Since the previous November I had kept a large bath-towel and complete set of spare clothing aboard *Martha*, so David was soon dry and back in the cockpit for tea.

'Perhaps you'd better have a drop of rum to warm you up?' I suggested; but the hissing and groaning noises became so deafening that I quickly amended it to 'Perhaps we'll all have a drop of rum in our tea!'

I broke the bottle of rum out of the bilges for the second time that day — it was becoming quite a habit — and the tea was lapped up with loud smacking noises to denote general approval.

The sky was as bright as heaven and the wind as warm as a tropical night. It was the summer half-term holiday so *Martha* was filled with children — no chance of sticking to the rigid 4-boy rule on such a day.

We set off at ten o'clock that morning, bound for Greenhithe — *Martha's* farthest ever voyage downriver with the boys aboard. Our favourite lock-keeper lowered the water very gently when he perceived the number of legs hanging over the gunwale and the monkey-house noises issuing from the old boat. 'Have a good time,' he called after us; 'and watch out for all those big washers!'

Philip and Mark were the first pair to occupy the steering position, making it clear to all of us that extra people down that end of the boat would get in the way of their powerful thrusts at the tiller.

'I rely on you to watch the river for shipping and make sure he steers properly,' I whispered to Philip rather anxiously.

Mark was wearing his cherub's expression — gleaming eyes the shape of sugar-almonds shaded by a thick blond fringe, a round pink face with mouth turned up at the corners and strong white teeth — widely-spaced, which accentuated his look of total innocence.

'Perhaps he really is like that and we all misjudge him?' I suggested to Emily; but the noise which erupted from her throat soon put an end to such a fanciful notion.

After Erith, with its chimneys and church spire, and its moorings filled with small craft and thundering lighters (each time a big wash swept beneath them), we sailed past the lighthouse on Crayford Ness and through a swirling tide-rip into Long Reach.

'Look, Auntie!' Stephen tugged at Emily's arm; 'there's the place where we roared down that sand-hill an' you roared fastest of all!'

'Remember Texel jumpin' about on top of us an' the wicked time we had in the sand-pit?' David chimed in.

Mark swung round to stare at us with green sparks flashing in his eyes — his group had never been to Purfleet — and Ursula raised one eyebrow a fraction of an inch and gave us a rather old-fashioned look. But the Good Lord came to our rescue at that moment by arranging for a dredger to appear in front of us.

'See that signal?' I pointed to the two red balls with a white diamond between them suspended from the vessel's yard-arm. 'I'll give a prize to the first person to tell me what it stands for!'

The prize was a ball of oiled twine — an irresistible possession for some of the boys because of its delicious smell and its close connections with the boat. I forget who the winner was, but I distinctly remember our sail down Long Reach with the warm breeze on our starboard quarter and the shrieks of delight each time a big 'washer' came our way and several pairs of legs were drenched with spray.

We moored *Martha* at the pier behind the old training-ship, *Worcester*, at Greenhithe, and laid out our sandwiches and fruit in the cockpit for lunch. Peter and Victor took theirs on to the foredeck, and every so often I looked up and noticed their rapt expressions as they watched the whalers filled with cadets running between the shore and the *Worcester*.

'What's that big house half way up the hill, Rozelle?' Victor asked, pointing to an impressive white building overlooking the bay.

'That's the Merchant Navy officers' training college, I think. It's run by an old friend of Captain McLaren's, the man who's coming to give you all an exam one day soon.'

He peeled a banana thoughtfully, then bit off a large chunk while he contemplated the building with a far-away look in his eyes.

The wind had veered northerly and freshened during lunch, and it was blowing quite hard by the time we were ready to sail back home. We motored out of the sheltered bay and pointed the bows towards Stone Ness Lighthouse to hoist the mainsail.

'It feels quite different down here,' Emily remarked. 'Real big-ship stuff with all those cranes and masts and funnels over there — that's Tilbury Docks, I suppose? Even the waves seem bigger and the smell of the sea stronger than what you get up Gallion's Reach.'

Some of the children swung round towards the east and inhaled noisily, beating their chests with their fists, then flapping their arms up and down to pretend they were seagulls. While this was going on Peter grabbed the tiller, hauled in the main and jib sheets and set a course of 310° straight up Long Reach. *Martha* heeled far over on the starboard tack, the water foaming along her lee deck and the wind singing a Viking war-chant in her rigging. The sails were hauled taut — not a wrinkle to be seen in the new mainsail — and Mark and Victor perched on the cabin-top, attached to the guard-rail by their safety-harnesses, bellowing like bulls each time a wave broke over the bows and drenched them with spray.

Peter was poised on the stern-deck, one hand grasping the tiller and the other holding the mainsheet — ready to let it fly if an extra strong gust threatened to knock us flat. His profile was carved out of granite — no childish softness nor indecision in that outline. And *Martha* seemed to know that she was in firm hands as she rose and fell to the rhythm of the waves.

It was a grand day for sailing, and suddenly it struck me that this was our first anniversary and the sky was even brighter than on the day it all began. The eight boys, Emily, Ursula and I were still together — John had come back with the swallows to rejoin his group — and there had been no big dramas nor quarrels nor accidents to spoil our venture. Each Tuesday, in fact, I had the strangest impression that we had become one big family; and it grew stronger and stronger as the months sped by.

★   ★   ★

PART II
GROWING UP

Chapter 13

'*Come and see me!*' There was no mistaking those four words discreetly etched by some small finger in the dust on the side of my car-bonnet.

'Who wants whom to come and see them?' I asked myself with some curiosity as I sped along the A13 towards North Woolwich.

A short pause at the little shop in Cyprus to buy some cakes for tea confirmed the rumour that young Albert ('the best lad as ever drew breff', according to his brother) was in trouble again.

'Know what 'e's gorn an' done this time, love?' Madge asked me in a theatrical whisper as she leant across the counter to give me my change.

'I can't imagine.'

''E's got 'isself nicked fer usin' choice langwidge up the Social Skewritty! Don't know what this world's comin' to, I reeliy don't, when folks can't 'spress themselves no more when the urge comes over 'em, like. Makes you bleedin' scared ter open yer mouf nahadays!'

She was cut short by the shop door opening wth a thunderous clang to admit a huge black man.

'You got some of that Pecadillo Sauce, Ma?' he demanded, the whites of his eyes gleaming hopefully as his eyeballs swivelled right and left, scouring the contents of the shelves.

Madge and her sister retreated into their protective shells, like a pair of old tortoises confronted with a boa constrictor. 'We never 'ave no call for them fancy sauces rahnd Cyprus,' she announced with pursed up lips and a dead pan face. 'Better try over Silvertown way.'

'Load of pony, what you got on them shelves, Ma!' the black man snarled, making a rude gesture at her with two of his fingers.

The shop door opened again just then to reveal the sensational outline of the docker, young Albert's brother; so I felt the moment had come for me to fade quietly away! Back aboard *Martha* I just had time to look up 'pony' in my little book before the children arrived. 'Pony = pony and trap = crap,' it told me.

There was a heatwave during much of June but, as luck would have it, the lock gates of the Royal Albert Dock Basin had developed some serious troubles which meant that we could not escape to the river for two Tuesdays running. The engineers, meanwhile, clad in bathing-trunks with holidaytype grins spread across their faces, tinkered lethargically with the mechanism of the gates while we sweltered inside the basin and ground our teeth with frustration.

On the first Tuesday — the day of my visit to the shop — we had three boats under way simultaneously: *Martha*, *Water-Rat* and *Pacific Star*, a model yacht that Dick had brought down the previous week for the boys to sail when nothing more exciting was happening.

Philip, David, Stephen and Jeff had come with Ursula that afternoon, and they took turns at sailing *Martha* under her genoa and engine, or rowing *Water-Rat* with powerful swipes of the oars in pursuit of *Pacific Star*. The afternoon, having started on a serious note with a test on the various parts of a boat and their uses, gradually deteriorated into a noisy junket as the two boats converged on the toy which was sailing briskly around the basin as if it possessed an invisible helmsman and a secret life of its own.

'What the 'ell's goin' on down there?' boomed an angry voice from the dockmaster's office. 'I'll 'ave a word with Mr Cohen about you lot if you don't be'ave yourselves. This basin is meant to be an 'aven of peace for decent folks to keep their boats in, not a playground for the likes of yous!'

'Miserable arsehole!' Stephen muttered; 'throwing a wobbler whenever we start to have a good time.'

Luckily a diversion occurred at that moment, as we noticed Emily and someone I did not recognise waving to us from the far side of the dock.

'That's Auntie Em's mother,' David told me, as we set off with all our fleet (*Pacific Star* towing behind *Martha*) for the far side of the dock.

Emily's mother had come over from Ireland for a week or two to stay at the Edith Moorey Home, and all the children were on very friendly terms with the old lady and clearly enjoyed her company. We had a big tea-party that afternoon — eight of us in the cockpit or perched on the cabin-top — and I soon grew to appreciate the quiet sense of humour and charming manners of our guest.

Ursula and I lingered on for a few minutes at the end of the day, talking to Mrs Murphy after the boys had gone ashore. Ursula had left her car at Norwich Road, so I was to take her back there with David and Stephen, while Emily brought the others home in her Corsair. When we reached the car-park, however, I was astonished to find the boys already settled inside my car.

'I thought I'd locked it,' I told Ursula; 'how on earth did they get in?'

There they sat with downcast eyes and puffed out cheeks, trying to behave as if nothing unusual had occurred; but when he saw the expression on my face, Stephen began to bellow with laughter until the tears ran down his cheeks.

'It's no sweat for us to get inside any car we want to, Rozelle,' David explained to me quite seriously, as if he were lecturing a backward child. 'You just 'ave to learn a few special tricks, know what I mean?'

I seemed to be absorbing new tricks, phrases and ways of life every Tuesday. And when I had dropped off my passengers and finally parked the car outside our house, there was one more revelation to give me food for thought: just below the four words, *Come and see me,* that I had noticed on my bonnet earlier in the day, some fresh words had been inscribed which said '*We'll try and make it next week, Love, S. & D.*'

We were doing the washing-up after supper that evening when I heard cooing and tittering noises in the street below. I raised the window silently and leant far out over the pavement where I perceived two little girls from the block of flats across the road squatting beside my car; and they were busily rubbing the bonnet with their pinafores to remove all traces of the messages in the dust!

After another hot Tuesday spent circling the dock, we celebrated the reopening of the lock gates by sailing all the way to Tower Bridge and back.

We sailed past our house in Limehouse Reach.

It was the summer half-term holiday and a few of the boys had gone camping, but Peter and David had refused all other engagements so that they could make the voyage upriver.

Martha ran before a fresh south-easterly breeze, the flood tide hurrying her westwards while the sun blazed down on her happy crew. Whisked through the gap in the Woolwich Barrier, we sailed round the loop of the Isle of Dogs, past the Greenwich Naval College to port and, a short while afterwards, our house with its feet in the river to starboard. Beyond the tall warehouses and River Police Station at Wapping, I brought the boat alongside St Katharine's Pier to land the boys for a short run ashore.

The wind had risen to Force 6 by the afternoon, and we met the full force of the spring flood tide as we beat down Limehouse Reach on our way home. *Martha* was hard-pressed in the rough and tumbling seas off Cuckold's Point and there was no room to heave to and reef the mainsail on that narrow stretch of the river; but Peter, who was steering at that time, had his teeth firmly clenched together and one hand clamped around the nearest stanchion to steady himself as the boat heaved and rolled dramatically.

Just before we reached the bottom of the U-shaped bulge formed by the Isle of Dogs, David gripped my arm and pointed to the shore. 'Look at that funny old boatyard wiv the green shed and slipway for pullin' boats up,' he said. 'Wouldn't that be just the place for pullin' *Martha* up next time you

A derelict yard with one boat on the slip.

wanted to look at her bottom? Better'n hirin' the old crane round the marina each time?'

The place he was pointing at was next to the lead works, a derelict yard with one boat on the slip and a couple of dinghies in the corner. I had noticed it before on a nineteenth century map of the river, showing that it was where the chain-ferry used to cross from Greenwich to the Ferry Inn on the Isle of Dogs. We were soon so busy easing sheets and changing helmsmen that I forgot all about the place — until a few years later, when it began to play an important part in our lives.

After the Woolwich Barrier, Emily took the helm and tacked *Martha* back to Gallion's Reach under mainsail alone as I had decided to hand the jib by then. We entered the lock at dead low water, scraping our keel over the gravel just outside the gates. But our friendly lock-keeper was waiting on the bridge with Dick to receive us, and *Martha* rose steadily up the wall while the boys used the boat-hook to poke at bugs and limpets scrabbling about in the oily seaweed.

It was 8.30 p.m. by the time we had moored the boat and made her shipshape — both Peter and David were particularly helpful in furling the sails and tidying up the deck, while Ursula lit the stove and prepared our final meal of beef stew, banana and apricot jam sandwiches and mugs of coffee laced with rum (Dick's idea!).

The last words recorded in the log book that evening were: 'It's been a glorious day.'

A new cable for the throttle on *Martha*'s engine arrived one scorching day in July, and I spent a memorable afternoon struggling with it down in the bilges and trying to suppress its snakelike behaviour. It swivelled to and fro in the darkest recesses of the engine compartment, and refused to stay still for a moment so that I could fix it into position. Before very long I had dropped some vital clamps into the deepest part of the bilges, so was obliged to cross to South Woolwich on the ferry in order to buy a magnet with which to fish them out!

Fishing with the magnet became a popular sport after that, and I often caught the boys dropping bits of metal over the side just for the fun of seeing them emerge on the end of the magic horseshoe. Even Emily's car keys came up from the deep by magnet one afternoon!

The never-ending heatwave gradually reached its climax, and our last Tuesday before the summer holidays ended in a short period of intense drama. Ursula had come with John, Peter and Victor that afternoon, and the boys voted not to go out on the river in *Martha* as there was hardly a breath of wind.

Peter, Ursula and John cleaning Water-Rat's *bottom.*

I gave them a test in knots and hitches after lunch, then we hauled *Water-Rat* up on to the pontoon, turned her upside-down and scrubbed all the weed and barnacles off her bottom. This was a very popular task with the water-hose frequently directed at anyone who was foolish enough to turn their back on the work-force!

At three o'clock Ursula, Victor and I set off in *Martha*, while John and Peter followed in *Water-Rat* with *Pacific Star* towing behind them. We circled the dock for some while during which the sky turned black and yellow, like the backdrop to a Wagnerian opera, and I had an uncomfortable premonition that something nasty was about to hit us. We hurried back to our pontoon and had just begun to moor *Martha* when a blinding flash of lightning heralded the beginning of the storm. A moment later we were in the middle of a torrential downpour, thunder, lightning, hail-stones and sudden gale-force gusts of wind that churned the glassy surface of the dock into a seething cauldron.

John left the dinghy as soon as he could clamber ashore and dived into *Martha*'s cabin to change out of his soaking clothes. Victor and Ursula were already inside and I could hear John telling them how dangerous it was in the dinghy.

'O.K. if I sail round the dock once more, Rozelle?' Peter called to me from the far end of the pontoon; and, without waiting for my reply, he cast off the painter and *Water-Rat* shot across the dock like a guided missile. I stood there watching for a few minutes and marvelled at the way he let out the mainsheet in the strongest gusts, always in control of the situation when the little boat showed signs of capsizing. As she sped past our pontoon on her second circuit I realized that Peter was revelling in the storm and it would be cruel to call him in.

I felt a rope being pushed into my hands by a dripping figure beside me who stuttered through chattering teeth, 'I've come to help you tie up the boat!'

'That's nice,' I grinned. 'Thought you were changing into dry clothes and getting warm over the stove.'

'Well, I was, but it didn't seem fair to leave you out here on your own wiv all that thunder'n'lightning an' rain.'

Victor put the springs on *Martha*, tied the halliards to the guard-rails so that they would not slat against the mast, then helped me to furl the sails on *Pacific Star* who looked as if she might spring off the pontoon and go for a sail on her own, give her half a chance. Then Peter came back with *Water-Rat*, and I breathed a deep sigh of relief that the fleet was gathered in and there were still five of us to have a welcome mug of tea together!

By mid-August Emily and several of the boys had gone to a holiday home at Walton-on-Naze. They all enjoyed that week at the seaside and were looking

Waiting for the launch to take us out to Roskilde — *Ursula, Emily, Jeff, Stephen and John, and front row: Peter and Mark.*

sunburnt and relaxed when Emily brought them to meet Ursula and me at Walton Station on August 11th. She drove us to the Halls' yard where a launch was waiting to take us out to *Roskilde* on her mooring in the Walton Channel.

Roskilde was built on the lines of a Shetland sixareen, a much bigger and heavier boat than *Martha*, but Dick had trustingly said that we could take her out if the wind was not too strong.

Well, it turned out to be a dream of a day with fine settled weather and a light north-easterly breeze. Emily and the boys were wearing their smartest holiday gear for the outing and there was a Costa del Sol air about the whole party, even Ursula. I decided to use only the engine and working jib that day as our time was limited and the mainsail was large and cumbersome to handle. We let go our mooring at midday and set off along the Walton Channel towards Hamford Water.

The Walton Backwaters consist of a number of small uninhabited islands and a great many mud-banks with meandering channels between them. It is the haunt of countless sea-birds, a beautiful lonely region with immense freighters and North Sea ferries making for Harwich and Felixstowe just visible over the saltings away to the north. Until that day, the children had always pictured Walton as a crowded beach and noisy pier full of round-abouts and dodgems, amusement arcades and ice-cream parlours; and the big caravan park where Stephen and Mark's grandparents spent their holidays. But the Walton Backwaters was a new experience for them, and they were not quite sure what to make of all that empty landscape under an enormous sky.

We picked up a mooring between Horsey Island and Skipper's Island to have our lunch, then pumped up the rubber dinghy and John rowed Mark and Jeff ashore to do some exploring.

'This is a bit different to last time we was on a boat together, isn't it, Ursula?' Peter remarked. 'But I really enjoyed meself whizzing round the dock in *Water-Rat!*'

Ursula, who was sunbathing on the foredeck, half-opened her eyes to murmur: 'Give me a day like today, every time!'

'I seen a rabbit an' some big birds wiv long beaks, Auntie,' Mark bawled across from the island; 'an' there's a funny little house on legs over there...'

'The man in the launch told us it's what they use for watching the birds from,' John added.

Stephen at the helm aboard Roskilde.

Soon after the dinghy returned we dropped our mooring and motor-sailed along Hamford Water, then out to sea with Stephen at the helm. He reminded me of an ostrich stretching and curving its neck to see over the top of the high hatch-cover, but his face was alight with the beauty of his thoughts.

'It really suits me, this boat does,' he declared after a few minutes. 'All that space down in the cabin an' this great big tiller wiv a dragon's head on the end of it; an' the blue flag — very classy that looks. Real big-ship stuff, an' it makes you feel important sitting up here in charge of it all!'

He waved to a passing fishing-boat and I was just in time to grab the dragon's head and heave it over to starboard before *Roskilde* ran aground on the steep-sloping sandbank that flanks the east side of the Pye Channel.

There was a slight swell out at the Pye End Buoy which gave us all the grand sensation of being on the open sea at last. We sailed round the buoy then ghosted back towards the land. There were long low ridges on either side of us, strips of mauve and muddy-brown where the wet sand emerged from the shallow sea; amber glints turned to gold as the sun beat down upon the glistening banks, and beyond Stone Point a Thames sailing-barge stood out in sharp relief, a bold black outline with its mainmast touching the soft white clouds. Hundreds of sea-birds were twittering and squawking on the edge of the banks, and one solemn shag was perched on top of a wooden post. A thin mist drifted in over the land and the islands ahead became vague grey-green shapes, encircled by the gold and silver strands of the Walton Backwaters.

'I've never seen anywhere quite like this before,' John observed, shielding his eyes with one hand as he gazed along the path of the sun. 'Like a sort of dream-world, isn't it?'

The biggest thrills of all were caused by the dinghy rides on the way home, towing behind *Roskilde* in a welter of foam. Peter and Stephen were the first to sample this new mode of transport, and we could hear single staccato words coming from astern — Wicked...Evil...Brilliant...Cool — which reduced the steady thump-thump of the diesel engine to the murmurings of a dove.

Jeff was steering at that time, but he and Mark soon made it clear that they also wished to ride in the dinghy; so we picked the quiet anchorage behind Stone Island to exchange passengers. I pushed the throttle wide open for the last two miles along the Walton Channel and Jeff lay back in the stern of the dinghy, king of all he surveyed, while Mark trailed his arms in the bow-wave and emitted screams of excitement whenever the little boat bounced up and down over a 'washer'.

Jeff and Mark in the rubber dinghy, towing behind Roskilde.

An hour or so later Derek Halls who, with his brother John, runs the boatyard up Foundry Creek, came to pick us up in his launch. 'Had a good time, lads?' he asked the children as we motored back to the shore.

'I had a bewteeful day,' Mark acted as spokesman for the group. 'Best day I ever had in me life!'

Chapter 14

'I wouldn't never want to go for anuvver trip on *Larvik*,' David declared, his fists clenching and brows furrowing at the memory of his week's holiday afloat.

Larvik was an old Norwegian sailing pilot-cutter, a beautiful seaworthy vessel designed by the famous Colin Archer nearly a century ago. She belonged to Tower Hamlets Council who chartered her to various charitable organizations, so that children could have holidays aboard her and learn some nautical skills during the summer months. Her skipper was an ex-naval officer, and he and his wife were reputed to be fine sailors and good instructors.

'What was wrong with her?' Ursula asked. 'We pictured you having a marvellous time sailing around in the Thames estuary on such a splendid big boat.'

'I didn't say there was nuffink wrong wiv the boat, did I?' David glared at us like a cornered fox, very much on the defensive. 'It was the people what run it that made you feel so bad. Never mind how hard I tried to do somefink right, they orways used ter pick on me an' try ter show me up in front of all the uvvers. They had a way of makin' you feel really small an' uncomfortable — like some sort of insect.'

It was mid-September, the autumn term had already started and we were back aboard *Martha* in the London Marina, anxious to hear what the boys had to tell us about their sailing holidays.

'They sound like pigs to me! We'll make sure you go on one of the other boats next summer,' I tried to comfort David.

Peter Cobb, Dick and I, with the blessing of Newham Social Services Department, had taken a great deal of trouble to arrange holidays afloat for the six oldest boys that summer. We felt it was time they went to sea in larger vessels with more children aboard, and a proper watch-keeping routine to prepare some of them, perhaps, for future seafaring careers. The experiment had, clearly, not been a great success in David's case, but a week later we heard the other side of the story from Victor and John.

The Thames sailing-barge Thalatta, *belonging to the East Coast Sail Trust.*

'*Thalatta* was a bit of orright,' Victor grinned broadly; 'good skipper and the mate was cool — only a girl, she was! And the cook was O.K. as well.

'We set off from Mistley near Harwich, and sailed to quite a few places up an' down the East Coast. We used to drop anchor every evening, and me and Steve used to go for a swim over the side, then we'd climb back aboard and have a big tea, then play games or have a sing-song. We slept in hammocks at night — we slung them 'cross the place where we had our nosh — and there was a great big trunk what everyone was told to put their gear in. Well, one night some scumbag went an' left a valve open in the heads so the whole boat got flooded; the water came right up to your bum if you stood on the cabin floor! All our gear got flooded too, but it didn't matter 'cos we was havin' a good time, me and Steve.

'Before we came back to Mistley the mate got us to write up our logs: all about the boats an' birds an' seals what we'd seen on our trip, and the 'ventures we had and what we thought about it all.'

'It was wicked!' Stephen confirmed; 'but I never did take to sleepin' in a hammock. Some sod let go the headrope on one of the other kid's hammocks one night, an' he came a cropper on top of the trunk!'

Thalatta was an ageing Thames sailing-barge belonging to the East Coast Sail Trust, looked after with loving care by her mate, Jane Benham. She is still a queen among the East Coast sailing-vessels; only last summer, in fact, we passed her reaching down the Walton Channel with a swarm of children buzzing happily around the decks, the old barge as hauntingly beautiful as ever.

John, Philip and Peter had just reached the age when they were allowed to sail on *Arethusa*, a magnificent ketch belonging to the Ocean Youth Club. Her skipper, Jim Spencer, an old friend of ours, was a bearded Viking of a man who combined being a natural leader and very fine seaman with the patience and compassion of a saint. He took a real interest in the children as individuals which endeared him to all his crews; and, as we were soon to discover, these virtues were a rare combination indeed. Many of the skippers in charge of youth training schemes were accomplished seamen and good instructors, but lacked any particular interest in their ever-changing and sometimes disruptive crew-members.

All three boys agreed that it had been a splendid week but John, who saw things through wider eyes, was able to paint a picture of the voyage that made me feel quite envious.

There were twelve aboard the ketch, including the skipper and mate; three of the boys were police cadets, and there were two girls as well. Each crew-member was assigned a special task — John, for instance, was the bo'sun — but everyone was expected to take a turn at doing all the other jobs as well: steering, cooking, sail-changing, scrubbing the decks, climbing up the masts . . . John managed to climb two-thirds of the way up the mainmast, but he was not sorry to come down to deck level after a few minutes aloft with the spar swaying gently to and fro.

Arethusa sailed from Brightlingsea with a fair wind straight across the North Sea to Ostend. As she entered harbour, the long piers on either hand were lined with people who waved to the gallant crew and cheered them in; so the boys felt like conquering heroes at the end of their longest ever sea-crossing.

'Myself and Philip hired a pedal go-cart,' John recalls; 'and we pedalled round the narrow cobble-stoned streets and had a lot of fun. Also we stopped at a caff to have a big bowl of steaming mussels and chips. They were good, but not as nice as Ursula's banana and apricot jam sandwiches!'

Next morning *Arethusa* left for Holland, and a big crowd of men and women were still jostling each other for space along the narrow jetties to wave her goodbye. A few hours later she sailed into the West Schelde estuary and passed through Dutch customs inside the sea-lock at Flushing; then on up the Middleburg Canal to the little village of Veere on the north-east coast of Walcheren Island. As you turn the last corner on the canal you can see the immense church and exquisite townhall rising above the green fields dotted with black and white cows.

You can see the immense church and exquisite townhall rising above the green fields dotted with black and white cows.

Veere was a flourishing seaport in the fourteenth century, carrying on a brisk trade in woollen goods with Scotland. The harbour could hold seventeen merchant ships but, tragically, its prosperity vanished during a terrible storm in the seventeenth century when most of the town was destroyed by floods. The church, however, stood its ground and was later used as a hospital by Napoleon's soldiers when he made his headquarters in the little fortress, now a hotel, guarding the harbour entrance.

By the time I first sailed into Veere harbour some forty years ago, it had

Arethusa *dropped anchor off the wooden jetty in front of the hotel.*

become a peaceful fishing village with a touch of magic in the air. This curious phenomenon affects many strangers who come there for the first time, casting a spell over them so that they are compelled to return, year after year!

John told me that *Arethusa* dropped anchor off the wooden jetty in front of the hotel, and the crew went swimming over the side.

'There were lots of tiny fish swimming all round us,' he said; 'and when I looked up I could see the old houses and the windmill reflected in the harbour, so you could see them upside-down as well. It was a beautiful place, and that evening we had a party in the yacht club with all the Dutch kids.'

Arethusa sailed straight back to Harwich from Walcheren Island. It was a rough and stormy twenty-four hour passage ending in thick fog near the Thames estuary. It must have been a worrying time for the skipper, and no fun for his inexperienced crew.

'It was very scary on the way home, with big waves crashing against the yacht and going clean over the top of us,' John recalls. 'It got very cold and foggy, and I had to keep on blowing the fog-horn so passing ships could hear. I remember seeing a big ferry go by quite near to us, and it made giant-sized "washers"!

'I was seasick on the way home, but wouldn't go below to sleep as it made me feel worse than ever. Also I couldn't eat anything, but Jim said if I didn't

eat and started heaving it would be worse than ever. It was 2 a.m. then and
all that was left to eat was cold custard from tea-time which I spooned into
my mouth, but you can imagine what that tasted like!'

Philip remembered Jim telling the boys on watch some terrific yarns about
his voyages and adventures he had had at sea, which helped to take their
minds off the waves crashing over the bows on that stormy night crossing.
Arethusa came home a day early, so there was plenty of time to sail around
the river estuaries near Harwich and watch the sun go down in a blaze of
glory from their anchorage on the River Orwell.

Peter recollected passing close to Ted Heath at the helm of his yacht,
Morning Star, and Jim asking *Arethusa*'s crew to line up on deck and stand to
attention while he dipped the ensign. He was peeling spuds in the galley
later that morning when he heard a familiar fog-horn blowing three
prolonged blasts, and rushed up on deck just in time to wave to us sailing by
in *Roskilde*!

With the exception of David, the summer holidays on bigger boats seemed
to have been a great success — a further incentive to work hard in preparation for the first nautical examinations next November, which were already
beginning to loom large on the boys' horizons.

★   ★   ★

'Only two months to go, and I've no idea what Ian's going to ask them. And how on earth will poor little Jeff manage to face an exam?' I appealed to Dick in desperation.

'Well, he was very patient and long-suffering when we were his pupils,' he reminded me; 'and I'm sure he'll find a few things that Jeff's good at, to bring out the best in him.'

By the end of September we had started listening to the 1355 shipping forecast on a Tuesday afternoon. The boys wrote down as much as they could, then we drew our own weather maps and made sure that everyone knew where to find the different sea areas mentioned in the forecasts; and, as a final treat, we studied the clouds sailing by overhead.

'There's a big soft white one shaped like a pig!' Stephen, who was lying on his back on the foredeck, shouted out; 'and 'nuvver one like a grey cotton-wool rabbit.'

'Aren't they called cumulus clouds?' Philip asked. 'Sort of fine weather clouds till they get dark an' heavy-looking?'

Everyone loved the fleecy white cumulus, but when the low stratus moved in with torrents of rain it was another matter.

'We done two hours' hard work inside the cabin today, Auntie,' I heard David trying to impress Veronica when I took them back home. ''Nuff ter burst your brains open, it was! First we done Rule of the Road and boys . . . '

'What d'you mean, "boys"?' Veronica interrupted.

'You know, B O Y S; funny-looking coloured shapes you get out on the sea to tell you which side the rocks and sandbanks lie, so you don't go an' hit one of 'em, see?'

'I bet you'd soon forget which side to go when the crunch came!' Veronica laughed.

'Then we did chartwork an' mejring distances — that's dead easy,' David continued; 'an' last of all knots an' splices. I'm really good at them!'

On October 12th we lit the cabin stove for the first time for some months to celebrate the approach of winter after spending most of the afternoon rowing energetically round the dock to keep warm. Ursula had just returned from a holiday in Italy, and she described the wonders of the Duomo in Florence, the opera in Milan and the art treasures of Venice while the children masticated her banana and apricot jam sandwiches and gazed at her with round eyes in total bemusement.

'My dad went to Blackpool for his holiday,' Victor volunteered; 'an' he said there was plenty goin' on there. Better'n bein' in Benidorm, he said. You aughta try somewhere like Blackpool next year, Ursula.'

Roskilde was on her way to the River Thames to spend the winter in the

London Marina. Dick and I had sailed her across to France at the end of August, but we ran out of time after rounding the North Foreland on the way home. We decided, therefore, to leave her in the charge of an old friend who kept the moorings at Harty Ferry on the River Swale until we had a free weekend to continue the voyage up to London.

On the last Tuesday in October Emily, Ursula, Philip, Peter, Victor and I drove to the lonely marshes north of Faversham and signalled to the old boatman who ran a launch up and down the moorings to come and fetch us. It was a cold wintry day with a low pressure system covering most of the British Isles but, as luck would have it, Sea Area Thames was in the middle of a temporary lull between gales, and a moderate southerly breeze greeted us when we got out of the car.

We wasted no time in gobbling down our lunch as soon as the old man had dropped us aboard *Roskilde*. It was that sort of day, when plenty of brisk action was required to still the butterflies in one's tummy. Philip let go the heavy mooring ropes and we headed out to sea under engine, mainsail and working jib. There was, however, a strong flood tide to stem — it runs at about five knots at spring tides — so it took us nearly two hours to reach the Columbine Spit at the entrance to the river.

The barometer had begun to fall by then, the wind was rising steadily and the vague outline of Whitstable on our starboard quarter seemed infinitely remote and inaccessible. Away to the north I could see a coaster making towards the Red Sand Tower, her navigation lights glowing in the rapidly fading daylight.

'It *is* bleak out here today, isn't it?' Ursula remarked, perhaps remembering that golden spring day more than two years ago when we had scattered Noel's ashes over those same waters.

'Sure it is!' Emily pulled her woollen cap with a bobble on top down to the line of her eyebrows and turned up the collar of her sailing-jacket.

We caught each other's eye and knew that we shared the same thought.

'We'll swing her round here and sail between Ham Gat and the Pollard Spit Buoys,' I announced; 'then straight back home.'

Peter pushed the tiller hard over to starboard while Philip and Victor hauled in the sheets, then had a boxing-match to keep themselves warm. *Roskilde* was close-hauled sailing back into the river, heeled far over on the port tack with the tide galloping along beside her gleaming hull. Away to starboard we could see the curve of Shellness, its sandy hook reaching down towards the narrow channel that hugged the eastern end of the Isle of Sheppey. Ahead lay a broad stretch of heaving nothingness, that most deceptive of river estuaries where the shallow patches lie just beneath the surface, ready to clutch at your keel the moment your attention wanders. Everything depended upon the sharp eye-sight and deep concentration of the helmsman: would he be able to pick out the tiny port and starboard-hand buoys flanking the Horse Sand, a treacherous bank that bulges south into the main channel near the entrance to Faversham Creek?

I had not taken into account that all three boys were adept at this type of navigation after their summer sailing holidays. 'There's the black one!' Peter and Victor shrieked at the same moment, dancing each other round and round on the foredeck in their excitement.

'I can't see a thing with you two fairies blockin' my view!' Philip, who was steering, bellowed at the others.

'Don't know which way's norf an' which way's souf, that's your trouble!' Victor stuck his tongue out at his big brother.

As soon as Philip had picked out the starboard-hand buoy and taken its compass bearing so that he would not lose it again, I handed the mainsail and Peter helped me to furl it and put on the sail-cover. Then we crawled back to the cockpit and all had swigs of rum to celebrate the fact that we had not yet run aground.

The five-knot tide had slackened by the time we reached Harty Ferry, so we picked up our mooring without any problem, washed down *Roskilde*'s decks and made her shipshape, then the old man came to fetch us in his launch.

'Rare old wind gettin' up,' he remarked, 'You lot are the only ones down here today. Gettin' a bit late in the season, know what I mean. Won't be sorry to get back to the old stove, I won't!'

We sat on the sea-wall eating cakes and drinking mugs of strong tea while the launch puttered away into the wintry twilight. A curlew called to its mate across the marshes and Victor said; 'Makes you feel good goin' to sea on a day like this — 'specially when you get back on land again!'

Chapter 15

Dick and I sailed from the River Swale in *Roskilde* at the end of October. It was a cold sunny day with a cutting edge to the north wind — a wrap-me-up-warm sort of day when a tot of rum to mark the rounding of various buoys was something to which we looked forward with keen anticipation. We sped out of the Medway and into the Thames, past Southend Pier, Holehaven Creek, Mucking Flats and the Piccadilly Circus of shipping between Tilbury and Gravesend. The wind petered out after Northfleet Hope, so we handed the sails and chugged upriver past all the familiar landmarks: the training-ship *Worcester* at Greenhithe, the Royal Hotel at Purfleet, the chimneys and church spire at Erith and the tall pylons on either side of the river at Dagenham.

It was a still dark night by the time we had passed through the London Marina lock and moored alongside the empty pontoon next to *Martha*. The smaller boat rocked gently to and fro to greet her big sister and I wondered if they would settle down to a friendly gossip about their summer voyaging after we had gone back home.

The first two Tuesdays in November were spent working unusually hard in preparation for THE GREAT DAY, which now had a ring round it on our calendar — November 26th. It had been selected by Captain Ian McLaren, Extra Master Mariner and Deputy Head of the Sir John Cass School of Navigation, for the boy's examination; and, although it was not a Tuesday, the various headmasters had willingly given their consent to this extra day of absence from school.

Ursula and Emily brought Number 2 group on the first Tuesday — all except Philip who had played truant from school so was not allowed to come.

David and Stephen put their hearts into reefing, hoisting and furling the mainsail after lunch; I was astonished at how well they could work when they knew that there were only three weeks left in which to improve their skills. Jeff was still unable to tie a reef knot, but he steered an unerring course out to the middle of the dock where several 'men overboard' were retrieved in quick succession. Inspired by his few moments of glory, as soon as David brought *Martha* back to the pontoon the little fellow succeeded in falling overboard when no one was looking!

We were all busy mooring the boat when a piercing shriek rent the air, and there was Jeff behaving like a frenzied flounder; but I was relieved to see that his head was well-supported above the water by his life-jacket. We soon fished him out and, after a good rub down and change of clothes, we gave him a sip of rum which brought a big grin to his face. Stephen and David, by contrast, were looking distinctly surly with so much attention being focused on to poor little Jeff.

'We'll move across to *Roskilde* as soon as we've had our tea,' I told them, remembering how Stephen felt about the bigger boat. 'Then we can use the cabin table for the rest of our revision.'

It had been agreed that there would be no more free half hours until after the exam, so we spent the rest of the afternoon doing tests on buoyage, Rule of the Road and knots. Jeff was much too absorbed in his own drama to concentrate on anything else, but David and Stephen worked hard and proved, once again, that they were quite capable of understanding and solving the problems I had set them.

The following week Peter, Philip and Victor came and we had lunch aboard *Roskilde*, then each boy took charge of *Martha* in turn, motoring round the dock, giving orders to the crew, coming alongside, mooring the boat and, finally, reefing the mainsail. When they started these manoeuvres I gripped the guard-rail anxiously, a tense bag of nerves waiting for the first nasty crunch!

'Wha's matter, Rozelle?' Peter bared his teeth at me and waggled the tiller to make me flinch.

'You wait an' see if we aren't all good as gold today — three sea captins in the makin'!' Victor proclaimed.

And they were too. I found it hard to pick a fault with any one of them nor the assured way in which they handled *Martha*.

Back aboard *Roskilde* we settled down to the test I had prepared, while Emily and Ursula laid out the tea things.

TEST

1. What would you do if you were out at sea and heard a gale warning on the radio?
2. What preparations would you make before entering harbour?
3. What would you do if one of the crew fell overboard out at sea?
4. What would you do if the boat ran aground on a falling tide?
5. What is the difference between spring and neap tides?
6. Look up the time of high water at Sandwich on May 2nd, 1976.
7. What time could you enter harbour if your boat drew five feet?

8.   What are the twelve most important items of equipment on a sea-going boat?
9.   If you were at sea in a fog and heard the following signals, what do they mean and
     what action would you take?
     (a) Two prolonged blasts at intervals of not more than two minutes?
     (b) One long and two short blasts?
     (c) A bell ringing rapidly for about five seconds?
10. If you see high cirrus clouds moving in from the west across a clear blue sky, what
     type of weather can you expect?

We were to do many such tests after that first one, some of them covering a
three-part voyage from Dover to Rotterdam, for instance, with a whole range
of problems to solve and disasters to be averted along the route. They were
quite popular among the older boys, and helped to put into context some of
the many isolated facts they were expected to learn. That first test done by
the light of two paraffin lamps in *Roskilde*'s cabin was, however, something
of a novelty, and Ursula remarked that the scene would have made a good
subject for Rembrandt to paint: the surrounding darkness with three heads
illuminated by the glow of the lamps, the deep concentration and tense
fingers clutching pencils that would soon be writing down those vital
answers...

'Tell me the secret of how you keep them quiet as angels like that, will you
now, Rozelle?' Emily broke the spell with a deep-throated chuckle; 'and
you'll be my friend for life!'

★   ★   ★

Roskilde *running before the wind.*

We had all been looking forward to Sunday, November 14th, when both boats were to make a voyage in company down the river to Grays Thurrock. Emily, Peter Cobb, Dick and all the boys except Philip came, and we set off at nine o'clock with a good forecast and a light breeze from the north.

Emily, David, Stephen and Jeff came with me in *Martha*, while Peter Cobb and the other boys were Dick's crew aboard *Roskilde*. We had passed through the lock by 0930 and hoisted our mainsails and genoas, but the wind was so light that we were soon compelled to run our engines as well.

Jeff resembled a miniature polar explorer clad in a range of multi-coloured woollen garments, most of them far too big for him. An hour or so later he was sitting on the bows with his feet dangling over the side and arms clasped round the pulpit, when he reported that *Roskilde* was 'acting strange' over on the starboard bow. Stephen grabbed the binoculars and focused them on to the unfortunate vessel which had just run aground and was making secretive efforts to come unstuck before we should notice!

David promptly pushed our tiller hard over to port and opened the throttle wide, so we were soon within shouting distance; and a lot of nasty insults went hurling through the air while Big Peter and John pushed hard with the boat-hook and Dick ran the engine full astern.

'We only come in here to look for somewhere to eat our dinner, you load of shit!' Victor yelled back, as *Martha*'s big sister rose on the crest of a 'washer' and spun round stern-first into deeper water.

Mark shouted a few choice words at his brother while John resumed his position right up for'ard — like some Viking figurehead. He had been put in charge of *Roskilde*'s log-book and had already noted that 'Dick was Captain and John Munro was First Mate. It was a foggy morning and they'd put the sails up at 20 to 10, just as they'd come out of the lock, and taken them down near Purfleet. When *Roskilde* reached the moorings at Thurrock he mentioned that we were going to moor both boats together for dinner, but a bloke came out in a dinghy and said it wasn't allowed. Mark told him to piss off, but we'd already picked up another mooring by then and were close enough to shout to one another across the water.'

After our meal we motored alongside *Roskilde* to change crews and I took John, Victor and Mark aboard, while my crew clambered on to big sister. A thick grey fog was gradually creeping up the river, clutching with icy tentacles at everything within its grasp. Although it was only one o'clock we decided to get under way as the tide was just beginning to turn. We switched on our engines and set off upriver at a good speed.

Little Peter, who had remained aboard *Roskilde*, took charge of her log-book on the way home. He recorded that 'Dick Rains was Caption and all the crew were well and ready at 1300 hours. The staysail was packed away and the mainsail in its crutch, and they were dew home at 1530 hours.'

We had an unfortunate accident on *Martha* during our run upriver. We were motoring past Erith at the time, and went over a big wash caused by one of the Sun tugs which was hurrying home to Gravesend. Victor, who was on the foredeck making faces at Stephen aboard *Roskilde* at that moment, fell on top of the anchor and hurt his knee rather badly.

Both boats arrived outside the London Marina just after three o'clock, but the lock was not due to open for another half hour; so we decided to motor on to Woolwich Reach, rather than hang about off Gallion's Point.

Peter reported that 'the fog was still in the air and it was very cold. We took the sails down because we could not catch the little bit of wind.'

By four o'clock both boats were back inside the London Marina, their crews devouring an enormous tea in *Roskilde*'s cabin.

'My face is all pink an' burning, Auntie!' Victor announced, limping towards us after peering at himself in the mirror; 'but it's bin a brilliant day. Even ole Skunk's enjoyed hisself, haven't you, mate?' he said, giving Jeff a tickle in the ribs.

★   ★   ★

Two days later Ursula met me at the London Marina to help strip *Martha* of all her gear. It was a miserable damp day with the raindrops pattering down on the cabin-top in sympathy with our mood. We felt sad that our old friend was going away to Walton-on-Naze to spend the winter in a shed far away from us all, but knew that it was time she had a proper refit after nearly two years afloat.

We had lunch together in the cabin and a few quiet moments to review our boating project over the past year. Then we covered up *Martha*'s cockpit and drove to Norwich Road. I had promised to give the boys as much revision as possible before November 26th, and it seemed a good time to catch most of them at home after school.

I rang the front door bell and Veronica let us in; but no sooner had we crossed the threshold than I sensed an unusual atmosphere — something electric in the air on which I was quite unable to place a finger! Ursula had the same impression, as I saw her glance at me with arched eyebrows which clearly inquired, 'What's going on in this place?'

We started with the Rule of the Road, using the big table in the boys' sitting-room as a harbour, with the pepper and salt-cellars acting as light-houses to guard the entrance and our model buoys placed just outside in unexpectedly difficult positions. I handed the little yellow tug to Mark and asked him to steer it safely out of harbour, as far as the edge of the table which represented the open sea.

He grasped the toy boat and sped out of the port at top speed, colliding with a ship about to enter, running aground on a crop of rocks, scraping over the top of a shallow wreck and giving the sound signal for a vessel going full astern while he was forging ahead on a collision course with a homebound liner!

'You didn't make one single correct move!' Ursula chided him; 'and I've often heard you boasting to people about how clever you are at the Rule of the Road.'

Peter, meanwhile, had been asked to look up the time of high water at Wivenhoe that morning. He appeared studious enough, his glasses perched on the end of his nose and his head buried in Reed's Almanac; but he added an hour for British summertime (it was now November) and subtracted the wrong tidal constant from high water Sheerness, so the answer was completely incorrect. I opened my mouth to warn him that he would have to pull up his socks before the 26th, but stopped in mid-sentence when I noticed him staring at me in a vacant sort of way, then exchanging with Victor what I would describe as a conspirator's leer.

More mystified than ever, I pushed the Dover Straits chart across to Victor and asked him to estimate the compass course for a ship to steer from Folkestone to Boulogne, allowing for variation and tide at 1600 that

afternoon. He loved that type of problem so I awaited his solution with
confidence; but the course he produced, after gnawing the end off his pencil,
would have placed the ship in the middle of the Varne shoal on a falling tide!

Ursula began to look thoroughly depressed and I felt like a time-bomb,
waiting for the right moment to explode. 'We've spent one and a half years
trying to instil a few simple facts into your fat skulls,' I began; 'and there are
only ten days left before your exam and...'

The kitchen hatch was flung open at that moment to reveal Emily's
smiling face. 'It's all ready, boys,' she called out, 'Bring her in!'

Suddenly everyone was on their feet, some carrying chairs and others
hauling me along with them into the kitchen: and what a beautiful un-
forgettable surprise I found waiting for me inside!

The whole place was festooned with balloons and coloured streamers and,
in the middle of the table which was laden with sandwiches, scones, brandy-
snaps, fruit, nuts and all sorts of other delicacies, towered a magnificent pink
birthday cake with a great many candles, all burning brightly. And, as if that
were not enough, a number of small parcels were carefully positioned in
front of my place at the tea-table.

'Me and Steve got you that when we was on holiday up at Walton!' Mark
exclaimed, as I drew a lovely pendant fashioned from a 1957 half penny piece
out of its box.

'I made this speshly for you wivout any 'elp from teacher!' Jeff proudly
held up a little wooden boat painted blue. It has been one of *Martha*'s
treasured mascots ever since that day.

'I made these for you in needlework,' Victor mumbled, turning a brilliant
shade of puce.

They were a pair of tiny table-mats, skilfully crochetted in navy, white and
blue wool — something so out of character with the Victor I knew, and yet so

attractive that they have sat on my dressing-table for the past fourteen years.

'How did you know it's my birthday?' I gasped, unable to find adequate words to thank them for giving me such a wonderful treat; and suddenly I remembered how horrid I had been to some of the ones who had shared this secret and could not concentrate on their lessons because of the excitement of it all, before Emily opened the hatch.

'*November 22nd*

0900 — I started up the engine and motored round to the quay below the crane. Soon afterwards the mast was pulled out, then *Martha* was lifted out of the water. Mr Whippatt took her away on his trailer to Walton-on-Naze for the winter.

There were no dramas, and she arrived safely at the Halls' yard at Walton about 1400. The engine has now done 86 hours running.'

Thus ended *Martha McGilda*'s story for the year 1976, but the Tuesday boys still had their big day to come.

November 26th got off to a bad start. Mentally, I had carefully stage-managed the whole day, but how was I to guess that Ian McLaren would arrive half-an-hour early in pelting rain, and that I would drive up to the London Marina and find him sitting in *Water-Rat*, baling her out and cleaning her thwarts with a soggy floor-cloth!

I soon persuaded him to step aboard *Roskilde* where the decks gleamed like virgin snow, and the ship's lamps, barometer, clock and copper stove glittered magnificently from the previous day's fierce application of Brasso.

'I can see someone's been hard at work aboard this vessel!' Ian commented with a dry chuckle. 'I've brought your log-books back and they make impressive reading for such a young group. Believe it or not, some of my Second Mate students still don't know how to apply variation and deviation correctly to get a compass course.'

'Well, I wouldn't be too sure that my lot will get the answers right either, except by a lucky fluke,' I laughed, pouring him out a mug of coffee.

At one o'clock sharp the whole gang arrived, eight inquisitive noses pressed against the steamed up window-panes of Emily's Corsair. They did not look at all nervous — I was the one who suffered agonies of doubts, just as I had when Miss O'Brien came for the afternoon.

'Hello, Captin!' Mark barged into the cabin ahead of the others, a grubby paw extended towards the great man. 'Me an' my mates bin lookin' forward to meetin' you.'

Ian, who was rather a shy person, was clearly taken aback at this early social thrust from the smallest child in the group. It cleared the way, however, for a convivial lunch-party in which none of the boys appeared to be suffering from withdrawal symptoms. As usual, I was the only one who could hardly swallow my sandwiches while I listened anxiously to the rising south-westerly wind whistling in the rigging.

The exam started at half past one. David, Stephen, Mark and Jeff were asked to get *Roskilde* under way, bring her alongside the fishing-boat on the far side of the dock, hoist the mainsail, pick up several 'men overboard' and, finally, bring the boat back to the pontoon and secure her. Then the four older boys were invited to do the same manoeuvres which, on this occasion, included reefing the mainsail.

The wind was blowing a good Force 6 by then, and it seemed a miracle to me that no one had bungled their come-alongsides nor crashed into the main pontoon. Clearly they had iron nerves and knew more than I gave them credit for. The remainder of the afternoon was spent on dinghy handling, chartwork, Rule of the Road, buoyage, knots and splices and general knowledge.

Ursula arrived at four-thirty with a bagful of her special sandwiches. As soon as the last boy had finished his individual oral exam inside the cabin we all crowded in, twelve of us altogether, and had a very cheerful and noisy tea-party.

'Now I want all you lads to go for a run round the dock,' Ian said, when we had finished; 'and don't come back till I hoist this red flag. Then I'll tell you your results!'

He had taken many notes during the tests, and there was a great deal of totting up of points allotted for each manœuvre or question to be done. Ursula and I, meanwhile, sat silently on one of the bunks and she darned a hole in a beige garment with small rhythmic stabs of the needle while I gnawed several finger-nails to the quick. Emily was outside, making sure that no one blotted his copy-book at the last moment.

After what seemed like a hundred years Ian looked up and peered at me as if I were a ship on some far horizon. 'The results are quite surprising,' he murmured, scratching his head with the non-writing end of his biro ... pause.

'God, I bet they've all failed,' I groaned inwardly; 'every single one of them!'

'...Considering their ages and complete lack of boating background,' he continued. 'You see they've all passed with merit, and three of them I've marked "commendable" as their general knowledge and mature way of handling the boat was really quite remarkable!'

That was by no means the end of all the glory that we lapped up like a litter of kittens faced with a bottomless trough of cream. A few days later the

MARTHA MᶜGILDA

CERTIFICATE   of   SEAMANSHIP

This is to certify that   I have tested
VICTOR HENRY aboard the vessel *ROSKILDE*
in the elements of *BOAT HANDLING (POWER) SAIL SETTING*
REEFING, BUOYAGE, RULE OF ROAD ETC.
and found his knowledge to be *COMMENDABLE*
for his age and experience.

signed: *Ian McLaren,*

Captain Ian MᶜLaren
Extra Master Mariner

MARTHA MᶜGILDA

CERTIFICATE   of   SEAMANSHIP

This is to certify that   I have tested
JEFF JESSON aboard the vessel *ROSKILDE*
in the elements of *BOAT HANDLING, SAIL SETTING,*
DINGHY WORK, KNOTS ETC.
and found his knowledge to be *VERY GOOD INDEED.*
for his age and experience.

signed: *Ian McLaren.*

Captain Ian MᶜLaren
Extra Master Mariner

Newham Recorder ran an article on the amazing kids from the Edith Moorey Home, together with one of my best photographs of Peter, John and Victor out on the river in *Martha*. Then Mr Mathews, the Director of Newham Social Services, issued a dry report entitled 'The Use of Volunteers in the Child Care Service — 14th December, 1976' which read as follows:

★ ★ ★

This report informs the Committee of the progress of a venture with children in residential care. Some two years ago the Department was approached by Mrs R. Raynes, wife of a previous Deputy Medical Officer of Health for the London Borough of Newham, regarding the possibility of arranging for a group of boys to learn the art of sailing and to study forms of navigation. The boat used for the practical sailing was owned by Dr and Mrs Raynes, and moored at the London Marina. At the outset it was felt that the experiment should be task orientated. All the boys were from the Edith Moorey Home, their ages ranging from 9 to 13 years.

The boys were in two groups, spending half a day each fortnight under the guidance of Mrs Raynes. This was made possible through the co-operation of the school staff at each of the schools attended who, on each games afternoon, allowed the children to be released from school.

During the first year the boys, none of whom had previous sailing experience, became aware of the many facets of the equipment of a boat, knots, personal and corporate safety, etc., which was related to trips on the boat in the Marina and on the River Thames. During the winter the academic aspects of navigation, rules of the sea, etc., were undertaken both on the boat and in their home.

During the year, the boys spent a day on the bridge of a cross-Channel steamer, taxing the Captain and crew on the operating of a large ship, and especially on basic navigation methods which they had learnt during the previous period.

Progress was such that some of the boys were sent on courses on training ships, namely the *Larvik* and the *Arethusa*, where they, together with other boys, formed the crew on ten day trips to the Continent and around the coast of this country.

The project is continuing and I am informed by my Advisory Staff that there has been a marked change for the better in the boys. There is no doubt that their confidence and independence have improved as a result of this experience, and it has given them a new outlook on life.

A few weeks ago a test was arranged for them on the practical and academic aspects of seamanship. The examiner was Captain Ian McLaren, Deputy Head of the School of Navigation, and you will be pleased to know that three of the eight boys gained a distinction, and five passed with merit. I would like to record my thanks to Mrs Raynes who has spent endless time and energy in making this venture possible, as well as to Miss Murphy, the senior Houseparent of the Edith Moorey Home, who has participated in the venture to the full, including undertaking courses in her own time and at her own expense to support the boys.

R. H. Mathews
Director of Social Services

★ ★ ★

The last boating Tuesday in 1976 turned out to be a fitting climax to the autumn term. A Force 9 gale was forecast, together with a visit from Jim

Spencer which was greeted with great pleasure by the boys of Number 1 group. Philip even managed to bribe Mark to do a swop with him so that the three children who had sailed on *Arethusa* last summer were there to welcome their skipper.

The combination of Jim's presence and the strength of the wind encouraged the boys to show off in the most frivolous ways, tearing round the dock in *Water-Rat* inclined at an angle of 60°, then producing their certificates (some of them already framed) at tea-time for his inspection and admiration.

Jim left us in the middle of a dramatic thunderstorm, turning round as he leapt ashore to shout to the boys: 'I promise to take as many of you as possible on *Arethusa* next summer!'

★   ★   ★

A cold wrap-me-up-warm sort of day — me at the helm of Roskilde.

Chapter 16

Stephen was inside the cabin pushing the chamois-leather lethargically backwards and forwards over the curved brass frame of the barometer; and humming that tuneless dirge again — like an Eskimo on an ice-flow, drifting far away into the never-never land.

'What's on your mind?' I asked him, laying out a chart of the North Sea for the afternoon's study.

'What d'you think's goin' to happen to me and Mark next weekend?' he countered, ignoring my question.

'No idea.'

'Well, our mum's come back after all these years. Married again, she is, wiv another new kid; wants us to go an' spend the weekend in her place, to see what she thinks of us now!'

'Well, isn't that exciting...' I began; but a glance at his face cut me short. Perhaps it would be, or perhaps it wouldn't?

A week later Emily gave me a rough idea of how things had turned out. Mum, it appeared, had gone up in the world, with white Indian carpets and middle class surroundings; and Mark, in particular, didn't care for this new set-up with the prissy little kid behaving as if it owned the place. So he had cast maggots into the cooking-pot, so to speak, by wiping his muddy boots on the white carpets and making it quite clear that she was not doing them any special favour by inviting them to stay.

On Monday morning she telephoned to Ken Boyce in his office at Newham Social Services Department and said, 'I've changed my mind. I don't want to see the boys any more. They remind me too much of their father!'

So that was that. But why come back at all and announce to people that she was going to invite her sons to stay for a few weekends, with a view to having them back to live with her eventually? Did she expect them to be sitting quietly in a corner for four or five years, waiting for this wonderful moment?

A number of changes were taking place in the Edith Moorey Home about that time. As the boys grew older they became harder to control, and Emily began to hint at the need for a home of her own; somewhere to which she could escape when she was off duty where no one could find her — except a few close friends who would never divulge her whereabouts.

She suffered not only from the boys' behaviour at times, she told me, but also from some of their parents who enjoyed coming round to Norwich Road to create a noisy disturbance. One such parent was a mentally-disturbed West Indian mother whose son, a charming boy with an excellent character, was put in Care for a short period along with the rest of our gang. George's mother made a point of turning up unexpectedly at all hours of the day or night, announcing her arrival by a fanfare of dustbin lids being hurled against the front door, followed by a lengthy diatribe of abuse roared through the letter-box at those inside who had 'stolen her son'.

A gentle bearded house-father, Dave Morton, straight from the Salvation Army, had recently joined the staff at No. 26, and although he and Emily did not always see things through the same pair of spectacles, he was very popular among the boys once they had come to terms with his religious outlook and discovered that he was an ace at unarmed combat. He challenged several of them all together soon after his arrival, and defeated them *en bloc* in less than five minutes. This assured him of their respect and affection for the length of his stay at the Edith Moorey Home.

After the triumph of their first nautical examinations had died down, there was a sharp division among the boys who were really interested in seamanship and navigation and saw it as a ladder to climb towards their golden futures, and those who liked to loll about on the boat in sunny weather, but preferred to rest on their laurels till summer returned or there was a chance of going on some amusing outing at half-term.

Peter and Victor from Number 1 group seldom missed a Tuesday, nor did Stephen, David and Jeff from Number 2 group. In some ways these smaller groups worked well for everyone, as there were fewer distractions during their winter studies and Peter and Victor, in particular, devoured everything I taught them like hungry wolves. They had both set their hearts on joining the Merchant Navy.

Stephen and David were, perhaps, the most unlikely ones as little Jeff, encouraged by his unexpected certificate, still saw himself as a budding Sea Captain! But Stephen had never shown any special desire to become a seafarer and David — well, I am not sure how he saw his future; so I came to the heart-warming conclusion that they both enjoyed their Tuesday outings and did not wish to stop coming, whatever the end results might be.

I bought a new set of model buoys in January, as the IALA had just begun to change the buoyage system all over Northern Europe so the children had to learn the new cardinal system as well as a change of colouring in many of the old channel-marking buoys. The new set cost over £100 but were objects of great beauty, and the old ones made splendid mantelpiece ornaments later on.

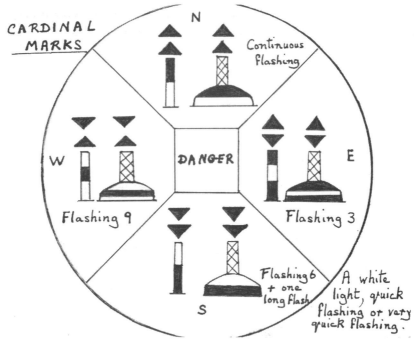

The Cardinal Buoys and their lights.

A fierce grey coldness gripped the London Marina for several weeks, but we were warm enough inside *Roskilde*'s cabin with the charcoal stove glowing in one corner and the boys clustered round the chart table, vying with each other to get the best answers. We planned a passage from Ipswich to Woodbridge one Tuesday, and there was much consternation when Peter's vessel ran aground on the off-lying shoals at the entrance to the River Deben on the top of high water, spring tides.

'I orways said you didn't know nuffink about tides — how to work 'em out an' all that!' Victor gloated happily, turning the pages of the tide tables with a conceited smirk on his face.

'You shut your trap you silly turd,' Peter snarled crossly; 'an' wait to see how I'm goin' to get off the shoal wivout shoutin' for help, like you'd be doin'!'

He inhaled noisily then informed us that he'd get the sails down straight away, so as not to be blown further on to the bank; blow up the rubber dinghy at top speed, put the anchor and all the crew into it (except himself) to take some weight out of the boat, then order them to row like hell towards the deep-water channel and drop the hook; meanwhile he'd bounce around from one end of the boat to the other and waggle the tiller to see which end was stuck fast; and if another boat came by causing a big 'washer', he'd have the engine running all ready to go full speed ahead (or astern, depending on the bank) when she rose on the crest of the 'washer'!

'Brilliant!' Ursula and I exclaimed, both amazed at the thought and understanding he had put into this very difficult manoeuvre.

'I think you get top marks for that and we'll forgive you this once for running the boat aground,' I added.

Apart from passage-planning, we worked hard on the Rule of the Road, the new buoyage system, and how to apply variation, deviation and leeway to our courses, so that the answers came as second nature and not just inspired guesswork. Whatever the weather, Peter took *Water-Rat* out for a sail before tea. And when it was Number 2 group's day, David often volunteered to scrub *Roskilde*'s decks or clean out the dinghy or polish the brasswork.

Dick and I went to Walton-on-Naze at the weekends to paint *Martha*'s hull, and the days sped by full of hopes and plans for the summer voyaging.

'What kind o' tramp you goin' to be tonight, Rozelle?' Mark inquired.

I was half way up a ladder in Durning Hall, trying to secure one end of a paper garland to a projecting nail. But before I had time to answer he began to tell me about the straw hat belonging to Auntie Em that she said he could borrow; and what did I think he should wear below it? A 'normous white shirt on loan from Dave Morton, or a brown tweed skirt and torn lace blouse to make him look like an out-of-work Social Worker?

He danced around beneath my ladder, making a pantomime with his face and hands to show me how he would look; and very nearly caused me to fall to the ground with laughing at the absurd pictures he drew for me.

Peter Cobb had organized our Tramp's Dance to help make some money towards the boys' sailing holidays which had proved such a success the previous summer. And the Reverend Jimmy Froud, a remarkable man who ran the Aston Charities in Newham, had lent us Durning Hall for the evening. By the time we had decorated the walls with brilliant-coloured posters and hung paper garlands across the ceiling, the place looked fit to receive the Queen.

Everyone was there by eight o'clock: all the Newham people whom Peter had induced to buy tickets for themselves and their friends, the teachers and social workers, the friends and relatives of some of the boys, the house-parents and, first and foremost, the boys themselves, if you could recognize them prancing happily around in the pink glow of the special lighting effects. There was to be a prize later on for the best-dressed tramp, so most people had taken a great deal of trouble over their appearance.

Philip wore a black felt-hat adorned with autumn leaves.

Philip, who wore longish hair according to the fashion of the late 1970s, had topped it with a black felt hat adorned with autumn leaves. Below this he made a striking impression with a loud check tie on a floral shirt under an ancient black waistcoat. Victor had affected the French onion-seller look, wearing a black beret at a rakish angle and a dark jersey under a shabby duffel-coat. John, whose hair was even longer than Philip's, wore a girl's beret above a tramp's suit of the country lane variety; and David wore a red and white woollen cap above a blackened face (very startling!), with a torn shirt and ageing trousers well-aerated with holes. Peter appeared to be some kind of Chinese tramp with bits of fur dangling from a white titfer; and Stephen wore a Scottish beret surmounted by an enormous pom-pom, a long

Back row — *Philip, John and me.*
Middle row — *Winkle, Victor and David.*
Front row — *Mark and Jeff.*

scarf thrown about a check female jacket, and large baggy trousers that showed a tendency to descend at unexpected intervals. Finally, the two little ones were by no means insignificant: Jeff, buried beneath a tall black Welshwoman's hat, had decided to wear his Scout's uniform with some unusual additions; and to half-blacken his face. Mark, on the other hand, had gone the whole hog; only the whites of his eyes and his big front teeth gleamed under Auntie Em's immense straw hat, the crown decorated with a striped tie and a red flower. He had, perhaps wisely, given up the Social Worker idea, and draped his small body in a torn white shirt with a long tail suspended over the back of his ragged trousers, and his wrists were clutched in with bits of string.

Durning Hall was like a Turkish bath by ten o'clock. The music was loud and cheerful, the food prepared by Peter Cobb and his wife, Carol, plentiful and delicious, and everyone appeared to be having a wonderful time.

The winner of the best tramp's costume was to be announced at eleven o'clock and, as the minutes ticked by, the children wore expectant looks and could be seen preening themselves in front of a big mirror in the gents'.

Dick was dressed as a derelict fisherman and I was a down-at-heel flower-seller, but we had to admit that there were two unknown tramps who had the edge on all of us. One was a big tramp wearing a bowler hat on top of a red

Dick and Peter Cobb at Durning Hall.

wig, dark glasses and a white beard that divided into three sections round its lower edge. A loud check jacket and plus-fours completed his costume, and the boys were convulsed with laughter each time he sidled up to them. The second tramp was quite different: he was an under-the-arches type of tramp, his face concealed beneath a filthy old hat. He was just a typical, rather tragic old tramp.

'Who *is* that scumbag?' Stephen asked me in a peevish whisper. 'He got here late an' no one knows who he is or where he comes from.'

The rest of the gang collected round us, hoping that we could throw some light on the origin of this strange tramp. But he was as much of a mystery to us as he was to Peter Cobb who knew almost everyone in Newham, especially those who had bought tickets for our dance.

'All will be revealed at eleven o'clock,' Dick told them soothingly. 'It's no use letting jealousy ruin your evening!'

At last the great moment arrived and the judges were seen to be deliberating fiercely behind a makeshift screen. They had been carefully selected from among the more serious citizens of Newham who had no axes to grind — no one who had a friend at the dance would have been contemplated. And sure as white mice thrive in small boys' pockets, they picked the poor old tramp as winner of the competition!

'Effing stranger!' Philip muttered; 'It's not fair comin' in late an' sweeping up the prize like that!'

Then the most extraordinary things began to happen. The judges suddenly announced the winner of a second prize — a bottle of sherry had been hastily smuggled on to the platform by Peter Cobb — and it turned out to be the big red-headed tramp who bared his teeth and danced a little jig, then tore off his wig and beard to reveal Auntie Em beneath!

Meanwhile the winner of the first prize had advanced towards the group of bad-tempered children and removed his outer garments . . . and there stood none other than our own Jim Spencer!

★   ★   ★

The sun shone warmly on the London Marina during the latter half of February, and some of the children worked like beavers at drawing weather maps from the shipping forecasts, plotting positions on a chart, using the Rule of Twelfths and transit bearings to find out when and how to enter

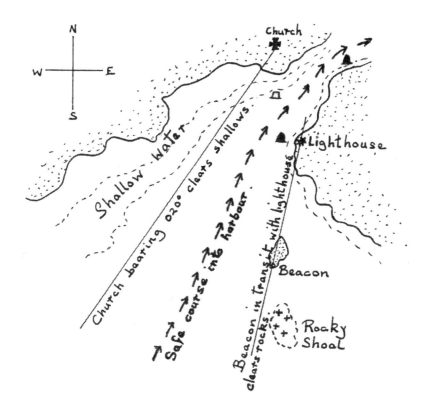

some drying-out harbour and planning exciting passages across the Channel and North Sea.

David, Stephen and Jeff did some eye-catching manoeuvres round the dock in *Roskilde*, causing a buzz of admiration in the dockmaster's office; and Peter frequently announced that he had quite made up his mind to join the Merchant Navy. His chartwork had improved a great deal since the previous year, and Victor was no longer able to point out his mistakes when they were working out tidal problems or turning true courses into compass ones.

On February 22nd, however, we abandoned all thoughts of coastal navigation as it was the half-term holiday — the long-awaited Tuesday for a mystery expedition into the blue! Ursula, Dave Morton and I were to take five of the boys out for the day, and I remember that we opened a map of Essex at random, spotted a place that was marked 'Ruins of old Castle', with a reservoir nearby, and said: 'Let's go there, shall we?'

It was a day cut out for exploration and adventure with huge cauliflower clouds, glittering sunbeams and a strong west wind. So we drove to Pleshey Castle and spread out our picnic lunch on a steeply sloping hillock, then the boys clambered about among the ruins and Peter, Victor and Stephen stood on a ridge outlined against the sky. They were wearing smart new jackets

We spread out our picnic lunch on a steeply sloping hillock. L–R: Back row —
Philip and Stephen. Front row — Ursula, Mark, Victor and Peter.

Peter, Victor and Stephen on the ridge, outlined against the sky.

made of some navy-blue shiny material, with red and yellow stripes down each arm, and they looked like valiant knights about to launch a surprise attack on the castle.

'How about coming with us to look at the old church?' Ursula called up from below in a deflationary tone. She never cared for these exhibitionist displays.

'What a good idea,' Dave Morton chipped in, just as Stephen had begun to tell us that he was not in the habit of going inside churches, 'like as if they were caffs or 'musement arcades, know what I mean?'

'Well, it won't do you any harm for once,' Ursula told him; so we slid down the hill and wandered round the peaceful old church with its grey stone tower and fine stained-glass window over the altar. The boys' faces expressed a variety of thoughts and impressions — like a jigsaw puzzle with a few bits missing.

We drove on, after the church, and soon came to the big reservoir which proved a popular place to visit. First there were some hefty swings and see-saws on which to work off the effects of lunch and the church; then the reservoir itself, with a narrow jetty leading you out towards the middle. Philip picked up Mark and threatened to throw him into the water, which soon brought Peter and Victor running to his rescue. Piercing shrieks rent the air and a water-battle ensured, with much noise and laughter. This was followed by total silence, while the boys sat in a row on the end of the jetty waiting for the fish to rise.

'Let's go to the seaside now,' I called out from the shore, as Dave had just said he did not think it was the right sort of weather nor time of day to get a fish to rise.

We were soon packed inside the two cars, heading towards Leigh-on-Sea. I kept a sharp eye on the rear windows in my driving-mirror to check for any racist gestures; but the boys, who were also keeping a sharp eye on me in the mirror, behaved like a covey of angels.

It was high water at Leigh-on-Sea, with the bawley-boats swinging to their anchors and the dark wedge of Canvey Island tracing a strong line across the horizon between us and the cranes and chimneys of Gravesend. We had tea on the beach: banana and apricot jam sandwiches, scones, Swiss roll and Mr Kipling's cherry slices washed down with hot tea or cans of coke, according to taste. Then the sun set in a bed of purple and black clouds and a chill wind blew in from the sea, while scores of buoys out in the Thames estuary winked their red, green and gold eyes to tell us where the sandbanks lay. It was the magic hour, the time of the afterglow, when mysterious black ships moved silently downstream on the first of the ebb and the children hopped about like fleas on the seashore.

'I prefer this place to Southend,' Dave observed, as he helped us pack up the picnic-basket. 'Nice and peaceful here, and no skinheads about!'

'I so agree,' Ursula replied; 'and even the children don't look as if they're missing the roundabouts and fruit machines, do they?'

We stood up to go and I noticed a look of wonder on Victor's face as he turned towards the open sea to watch a freighter heading out into the night.

'Ave you 'eard the latest rumours, doll?' Madge lent across the counter with an anxious look in her eyes and gave me a sharp rap on the knuckles to focus my attention.

'No, I haven't heard any rumours just lately,' I replied defensively. 'I've been rather busy working for an exam this winter.'

'Exams! At your age?' she peered at me with open disbelief.

'Yes; my husband and I are working for our Ocean Tickets,' I tried to explain; 'you know, all about finding your way out at sea when there's only the sun, moon or stars to tell you where you are.'

'Cor, love-a-duck!' she gasped; then there was a longish pause.

'That rumour you mentioned?' I prompted.

'Well, what our Albert tells me is this,' she began, spreading her elbows across the counter as she warmed to her theme. "E was told by some geyser up the 'ousin' orfice as 'ow Cyprus is goin' ter be swept clean orff the face of the map ter make way fer one o' them fancy 'ousin' estates an' a big new road. An' all rahnd 'ere's goin' ter change so you wouldn't recernize it no more in a few years' time. Bleedin' shame I calls it, when you 'members the good times we've all 'ad in ole Cyprus, even if it ain't no more'n a shanty-town, like they keeps tellin' us.'

She looked on the verge of tears which made me feel quite weepy as well — even though Cyprus was not my home. But I could hardly bear to think of the London Marina, the old Gallion's and the little shop being swept away — just a few heaps of rubble and some stagnant water left behind, where there had been so much sunshine and laughter...

The month of March was full of ups and downs; painting *Roskilde* and *Martha* for the new season — cold hard work, but very satisfying when the finishing coats sparkled in the spring sunlight; then there was the new miniature outboard engine which enabled us to circle round the dock for a whole hour in *Water-Rat* one Tuesday, to keep David and Stephen out of mischief. Alternate Tuesdays Peter and Victor worked at endless tidal problems, fog signals, plotting fixes, fire-fighting theory, laying off courses on a chart and an occasional visit to the London Dungeons or St Katharine's Dock to reward them for their labours.

By the middle of March I had succeeded in running *Roskilde*'s battery to a standstill.

'Never mind,' I tried to soothe Dick who had joined us all for lunch that day. 'I'll bring it home in the car tonight and ask Mr Barlow to put it on charge for us.'

Following a hectic afternoon and an argumentative tea-party, I stayed on after the boys had left to struggle with the battery in peace. It came out of its box like a dream, with two lengths of rope tied right round it attached to a clever block and tackle arrangement I had rigged to the boom, then led back to a sheet winch. It was a cold windy evening and *Roskilde* plucked at her mooring ropes just as I had begun to swing the monster round on to the side deck. The boat heeled to starboard and the battery tipped a fraction of an inch, escaped from its loops of rope and plunged dramatically into the London Marina, soaking me with icy water to celebrate its final journey to the bottom of the dock!

I arrived back home late, wet and in disgrace; but the following evening was to be the written exam for our Ocean Master's Certificates, so there was little time to dwell on the missing battery.

We both did rather well in the examination, much to Dick's surprise, as most of the questions were way beyond my comprehension. But somehow I managed to solve the PZX Triangle (an imaginary spherical triangle in the sky) by means of the Marcq St Hilaire method, using the spherical haversine formula; or, in plain language, I pulled a jumble of figures at random from the Nautical Almanac and Norie's Tables and combined them with some sextant shots of the sun, moon and stars plus a few readings of the chronometer, to calculate my position, give or take a few miles, in the middle of the Atlantic Ocean!

'You'll find it particularly useful in the Thames Estuary!' remarked a facetious engineering student in the canteen later on that evening.

He would, however, have been surprised to know that I did — only a few days later. Peter Cobb and I were paying a visit to the Sea Training College at Gravesend to try and secure places there for Peter and Victor when they left school. And the Captain-in-Charge was so impressed with my new certificate (which had, by chance, crept into my handbag that morning) that he promised to make a special application for our boys to come to his college as soon as they were old enough.

A week or two later we visited the Careers Officer in Prescott Street, an uncompromising person who handled all applications to join the Merchant Navy. I had brought photo-copies of Peter, Philip and Victor's certificates to show the man, and was just beginning to enjoy his flattering comments about ones so young having absorbed all that knowledge, when he fixed Peter Cobb with a stern gaze and said: 'I take it all these lads have perfect eyesight if they're considering applying for the Seamanship Branch?'

'Well, one of them does wear glasses,' Peter admitted warily. 'But he's the hardest worker and the keenest of all the boys.'

'Makes no difference.' The man's profile reminded me of a granite crag. 'If he needs to wear glasses, the only branch of the Merchant Navy who'll consider him is the Catering Branch. Stands to reason you've got to see properly if you're on watch on a ship's bridge in murky weather.'

Peter muttered that he thought all that watch-keeping lark on open bridges was old hat, and now they only had to look at their radar screens to find out what was likely to hit them.

The man dismissed us with a don't-waste-my-time expression on his face, his eyes as cold and hard as ice-cubes. But once outside in the street, Peter said: 'Let's not say anything to little Peter just yet. It will be a terrible blow to him if he knows, and there may be some way round it like the fishing-fleet or tugs or coasters, what d'you think?'

'Yes, I agree. It would wreck his future life to be told there's no hope of going to sea — and I know he'd hate to be a steward. Let's do all we can to find some other way of sending him.'

On March 29th we took *Roskilde* for her first voyage out on the river that year. Ursula came with Peter, Victor and Mark, all dressed like polar explorers to repel the icy north wind. It was a day of immense cotton wool clouds and brilliant shafts of sunlight, of white horses galloping across the river and a gleaming golden runway from Gallion's Point on the north bank to Margaret Ness Lighthouse over on the Kentish shore.

We hoisted the mainsail and working jib and sailed briskly downriver, each boy steering for ten minutes, then diving into the cabin to get warm again.

'It's the best day I've had on the boat this winter!' Mark poked his head out of the hatch to tell me.

'Because it's the only day you've had on her, that's why! What about all those other days when we were working hard with the charts and tide tables inside the freezing cabin?'

Mark's tongue appeared briefly between his big front teeth, then his head vanished below the hatch.

We sailed up and down the river for two hours or more, and Victor declared that it was wicked and Peter said he would try to mend one of the switches on *Roskilde*'s dashboard when we got home. At four o'clock we were approaching the lock gates which began to open at that moment, so there was a rush to furl the sails and get the fenders and mooring ropes ready.

'Phew!' exclaimed Ursula, as we threw a line to the PLA driftwood boat, already secured inside the lock, and the gates closed with a wham behind us. 'That *was* a near thing.'

'All them kids yours, love?' asked the driftwood captain, examining the boys with interest. 'They know a thing or two about moorin' a boat, I'll say that for 'em.'

The three in question puffed out their chests, while self-satisfied smirks spread across their faces which made Ursula wish to disown them. But she was saved from answering the man's question by a shout from the inner bridge. Emily had come to join us for her birthday tea-party aboard *Roskilde*.

Peter steered the boat out of the lock and brought her alongside our pontoon without a bump, then he and Victor moored her and made everything shipshape, glancing over their shoulders at intervals to see if the driftwood captain was still watching. Mark, meanwhile, made a big show of taking down the burgee and blue ensign, at the same time emitting a high-pitched whistle to announce their descent.

Ursula had lit the candles on Emily's birthday cake and placed some small parcels on her plate, and we poured a big tot of whisky into her mug of tea when she was looking the other way. Outside it was a dark cold evening with frost beginning to form on the rigging; but the snatches of song and 'Happy Birthdays!' filtering out of the for'ard hatch brought a touch of magic to our pontoon.

★   ★   ★

Number 2 group were very jealous when the others came home and gave a vivid description of their afternoon.

The following Tuesday was not suitable for taking Stephen and David out on the river, so we gave them a brief lesson about fog signals — each person pretending they were a ship making the appropriate noises, while the others had to take avoiding action. This proved a very popular way to learn the signals!

We finished studying early and drove to St Katharine's Dock where *Thalatta* was paying a short visit, and Jane Benham gave the boys a warm welcome. And, finally, we came back to my home for tea and allowed the children to spend as long as they wanted in the bathroom and to lie on the sitting-room floor playing with the Scalelectrix set.

'I reckon it's bin just as good a day as the uvver creeps had, if not better!' Stephen declared as they were leaving, much to my relief.

During the school holidays I hired a small van to take all *Martha*'s gear to Walton one Tuesday, and Emily brought four of the boys, Peter, Victor, Mark and George, to help me load up, then we drove in convoy to the coast and had lunch at the pier café. Afterwards we put the gear aboard *Martha*, and Peter and Victor helped me get her ready for sea; three hours' hard work, then we all had a picnic tea on the beach and built sand-castles with deep moats so that they were soon filled by the rising tide.

'I like this place,' Mark announced, with his chin thrust out and nostrils flared, drawing big gulps of North Sea air into his lungs. 'It's like a sort o' dreamland, what wiv the pier an' the funfair, an' the beach an' all that part where the wild birds live, where you took us last summer.'

Martha returned to the London Marina on Sunday, May 1st 1977. Dick and I had left Walton the previous day with a reefed mainsail and heavy black clouds to seaward. It turned out to be a day of hot sunshine and freezing squally showers, a day full of hopes and fears — like so many days at sea. But the weather gradually improved and we sailed across a glittering silver sea all the way from the Blacktail Spit Buoy to Southend Pier; and after Southend there were iridescent streamers shining out of holes in the clouds, beams of glory that lit up the dark freighters moving along Sea Reach on the flood tide.

We dropped anchor in Holehaven for the night, and set off in a thick white fog early next morning. A tug travelling at great speed almost demolished us a few minutes later, so we motored close inshore and attached *Martha* to a ship moored off Shellhaven till the fog lifted.

Late that afternoon we passed through the London Marina lock and noticed two small boys dangling their feet in the water on the end of our pontoon. Peter and Victor had been waiting there for most of the day to welcome *Martha* back home.

Chapter 17

May was a wonderful sailing month; also our last month together before the Tuesday boys began to disperse and the Edith Moorey Home eventually ground to a halt.

But we knew nothing of what the future held in store when we set off — thirteen of us — in both boats on May 8th. *Roskilde*, with Dick in charge, had Peter Cobb, Dave Morton, John, Philip, Little Peter and Stephen to man her; and *Martha*'s crew consisted of Emily, my cousin, Hugh Matheson (who had won a silver medal rowing in the last Olympic Games), David, Victor, Mark and me.

A fresh north-westerly wind was blowing but, not to be outsailed by her

Martha McGilda *leaving the London Marina, North Woolwich.*

big sister, *Martha* was wearing her full spread of Terylene. We hoisted the mainsail and genoa in Gallion's Reach and sped downriver at an exhilarating speed with *Roskilde* thundering along behind us. She threw up clouds of spray as she rose and fell to the steep 'washers' caused by passing tugs; but, hard as she tried, it soon became clear to my delighted crew that she was not going to overtake us. We passed through some violent squalls and heavy showers, but no one complained as we drew further and further ahead of the bigger boat.

''Citin', isn't it?' Mark observed to Hugh, squeezing the river-water out of his best pullover. 'Bet you bin wet a few times an' all, winnin' silver medals on a boat! What's it feel like bein' on telly wiv hundreds and fousands of people watchin' you?'

The other boys had lost their tongues as they gazed at Hugh with round eyes and reverent expressions.

'Any one of you could do the same if you worked hard enough at it,' Hugh told them. 'I might have a few days to spare this summer and I'll give you some training on a boat on the River Lea, if you really want to have a go?'

We were approaching Erith at that moment, so we handed the sails and picked up an empty mooring for our lunch stop. *Roskilde* arrived a few minutes later and selected the mooring next to ours which was also free.

'Them moorin's is private!' yelled an irate yachtsman who was doing a little Sunday pottering on his own boat nearby. 'They ain't placed there fer any Tom, Dick or 'Arry ter pick up.'

The boys emerged from the cabins and ranged themselves along the decks of their respective vessels — quite an impressive sight they made.

'Oo says so?' Victor fired the first return volley, with a contemptuous curl to his lips.

'I do, an' I'll get the 'arbourmaster out 'ere if I 'as any lip from you lot.' The man had assumed a ferocious expression but the boys knew, from past experience, that they had the upper hand as he had never expected to find so many of them aboard. At that moment Peter Cobb and Dave Morton, neither of them delicate china ornaments, emerged from *Roskilde*'s cabin and stood there, four-square plus two, gazing at the Erith yachtsman. This proved to be far more intimidating than anything he had experienced before; so he hastily seized a few belongings, locked his cabin door and, jumping into a small dinghy, rowed furiously towards the shore.

'*No* jeering or swearing, boys!' Peter Cobb held up a hand to cut short the 'Piss offs, etc.' that were erupting all round him. 'Just get on and eat your lunches fast, will you, before that ponce brings the harbourmaster back with him to have you all locked up.'

As soon as we had finished lunch we came alongside *Roskilde* to change crews; and both boats were soon under way, tacking upriver with dollops of greenish-brown water breaking over the bows and pouring along their lee decks. Everyone steered in turn, and John and Philip lay along the narrow decks on either side of *Martha*'s cabin-top, roaring with delight when some extra big wave came crashing down on top of them.

We were all having such a lovely time that we decided to sail on past the London Marina entrance and round Gallion's Point as far as the Woolwich Barrier. We tacked past a Russian freighter waiting to go through the Barrier channel, then ran before the wind on the last lap eastwards, only to find the lock gates firmly closed. So we landed John who scrambled up the iron ladder to the lock-keeper's house, but he was told there was some trouble with the mechanism of the gates and we might have to wait outside for nearly an hour. And that was when the water-battle first began . . .

Roskilde was turning in a tight circle close to *Martha* to hear what John had to report when David received a bucketful of water over his head, skilfully aimed at him by Stephen who had been lurking low down in our cockpit, awaiting his chance. Victor then scored a bull's-eye over his big brother, while Dick steered *Roskilde* round and round *Martha* to give his crew the best angles from which to drench us! Bellows of fury and excitement rent the air as the two boats spun round each other like a couple of whirling dervishes, and dripping figures leapt about on deck or hung over the sides with buckets to replenish their ammunition.

Some half-an-hour later Peter Cobb was crouching bad-temperedly inside *Martha*'s cabin, massaging the back of his neck with a damp bath-towel; and Hugh was similarly employed in *Roskilde*'s galley, his brows furrowed and eyes bleak. It was, perhaps, fortunate that the harbourmaster's launch came speeding towards us at that moment, with a man standing on her bows shouting through a loud-hailer who described us as 'a menace to navigation'!

Dick, who had never been referred to in such terms before, paused in the middle of his current circumnavigation of *Martha* to straighten the tiller and order his crew to behave themselves; but not before Mark had seized the opportunity to score a direct hit at Dave Morton.

The lock gates opened at last to receive the two boats manned by thirteen saturated mariners, much to the amusement of the lock-keeper.

'Looks as 'ow a good time 'as bin 'ad by all concerned!' he chuckled, as the gates closed behind us.

Despite the water-battle Hugh kept his promise, and later that month began to train several of the boys on the River Lea. Philip, Victor and David were the keenest, and as soon as they escaped from school they would make their way to the boat-house at Springhill Park in Clapton and spend a strenuous hour or two rowing or sculling on the river.

Philip rowing on the River Lea.

Martha, meanwhile, was out every Tuesday with her cargo of children who were pleased to have her back, and a few seemed eager to learn all they could from her. Time, however, was running short for two of the boys — John and Jeff.

Little Jeff was the first to go, a few days after he had excelled himself in charge of *Martha* doing a number of complicated manoeuvres round the dock. There had been a meeting of Social Workers — one of those serious affairs at which the fate of certain children is decided, for better or for worse. And it was decreed that he should go to a foster home as he was not doing very well at school nor in the Edith Moorey Home, so it was suggested that he might stand a better chance all round if he could rely on the individual attention of a good foster-mother.

Well, Jeff went to two foster homes, one after another, and that was the period when he started running away, sometimes walking for miles across London to get back to his mum's home. But as soon as she found him sitting on her doorstep she would ring up Newham Social Services Department and tell them: 'He's here again! Come an' fetch him soon as possible, will you, 'fore I do him an injury.'

Jeff still came back to Norwich Road now and then — in between foster homes and the boarding-school that he was sent to later on. He was devoted to his Auntie Em and to Philip, and he always looked forward to an outing in *Martha*.

John was the next one to leave, but this was for quite a different reason: he had asked himself to be transferred to a bigger place than the Edith Moorey Home. He did not like being the oldest boy in the home, and he wanted, he explained, to spread his wings a bit, meet a few girls and expand his horizon in a way that he felt was not possible at present. So they sent him to Violet Ayres Lodge at Buckhurst Hill, a mixed home with many more children; and it was there that he met the girl he was to marry a year or two later.

★　★　★

May 24th was, perhaps, the pinnacle of Number 1 group's sailing days on the river — the day they would sometimes remember when all other days had faded into a grey mist.

The previous Tuesday had been a difficult one; an afternoon of endless turns round the dock because the wind was blowing too hard — or so I thought — to venture out on the river. Stephen and David soon became bored and, instead of rowing *Water-Rat* across to their secret harbour, had disappeared on foot during their free half hour before tea. Then a policeman with angry eyes and a rat-trap mouth strode down our pontoon to tell me that the boys had been reported to him for 'loitering with intent' near the Gallion's Hotel!

'Loitering, perhaps,' I suggested. 'But I doubt if there was much intent round that old ruin?'

But he was an Officer of the Law, and not prepared to bandy words with stupid females. 'They're your responsibility, and if I ever find them over there again I'll have to apprehend you,' he warned.

'Better watch our Ps and Qs!' Ursula remarked, as he stomped back along the pontoon to have a word with Tony Cohen.

Well, that was last Tuesday. The east wind was blowing just as hard on May 24th, but the sun shone dazzlingly and the river called to us in a loud clear voice. Our party consisted of Emily, Ursula, Peter, Victor, Mark and me; and as soon as we had gobbled our lunch we got under way. Emerging from the lock twenty minutes later, I noticed that the river was seething with white horses and the wind whistling in the rigging in the most alarming way. I crawled cautiously along the cabin-top to hoist the double-reefed mainsail and Peter, who was helping me, said, 'There's the old *Sir John Cass* come to see if we know one end of a boat from the uvver!'

She circled round us once or twice and the cadets waved to us from their cosy glassed-in wheelhouse wondering, perhaps, how it felt to be outside on a wet heaving cabin-top, inclined at such an extraordinary angle.

Our three boys steered for ten minutes each, and water came roaring along the lee deck as we tacked downriver. The tide fought against the wind, there were ships on the move whichever way you looked and the waves broke all over us, extracting shrieks of delight from the children. I discovered later that the wind had been blowing Force 6–7 from the north-east that afternoon.

We turned right round between the pylons on either side of the river at Dagenham, and I took the helm as *Martha* surged upriver, the wind threatening to cause an unexpected gybe each time a tall building interrupted its violent gusts. I was thankful to reach the London Marina entrance without any accidents and I recorded the next few minutes in the log-book as follows: 'Circling under engine outside lock gates; the boys hauled down the sails very fast despite the rough water and fierce gusts of wind. Entered lock at great speed and stern mooring rope wrapped itself round the tiller; it nearly broke the backstay and pulled Ursula overboard! Once the gates had closed behind us, there was glorious peace!'

With his mouth full of banana and apricot jam sandwich, Victor announced during tea that it had been the best day he'd ever had out in *Martha*. Peter nodded his head in agreement and Mark discreetly removed some half-chewed bread from his mouth to add: 'My 'pinion's the same as Stitchum's; it's bin the kind o' day we won't never forget.'

Roskilde left the London Marina early in June, and we sailed her back to Harty Ferry in preparation for her summer voyages.

The following week was the Queen's Silver Jubilee and the boys, who had a holiday from school, came to our house to watch the river pageant and to wave flags from the balcony as the Queen and Prince Philip passed in the Royal Barge. Unfortunately neither of them were visible at that moment — after a hectic reception at Greenwich and Deptford they were, perhaps, resting in the cabin. The boys, however, were very disappointed and started using foul language, so Dick promised them he would write to Buckingham Palace to complain!

A week later we celebrated Peter's fifteenth birthday. Ursula, Victor and Mark came with him that Tuesday, and it turned out to be a grey thundery afternoon without much wind. We all agreed that it was not a river day, so we planned to finish work early and pay a visit to H.M.S. *Belfast* as a birthday treat.

I gave the boys a test on fog signals and lights, distress signals, changing magnetic bearings to true, chartwork, weather signs, tidal calculations and boat's equipment; and Peter and Victor excelled themselves, Peter getting top marks. Then we drove to the City and the boys had a lovely time exploring the great warship.

'What the 'ell d'you think you're doin' down the engine-room?' roared a Petty-Officer, perceiving our charges through an open hatch, happily engaged in fingering some enormous spanners.

'Just checkin' up on your tool kit,' Peter shouted back. 'Makin' sure you've got all the right spanners for the job!'

'*Out!*' ordered the Petty Officer. 'And never let me catch you down there again.'

We drove back to Limehouse for fish and chips and birthday cake; and Dick arrived home simultaneously, so he was able to join the party and challenge Peter to a race on the Scalelectrix set.

For many years we have owned a small cottage called Dolphin's Leap which stands high up on the Dover cliffs, close to the South Foreland Lighthouses. Originally the upper and lower lights were used in transit to prevent ships from running aground on the Goodwin Sands; but when the three lightvessels and numerous buoys were placed around the sands in the 1920s, the lower light (the one in our garden) became redundant. It is usually referred to as 'the old lighthouse' on account of its antique appearance and the crop of wall-flowers that sprout haphazardly from the stone-work on the upper ledges.

Dolphin's Leap is the nearest house to France in England, and the garden is a magic place where the gulls build their nests below the edge of the cliffs and the rabbits and foxes rear their babies without fear, while far below them innumerable ships pass through the Dover Straits, day and night.

The old lighthouse in our garden on the edge of the cliffs.

We had often discussed the idea of a camping weekend there with Emily, and the day at last arrived when she and Veronica with seven of the boys drove down in her Corsair, the roof-rack piled high with tents.

'I'm going to give you a serious lecture before Auntie Em releases you,' Dick greeted them. 'That's the edge of the cliff over there, just beyond the old lighthouse, and it's a 350 foot drop on to the rocks below. As you can see there's no fence in front of it, so I want you all to give me a solemn promise that you won't go playing games near there nor peering over the edge to see where the rabbits and gulls live?'

There was a moment of total silence, followed by a gabble of promises so that they could escape from the car. Dick led them forward to look over the edge themselves, to see that he was not exaggerating.

Next came the serious business of selecting places to erect the tents. Emily and Veronica were going to sleep in the house and the boys conceived the idea of putting themselves as far away from us as possible; but Veronica persuaded them to settle for a little walled garden nearby. 'You'll be scared stiff when night falls,' she predicted, 'and all the wild animals come out of their burrows to visit you!'

As soon as the tents were up we walked down to the beach over the springy grass that grows on top of the cliffs. It was full of wild flowers and rabbit-

The 350 feet drop to the rocks below.

Next came the serious business of selecting places to erect the tents.

holes, the latter arousing great excitement in David who threw himself on the ground from time to time, to try and catch a glimpse of some baby rabbits inside.

'You sit at one end, Rozelle,' he ordered me, 'an' don't make a noise! An' I'll puff a fag down the uvver end an' try to smoke 'em out.'

'You wait till Auntie Em catches you smoking!' I began; but Stephen, who had been busy tearing up tufts of long grass, crept up behind me just then and tried to push it down the back of my neck!

As soon as we reached the beach, Philip and George led a climbing party to explore the caves that were dotted about on the cliff-face in tempting positions. All the boys had soon disappeared from sight and we could hear cries of 'Isn't 'arf dark in 'ere! Wonder if the smugglers use this one? We'll leave Gums in 'ere for the night, then 'e can tell us termorrer!'

Mark was the first one to emerge with his trousers covered in chalk and his eyes rounder than usual. 'You aughta climb up 'ere, Auntie!' he called to Veronica. 'It's kind of eerie — jus' the sort o' place you'd love!'

'Can you picture me climbing up that crumbling old cliff!' she roared with laughter. 'Not on your life, boy. Go and get the others, will you, as we're going home to make a big fire for the barbeque.'

An hour or so later smoke was beginning to rise from the eight bricks covered with chicken-wire enclosing a mound of twigs, charcoal, pine cones

Stephen, who had been busy tearing up tufts of long grass, crept up behind me just then . . .

and odds and ends. The boys had washed their faces and hands — wafts of some powerful after-shave lotion came from one group — and drawn up benches or planks of wood resting on logs all around the scene of operations.

We had three guests: Captain Jack Dawson (who used to be my Captain aboard the car-ferry, *Free Enterprise*), his wife, Miriam, and Jean Melhuish, an old friend from Yorkshire who took such a profound interest in what the boys had to tell her that they forgot to give her any of the hostile stares they often reserved for strangers.

'I like Jean,' declared David, helping me to carry the baked potatoes out from the kitchen. 'We've only just met her but she seems like an old friend, know what I mean?'

There were five or six toasting-forks with which to spear the bacon, sausages and lamb chops, with seven hungry children to wield them.

'Mine's ready first!' announced Stephen, brandishing a charred morsel for our inspection.

A curl of blue smoke arose from the fire while the purple fingers of twilight enclosed us. The lights on Cap Gris Nez and Calais harbour entrance began to flash their warning signals; then the great beam of the main South Foreland Lighthouse, only five minutes' run up the hill, swung round above our heads — a triple-flashing light every twenty seconds — illuminating the little white windmill to the east of us so that it gleamed, on and off, like an ivory miracle.

The children were unusually silent as they munched their food and poked at the fire to make it glow. But their eyes were everywhere, drinking in every tiny detail of this strange new landscape.

'Not a bit like Clacton, is it?' George voiced the general opinion. 'But it's orright here ... kind o' wild an' excitin', when you start to wonder what's lurkin' in that wood!'

Presently the moon rose from behind a windswept tree on the cliff edge, a red-gold Chinese lantern shimmering over the dark waters of the Dover Straits. The large alcoholic trifle I had made for 'afters' had all vanished, and the grown-ups were drinking coffee and glasses of brandy while Victor and Mark, who had just climbed to the top of the old lighthouse, came running back to share their discoveries with the rest of the party.

'It's wicked up there!' Victor panted; 'you can see all the stars in the sky an' the ships goin' in an' out of Dover, an' millions of uvvers out on the sea. Me and Mark could see right inside some geyser's house over in France!' he added, to whet the appetites of those who had not yet been up the lighthouse.

Peter, meanwhile, was deeply engrossed in conversation with Jack Dawson who, sensing how very important it was to him, had promised to put in a word for him at the Mercantile Marine office in Dover.

'Jack won't forget about it,' Miriam reassured the anxious boy. 'He'd like to stay at sea till he's a hundred he loves the life so much, so he understands just how you must be feeling!'

Dick went into the house to put on a few of his best-loved records and open the sitting-room windows so that everyone could hear the music. Then the boys played some of their favourite tapes and Emily produced hers — the songs of Elvis Presley.

The moon vanished behind a bank of clouds around midnight and a fine rain began to fall; but no one seemed anxious to go to bed, so I brought out a selection of old umbrellas for those who were still sitting round the dying embers of the fire. Jean had listened to the life-stories of three of the boys by then, and Jack and Miriam had made friends with Stephen and Peter. Dick, whose turn it was to choose a record, had just put on Beethoven's Ninth Symphony; and Victor sat under the evergreen oak tree, just outside the circle of light, with a serious expression on his face.

'I've never listened to music like that before,' he murmured. 'It's quite different to what we play at 'ome.'

When the party finally broke up about 2 a.m., Mark announced with a theatrical shudder: 'I'm not sorry you got us to put the tents near here, Auntie; it looks quite spooky now the moon's gone be'ind the clouds!'

I awoke at daybreak on Sunday morning to the sound of pattering feet and squeals of excitement as the children ran up and down the lighthouse tower, chased rabbits and went exploring — but only very short distances away, with infinite caution.

John, the deputy lighthouse-keeper of the main South Foreland Lighthouse, came striding down the drive just before breakfast to be confronted by the gang of seven, deployed across the lawn in a hostile manner.

'He's O.K.!' I shouted from the window; 'he's come down specially to invite you up the big lighthouse.'

This made a good start to the day; no time to offer assistance with the breakfast washing-up with such an important assignation to keep.

'The things you let them get away with, Rozelle — it shocks me to the core!' Emily shook her head disapprovingly as she helped me clear the table and make some preparations for lunch.

Dick suggested a walk across the cliffs to Deadman's Cove, so we collected the boys from the big lighthouse and walked along the cliff path towards Dover.

'I never seen so many wild flowers before,' Philip told me; 'an' very early this mornin' I seen a baby fox right on the edge of the cliff!'

Peter and Mark were full of what they had been shown inside the lighthouse: the huge bulbs and reflectors, and all the complicated machinery that made the light work. 'If they won't make me into a Sea-Captin when I grow up, Rozelle, I think I'll be a light'ouse-keeper instead,' Mark informed me, watching me closely for reactions to his latest decision.

'Good idea,' I murmured. 'Look! There's Deadman's Cove down there, with the wreck of the old fishing-boat lying on its side. It's supposed to be haunted on the night of the full moon.'

We descended a steep ladder to reach the seashore and the boys prowled suspiciously round the barnacle-encrusted hull, hardly daring to touch it after Mark had given them his version of my story about the ghosts. Then Victor suggested to George, 'How about burying Chums?'

Emily watched from the old gun emplacement above the beach, but I wandered across to the burial party to find only Mark's face visible beneath a mound of pebbles, with Victor showing off his handiwork to an admiring audience.

'You won't get any lunch if you don't hurry,' I said. Better appeal to their stomachs, I thought, if we want to extract him alive!

After lunch in the garden the boys played hide-and-seek round the little wood, then we all went down to the beach to hunt for crabs in the rock pools; and from there to a local farm to pick strawberries — each person with their own particular basket, to take home with them later that evening.

The day flew by and all too soon it was time to pack up the camping gear and get spruced up for going out to supper. Mark, who had sampled a generous squirt of Dick's after-shave lotion and washed his hair with some of my Almond Blossom shampoo, declared that he wouldn't mind staying at Dolphin's Leap for the rest of the summer. Victor sat on the edge of the cliffs gazing at all the ships going up and down the Dover Straits, and the other boys lay on the sitting-room floor racing cars round and round the Scalelectrix set.

Our last supper at the Wimpy Bar in Dover was rather a subdued affair, hemmed in by tired and crusty day-trippers. The freedom of the South Foreland was already a dream in the past.

Chapter 18

Back home in Forest Gate, the children mulled over their weekend at St Margaret's Bay and decided they had enjoyed themselves, and some of them began to harp on the question of when they could come again. It had certainly been different to their usual camping excursions or trips to the seaside, and Mark informed me a week later that he had written out a list of places to explore on his next visit which he had not been able to fit in on the first one.

The constant pressure exerted on us had become unbearable by September, so we arranged another weekend to which Emily and Veronica brought Victor, George, Stephen and Mark. It turned out just as much fun as the first one, with no great change of programme. I remember that we scrambled about on the beach and searched the rock-pools for crabs on Saturday afternoon, then cooked a barbecue supper under the stars to the sound of our favourite music; and on Sunday we walked across the cliffs to Kingsdown, with a helicopter rescue taking place out at sea to add a touch of drama to our day.

That particular weekend caused intense aggravation to Philip and David who had not been able to come for reasons I no longer recall — only their hurt and angry faces when they listened to the others enlarging on the beauties of their second visit! So Dick and I decided to issue invitations for a third, and final, weekend in November; but, because the weather was cold and wintry by then, we limited it to the two boys who were to drive down with us on Saturday morning, and sleep inside the cottage instead of in a tent.

After a visit to the beach and a delicious tea at Jean's house, we spent the evening racing cars round the Scalelectrix track on the sitting-room floor in front of a log fire. A fierce gale was blowing round the house and angry waves beat against the foot of the cliff, while the night was filled with rain and spindrift and the crying of gulls.

We had worried that the boys might find it rather dull with no barbecue and only the two of us to entertain them. But they seemed quite contented, and we awoke on Sunday morning to snatches of song issuing from the bathroom, together with a loud buzzing noise that I was quite unable to identify.

'Good God!' Dick suddenly exclaimed, leaping out of bed like one who has been stung by a wasp. 'That noise sounds exactly like my brand new electric tooth-brush!'

He roared along the passage and into the bathroom to find his worst fears confirmed; for there stood David with gleaming white teeth and a face like a

winter sunrise, holding Dick's latest toy in his guilty right hand.

Half-an-hour later the sun rose unexpectedly out of a nest of blue-black clouds; and our rather severe descent of the short staircase to cook the breakfast was arrested by the sweet smell of burning pine cones. Glancing through the sitting-room door we saw Philip and David on their knees in front of the fireplace which they had cleaned out and relaid, and a young fire was now crackling merrily while David worked the bellows and Philip held up a sheet of newspaper to draw the flames. Dick began to smile again inspite of the fierce emotions churning in his breast; and from then onwards the day soared like Concorde taking off from ground level, and the seagulls and rabbits round the old lighthouse suddenly seemed larger than life!

Directly after breakfast we walked across to Jack Dawson's house, and he

Captain Jack Dawson on the bridge of his new ship, the Viking Viscount.

took us to Dover to visit his new ship, the *Viking Viscount*. The boys were shown all over her by the quartermaster, then we had lunch with Jack in solitary state in the dining-saloon, as there were no passengers aboard at that time; and, finally, we spent a few sacred moments up on the bridge.

'Well, I hope that's given you some idea of how we live on a modern car-ferry,' Jack said to Philip; 'and I wish you every success when you go for your interview.'

We had not realized until that moment that Philip had also set his sights on the Merchant Navy; but, judging by the broad grin that spread across his face as his eyes swivelled from the Captain to the ship's wheel, we assumed that something was buzzing inside his head which Jack had perceived immediately. Perhaps the boy planned to spring a surprise on us all, to prove that Victor was not the only star turn in his family?

Sunday afternoon was spent playing hide-and-seek among the disused army huts behind the big lighthouse; an idea inspired by David which saw us lurking in dank corners, dodging through derelict rooms and running for dear life when one of our pursuers showed his head.

We drove back to London later that evening and dropped the boys off at Norwich Road.

'Sorry I tried your new toof-brush, Dickie,' David stood on the pavement waving us goodbye. 'But I reckon it's bin the best weekend of all — far bettern the uvver scumbags had!'

During that summer *Martha* still sailed on the river with a few of the boys each Tuesday, but the alternate weeks had taken on a different pattern as the children grew older. Number 1 group, consisting of Peter and Victor only, worked harder than ever — I felt sure they could have sailed the boat perfectly well on their own, without any grown-ups aboard, had they been given the chance. And when it was not a 'river day', they vied with each other to get the highest marks in the tests that I often set them.

'Your ship is five miles out to sea off the Yorkshire coast in a snowstorm, with almost no visibility, and you are making for a tiny harbour just north of Flamborough Head. How would you work out a compass course to lead you safely to the lighthouse on the harbour entrance?' That was the sort of question they seemed to enjoy, while they gnawed the ends off innumerable pencils and watched each other like lynxes to see how the other turd was tackling the problem! Inevitably they made a few mistakes, but they knew what they were doing and I was often amazed at the intelligent answers they produced.

One afternoon we were in the lock — Ursula, Peter, Victor and I — waiting for the water to rise so that we could go for a sail. Victor was in charge of the bow line and Ursula the stern line, while Peter fended off with the boat-hook amidships. He had seemed unusually preoccupied ever since he came aboard, and suddenly he swung round and asked us: 'D'you think it's really true that every kid who grows up in Care like us, is sure to end up in prison soon arter he leaves school?'

'Of course it's not true!' Ursula and I said simultaneously. 'What on earth gave you that idea?'

'Well, Auntie Em was talking to Mark's Social Worker last evenin', an' that's what they was sayin'. They was drinkin' a cup of tea in the kitchen with the 'atch open so we could listen to every word.'

'Well, it's a pack of lies!' I said, feeling very angry with people who have no qualms about making such statements in front of children. 'Everything depends on you yourself, how strong a character you've got and how hard you want to work to make a better life for yourself. I agree that it's much more difficult than it is for kids who have nice homes and understanding parents to fall back on; but it's also a greater challenge for you to work at. Why, look at our friend, the lock-keeper, over there!'

As if he were aware of the four pairs of eyes focused upon him at that moment, he turned round and gave us the thumbs up sign to show that the lock was about to open. We motored out on to the smiling green river with our friend waving to us from the swing-bridge above.

★   ★   ★

Alternate Tuesdays were quite different. Sometimes I used to dread them if the boys had decided to be bored or 'wind me up', as Emily described it; while other days were lovely memorable days when everyone tried hard to do their best and enjoyed themselves in their own special ways. Jeff's birthday, July 12th, was one such day. He was back at Norwich Road for a few days in between foster homes, and enchanted to find himself at the helm again, waving to the Captains of big freighters as we sailed downriver to Dagenham and back.

All three boys were in a good humour that day. David whistled a catchy tune while he rubbed the Brasso into the dirty winches, then polished them till they shone like burnished gold. Stephen pleased Ursula by asking her about the theatres she had seen that summer, and sucking his teeth noisily while he murmured appreciative words as she described the great dramas of the London stage. And Jeff just stood on the stern thwart wearing his enormous grin, the tiller clasped firmly in his right hand and the sunlight glinting on his ugly spectacles.

He revealed nothing of his life in the foster-home; his face, in fact, became quite blank if you asked him how he had got along there. But the happy grin persisted all through his birthday tea-party in *Martha*'s cockpit, and only began to fade when Emily whispered to us that they ought to leave early as she had promised to take him to his new foster-home before six o'clock. Suddenly his glasses misted over so that he had difficulty climbing ashore from the boat; and he seemed to have shrunk — or was I just imagining it — and to be no more than a thin waif of a child, lost in the savage jungle that surrounded him.

Dick and I went to Spitsbergen on an old Norwegian ship that summer. We were away for several weeks, delivering the mail and cargo to Bear Island and Longyearbyen, the capital of Spitsbergen, and visiting the edge of the pack-ice less than six hundred miles from the North Pole. Amid that glittering world of rainbow-coloured icebergs, whales, seals, Arctic foxes and millions of sea-birds, I often wondered what the children were doing, especially on a Tuesday; and whether *Martha* would look dirty and neglected by the time we came home.

I need not have worried for she was immaculate, and it was clear that Emily and the boys had been working hard on her to give me a lovely surprise. We continued with our sailing days on the river, but one Tuesday it was blowing so hard that we decided to take Stephen and David to the National Gallery instead.

'Seems a funny choice when you're meant to be teaching them seamanship!' Dick commented that evening.

'I know, but those two don't really absorb any of the theory, but they *do* show quite a talent for drawing and painting.'

'What did they think of the National Gallery then?' he inquired, with that maddeningly sceptical glint in his eyes.

'Well, they rushed through the rooms, then crept back to look at the nudes and spent a lot of time tittering together in corners!' I had to admit.

During the summer holidays most of the boys enjoyed a week at sea aboard the *Arethusa* or *Thalatta* again, and we took them out sailing in *Roskilde* while they were on holiday at Walton-on-Naze. By the end of August, however, the second nautical examinations had begun to loom large, and a date had already been set aside for them in November.

We had a telephone call one day in October from a captain who had been our instructor at the School of Navigation during our Ocean Master's course the previous winter. A pupil of his who was doing a refresher course in the college, he told us, owned a sturdy motor-fishing-vessel and was a very fine seaman. He had sailed her up to the Arctic Ocean several years running to do some research work, and was anxious to recruit a young crew for next season who already had some experience in coastal navigation and seamanship. Remembering about our boys and how much some of them longed to go to sea, the captain wondered if we would care to meet this man for a chat?

We thought of Peter, who knew by then that his eyesight would prevent him from joining the Merchant Navy; and Philip, who might or might not pass the stiff entrance tests; and, without pausing for further reflection, we said 'Yes, we would very much like to meet him.'

A day was fixed, and Emily came round to our house to form her own opinion of Mr P. who arrived in time for an evening drink. He brought with him a selection of photographs of his beautiful M.F.V., as tough a vessel as you could wish to see with extra strengthening around her bows and stern to resist the ice pressure. One photograph, I remember, showed a polar bear sauntering across the ice-floes towards her in a swirling snowstorm.

His plan was to try out the boys on the River Hamble first, then to sail them across to Cherbourg during the Christmas holidays to find out how they would respond to the open sea in wintertime; and later, perhaps, to offer jobs for the coming season to those who were old enough and had proved themselves good crew members.

He left after an hour or so, and we settled down to a serious discussion about the man and his project. Dick observed that he had a fine boat and was obviously an experienced navigator, but he felt that someone from Social Services should go to the Hamble to examine the boat in detail and interview Mr P. again, before any decisions were made. Emily said she thought he had come across as quite a decent guy and he was offering the boys the chance of a lifetime; but she was willing to go along with Dick's suggestion.

'What did you think of him?' she asked, turning to me.

'He gave me the creeps!' I replied. 'I've got no reason to dislike the man and I thought his proposals sounded very exciting — also he has a splendid boat, as far as one can judge from the photos. But there's something I can't quite put a finger on...'

We all agreed, however, that we could not turn down such a wonderful offer for the boys just because one of us had a hunch based on nothing. So we waited for the report from the experienced Social Worker sent by Ken Boyce to investigate the M.F.V. and her owner. It proved quite satisfactory, so plans were made for Peter and Philip to spend part of the Christmas holidays afloat, with the chance of permanent jobs aboard when they were sixteen the following summer.

A few days later Captain Ian McLaren came to the London Marina to give Peter and Victor their second nautical examinations. The four remaining boys had not wanted to chance their luck a second time feeling, perhaps, that they had not worked hard enough during the past year to pass with such good marks as the first time; better to rest on their laurels with at least one framed certificate to show for their efforts.

November 25th was a cold sunny day with a fresh north-westerly wind blowing, which made the first tests all the more difficult. A reef was taken in *Martha*'s mainsail, then we got under way with Peter at the helm and motored out into the middle of the dock. The boys then hoisted the mainsail and jib, switched off the engine and sailed round the dock several times with first one, then the other in charge. They gave demonstrations of tacking, gybing and heaving to; they did man overboard drill, tied numerous knots and hitches, restarted the engine, handed the sails and Victor brought the boat back alongside our pontoon in perfect style... And not a whisper from me during the whole performance.

'By Jove! You two lads have learnt a thing or two since I last saw you,' Ian exclaimed. 'If your theory is as good as this, you'll be getting higher marks than some of my Second Mate pupils who are in their early twenties!'

The remainder of the afternoon was devoted to chartwork — laying off courses, plotting positions, tidal allowances — followed by the Rule of the Road, buoyage, distress signals, safety precautions and a few general questions. Both boys achieved very high marks which caused Ursula and me to feel intensely proud of them.

Certificate of Seamanship & Navigation

This is to certify that I have tested

VICTOR JOHN CHRISTOPHER HENRY

in the Second Stage of Seamanship & Navigation in the yacht MARTHA McGILDA **and found him** very competent showing commendable advance from First Stage Test last year. **in SEAMANSHIP & NAVIGATION**

Making Sail, Reefing
Points of Sailing, Tacking.
Gybing, Heaving To, Man
Overboard drill, Leaving Berth.
Coming alongside a Berth
Knots and Hitches

Pilotage, Chartwork,
Tidal Streams, Tidal Heights,
Laying courses, Plotting Positions,
Buoyage, Rules of the Road at Sea
Distress Signals

Signed *Ian McLaren.*
Master Mariner   25" November 1977.

She and Ian's wife had joined us for tea and exam results. The paraffin lamps and stove gave a warm glow to the little cabin, while Ian sat in a corner munching scones and saying the sort of things that brought an even deeper glow to the children's faces. Outside there was a dramatic sky filled with purple and flame-red clouds, reflecting some of its glory in the murky waters of the Royal Albert Dock.

'Looks as if we've set the world on fire tonight!' Peter remarked, as he helped me tie the canvas canopy over *Martha*'s boom and cockpit before going home.

Stephen, David and Ursula became very keen on our painting sessions that winter. We had acquired a box of oil paints, some old palettes and brushes, and a few small canvasses; and I vividly remember one foggy afternoon when the artists had been working in silence at their various themes for several hours, refusing to let anyone see them till they were finished. Ursula did a portrait of David who was busy painting a model of *Martha* on my desk; and Stephen painted a big brown rabbit against a carmine background. Edward Wolfe, R.A., the distinguished painter who lived two doors away from us, happened to call round just then and he was so delighted with Stephen's rabbit that he whisked the canvas away with him, promising to find a frame to suit it.

The following week I took Philip and Peter to Putney to meet Mr P. The interview went well, and he was even persuaded to include Victor in his crew for the voyage to France, as the boy was becoming increasingly miserable at the thought of missing this wonderful adventure.

We had an early Christmas tea-party that December, preceded by an afternoon's skating at Queensway Ice Rink for six of the boys, Emily, Veronica and me.

'Why are you hanging about at the same spot in the middle like that?' I called out to Mark as I sped past him.

He waited till I was skating towards him again on the far side of the rink then, sidling close to me like a conspirator with dark revelations to impart, he whispered: 'Cos this is where we catches the birds, see? You jus' stick a foot out wivout anyone noticin'... "Must've struck a bit o' rough ice, love," you tell 'em as you goes to their rescue and helps to dust the ice off their jeans!'

Stephen had made us a splendid pair of miniature tugs in his school woodwork class as a Christmas present; and David had put together a wooden frame to set off his oil painting of *Martha*. A few days after the party Peter, Philip and Victor set off from Waterloo Station on their great adventure.

★ ★ ★

The latter half of the Christmas holidays passed very slowly. No postcards arrived from France — not a single word to tell us how the boys were enjoying themselves. I blamed this on the long delays caused by the Christmas mail; nevertheless, I worried incessantly, and it seemed as if some dark premonition was hanging over me like a cloud.

Just before the new term began Emily rang up to say that the boys were safely back; and very gradually we pieced together an account of what had happened aboard the M.F.V.

They joined the boat on the River Hamble, and the first two days were spent scrubbing decks, stowing ropes and other gear and making preparations for putting to sea. At last they were ready to cross to Cherbourg, with a fair wind on the beam and a moderate sea.

After an eighteen hour passage they secured to a buoy in the outer harbour and remained there for the next few days. It was, however, a long way to row ashore in the dinghy to buy fresh bread for breakfast, and they were usually soaked by the time they returned.

'Mostly we ended up eating biscuits for breakfast,' Victor recalled; 'an' the skipper wasn't best pleased wiv the salty meat an' veg we brought him!'

The bleak interval out on the buoy was followed by a week in dry dock. And the boys spent many hours each day scraping the barnacles off the hull, sandpapering the topsides and slapping on fresh coats of paint and anti-fouling. It was cold hard work, but they usually managed to slip away to the beach in the late afternoon to watch the French children enjoying themselves at a fairground close to the sea. A young West Indian boy and his sister often came to speak to them and, I suspect, did a little hero-worshipping of the three tough English boys who were real sailors in their eyes; for no one else they knew would brave the terrors of the winter storms to cross 'La Manche' to France!

We came to the conclusion that Mr P. had used the boys as cheap labour to rub down and repaint his boat, and only once did he take them ashore for dinner in a restaurant. Furthermore, it was revealed later that he had other unpleasant tendencies which was why he preferred to engage young boys as his crew. Fortunately there were three of ours together, and Philip had grown tall and strong enough to grapple with a rampant gorilla by that time.

The voyage back to England was quite dramatic. A gale blew up when the boat was half way across the Channel and waves like mountains reared up in the night and threatened to capsize her, but Mr P. emerged as a memorable skipper. He stood at the wheel, hour after hour, sometimes sipping a glass of red wine and sometimes endeavouring to calm the fears of his anxious crew by telling them yarns of the Arctic Ocean where his vessel had weathered far worse storms than this one.

'When all the rigging is coated with a thick layer of black ice, is the time to start worrying,' he told Peter. 'Because you know then that the boat is top-heavy, and if a great wave rolls her over there's not a chance in hell of her righting herself again!'

At last the dawn broke — a lemon-coloured sky streaked with thin black clouds moving east like racing-cars. But the worst was over by then, and a few hours later the storm-battered vessel and her weary crew dropped anchor in the peaceful waters of the River Hamble.

'I wouldn't mind goin' to the Arctic with him, 'cos I could handle him O.K.,' Philip told us a few weeks later.

But all the grown-ups said 'NO' to this idea, so Philip filled in his application form to join the Merchant Navy, and a few weeks later he was called up to Prescott Street for an interview.

'Well, what happened?' I asked anxiously on the telephone to Emily next day.

'There were about twenty kids there, he said, and only three of them got accepted for the Sea Training College. Some of them had never set eyes on the sea before and didn't know which was the front end of a boat from the back, can you imagine it?' Emily laughed.

'Yes, I can; but what happened to Phil?' I was beginning to feel quite desperate.

'Oh, he passed O.K.,' she murmured — keeping me on tenterhooks till the last possible moment.

Chapter 19

Philip was due to enrol at the Sea Training College at Gravesend just after his sixteenth birthday in June 1978. But a number of melodramas occurred at the Edith Moorey Home in the previous month — like the early rumblings of a volcano before the mountain erupts with molten lava.

The cold days of the winter term passed peacefully enough. Ursula invited six of the boys to go to the Islington Sports Centre for their half-term treat, and they all had a good time swimming, playing table-tennis and roaring round on skateboards. This was followed by tea at her home, a sumptuous feast of crumpets, drop-scones, rich cakes and, no surprise to anyone, a large platter of banana and apricot jam sandwiches!

'Look at the way she keeps this place — not a speck of dust on any of the furniture and everyfing shipshape, like on a boat.' Victor nudged my elbow and winked at Peter, as soon as Ursula was out of the room.

'Don't you start that business again,' I trod hard on his foot under the table; 'or I'll make you spend next Tuesday cleaning out *Martha*'s bilges!'

The following week we took Stephen's rabbit picture, beautifully framed by Teddy Wolfe, round to Norwich Road. And Dick played snooker with Mark while we were there, then took all the boys in turn for a spin round Forest Gate in his new Porsche Targa — a thundering monster that drew screams of delight from the children.

Martha emerged on to the river at the end of February with Peter and Victor as her first crew. We were running down Barking Reach with a fresh wind on the quarter when Peter announced that he had at last decided what to do with his life since the Merchant Navy had refused to take him because of his eyesight: he was going to become a shipwright instead.

We had already explored every other possibility we could think of : deep-sea fisherman (only local boys taken on the trawlers); tug crew or lighterman on the Thames (a seven year apprenticeship required to become a licensed waterman); coasters (good eyesight without glasses essential); North Sea oil-rigs (too young); etcetera, etcetera.

Ursula joined us for tea after our sail, and she and I helped him compose a letter to a boatbuilding firm, which he wrote the following weekend. He sent off more than twenty copies of it, in fact, to boatbuilders all over the country. Peter faced his new future without emotion. Although he was deeply disappointed about the Merchant Navy, his face revealed little of his inner thoughts.

A week or two later he had received a number of rejections: 'We regret to inform you that we have no vacancies at present . . . wishing you better luck elsewhere,' type of letters. An aura of gloom hung over the boat on alternate Tuesdays, and neither Ursula, Victor nor I could find a way to make him smile for suddenly he wanted to become a boatbuilder more than anything else on earth.

Towards the middle of April, however, Peter received a letter from Whisstock's, the famous builders of wooden yachts at Woodbridge in Suffolk, inviting him to go for an interview the following week. And on April 27th he telephoned me from a call-box outside the Yard, breathless with excitement: for he had just been offered a five year apprenticeship to start from the end of the summer term, by which time he would be sixteen.

We opened the bottle of rum on our next Tuesday together, and everyone had 'sippers' in their tea to celebrate this wonderful thing that was taking place. Two of the boys now had prospects — the chance to make a good life for themselves away from the dole queues and gang warfare of East London.

'That just proves you were wrong about all the kids going to prison when they leave the Home, doesn't it?' I told Peter with a satisfied smirk on my face.

He gave me a funny look and said nothing for a few moments; then he murmured, 'Let's 'ope you're right!'

Emily and Veronica brought Philip, Victor, Stephen and Mark to St Margaret's Bay for a night at the end of April, and next morning we met Peter Cobb and his wife and daughter in Dover, and all eleven of us crossed to France.

The boys had changed a great deal since their first invasion of Frogland. Philip and Victor both wore Number 2 hair-cuts which they assured me were nothing to get excited about compared with Number 1s (a skinhead crop); and Victor, who frequented a certain clothing shop at Aldgate whenever he had the chance and money, wore army trousers and a khaki jumper with immense German badges sewn on his right sleeve. Stephen and Mark had allowed their hair to grow to collar length and Stephen, in particular, had the appearance of a budding artist with his pale blue waistcoat worn over a dark pullover and patched jeans.

'Can we go up on the ole ruins to eat our dinner?' Mark proposed, before

Picnic lunch on the mounds above Calais harbour entrance. Victor and Stephen.

anyone else had time to put forward other suggestions.

So there we found ourselves soon after landing, with the boys hanging like bats from the rafters while the grown-ups laid out the picnic on the grassy mounds nearby.

'It's crucial this place,' Victor declared. 'Don't find many ruins like this round Forest Gate, wivout some arse'ole comin' along an' throwin' a wobbler soon as you starts havin' a good time!'

'You should see round the back of my dad's place,' Stephen offered, but Peter Cobb interrupted him to say that we hadn't all come to France to spend our day on a heap of old ruins, but if that's what they really wanted he was willing to lead them to the ancient citadel and ramparts of Calais after lunch.

'Might as well have a butchers,' Philip conceded, acting as spokesman for the gang — perhaps to soothe the grown-ups who were liable to turn funny as soon as you started having fun.

We were stumbling down from the harbour entrance after lunch, with tufts of grass attached to our clothing and mud all over our shoes, when who should rear up in front of us near the yacht club entrance but Monsieur le Président himself! Dr Jean Plancke was an old sailing friend of ours and, as such, had intercepted many scruffy arrivals of '*les types Anglaises*' on his native shore. But the sight of all eleven of us descending from the ruins, instead of ascending from rubber dinghies, almost rendered him speechless — but not quite.

'My dear friends!' he declared, throwing his arms wide open; 'I am ravished to welcome you and your big family' (one eyebrow had risen like a shepherd's crook) 'to our humble yacht club. But where is the brave *Martha McGilda*? I do not perceive her in the anchorage.'

Explanations and a few introductions followed, but Dick hastily declined his invitation to have a little glass of something in the yacht club by announcing that the children were enthralled with the ancient history of Calais, and could hardly be restrained from dashing off to explore the old fortifications. Mark glared ferociously at Dick, and ran his tongue over his lips to imply that a drink would go down very nicely, thank you; but Peter Cobb, who was bringing up the rearguard, hustled the boy from behind and I hung back to exchange a few polite words with Dr Plancke — and to remove a clod of earth from the seat of my trousers before exposing my back view to him!

We tramped for miles that day — all over Calais and up and down the venerable ramparts.

'Never thought I was coming to France to spend the day mountaineering!'

Peter Cobb and Dick outside a café in Calais.

Victor, Stephen, Mark, Philip with Peter Cobb, Carol and Nicky.

Veronica puffed, as she struggled to the summit of the penultimate battlement, to find the boys poised like goats on pinnacles of crumbling masonry, each one bellowing 'Look at me, Auntie!'

'How about visiting the shops, boys?' Emily called out, knowing one good way to get them down to ground level.

We walked the entire length of the main street, diving in and out of shops to keep an eye (some hopes) on our brood, and to utter a calming word here and there when some irate shop-keeper was beginning to screech with rage.

'I like shoppin' in this place,' Stephen declared, sipping his coke in the Café du Phare later that afternoon. 'You can really wind them up, those Frogs, if you know a trick or two!'

Peter and Carol's little girl, Nicky, gave him a level stare but said nothing. She looked so small and innocent in her pale pink woolly anorak, and I found myself wondering if she ever wanted to wind people up like the boys did.

When we reached Dover that evening, Emily and Veronica took Stephen and Mark back to London with them as the boys were to spend the Sunday with their grandparents. Philip and Victor, meanwhile, returned to St Margaret's Bay with us.

Next morning we overslept, and I awoke with a start to the pounding of a fist on our bedroom door. 'Come down quick, Dick, Rozelle!' Victor shouted

Dick advancing down the railway line in Calais with Philip, Mark, Victor and Stephen.

urgently. 'There's a load of strange men outside an' they're hangin' ivy all over the front of the house!'

'You must be crazy,' I called back, as I jumped into some clothes and ran downstairs.

But no; he was telling the truth. A television company who were making a new series called 'Telford's Choice' had arrived much sooner than we were expecting them and, wishing to make our cottage look more oldie-worldie and less white than it did, they had set to work hanging plastic ivy all over the front.

After breakfast Peter Barkworth and Hannah Gordon drove up in a shiny limousine and the cameramen got to work, using the boys to move props and do odd jobs for them. Then Jack Dawson arrived on foot to meet the great actors, and Victor whispered to me: 'This is really seein' life, mixin' with the telly stars as if they was ordinary people. Wait till I tell the uvvers what they missed!'

After a while everything quietened down because the director said the light was not quite right for shooting that day. Hannah Gordon and Peter Barkworth had coffee in our kitchen while Philip made friends with some of the cameramen who told him he ought to join them instead of going to sea.

Later that evening we drove back to London, dropping off the boys at Norwich Road on our way home.

I never found out how the other boys reacted to Philip and Victor's meeting with the Stars, because David's big drama swept all other thoughts from our minds. During the week following our voyage to Calais he was told by someone as a joke — someone with a strangely twisted sense of humour — that his mum had suddenly died in a car crash.

David, who still loved his mum above all other people, went on the rampage with one of his brothers, broke into houses and shops and stole a number of things. Then they climbed inside a ruined house at the back of Norwich Road and set fire to it, intending to stay there and burn themselves to death. Fortunately someone heard the sound of crackling timber before it had turned into the mighty blaze that the firemen had to tackle after they had dragged the two boys from the ruins.

Neither David nor his brother were badly hurt, but they were charged with arson when their case came up in Court and David was sent directly to Little Heath, a remand home with a very tough reputation.

During the months to follow Dick and I were occasionally allowed to visit the boy and take him out for a meal. And there was one Tuesday in July when Ursula drove to Little Heath to fetch him so that he could spend the afternoon sailing in *Martha* again. But he had close-shorn hair (not of his own choosing) and a closed face all that summer; and our David, the one we knew so well, had gone away into a far country . . . to somewhere that no one could reach him for a long long while.

The month of May was a bad time for the Tuesday boys — a month full of violent upheavals that struck at the very core of peaceful co-existence, so much a feature of life at the Edith Moorey Home in the past.

It was the time of the change in the size of one pound notes, and Peter was very proud of the fact that he had managed to save one of the original large notes. He kept it in a secret cache of prized possessions in his chest-of-drawers.

One evening someone told him as a joke (yes, another of those terrible jokes) that Victor had nicked it. He rummaged in the drawer where it was hidden and, not immediately being able to find it, he seized a photograph of Victor's mum and began to tear it in little pieces. This infuriated Victor who had not touched the pound note, so he leapt upon his adversary and pushed him up against the window with a view to sending him hurtling through the glass on to the conservatory roof below.

A young man who was a trainee house-father entered into the fray at that stage, and tried to separate the two boys who were fighting like enraged bulls. Emily then appeared on the scene and, not knowing who had started the fight nor what had caused it, she grabbed one of Victor's arms and screwed it round behind his back which gave Peter the upper hand.

Philip marched into the room at that moment and, seeing his little brother put to a disadvantage, he gave Emily a whack with his right fist and helped Victor to pummel Peter. The situation had certainly got out of hand when Emily rang for the police; but an unnatural quietness hung over the home by the time the flashing blue lights and urgent sirens swung round the corner into Norwich Road, bringing the neighbours scampering to their windows to find out what was going on. Formal statements were taken from all those concerned, and the other boys hung over the bannisters with rabbit's ears while the rozzers stood around in the kitchen drinking tea.

A nasty tense atmosphere lingered on after the fight and life in the Edith Moorey Home was never quite the same again. Emily, perhaps unfairly, was reprimanded by her superior who said she was worried that the police intervention, and threatened Court appearance, might impair Philip's chances of joining the Merchant Navy.

The last two Tuesdays in May passed rather peacefully, by contrast. Ursula and I took only one boy out sailing each time: Peter the first week and Stephen the second. Philip and Victor were busy moving out of the home to live with their mother who had just been given a Council flat in Stratford; and Mark was seldom allowed to come because he played truant so often from school.

On the first Tuesday we ghosted downriver in hazy sunshine, with the mainsail and genoa pulling well and Peter steering like an Olympic helmsman. He chattered happily about the kind of motor-bike he was planning to buy as soon as he was a working man; and Ursula and I listened to the chuckling waves running past *Martha*'s hull and held our peace. We both knew that he was going to have a hard struggle to make ends meet on an apprentice's wages once he had left the sheltered environment of the home.

The following Tuesday was a different kind of day. A strong north wind blew us into the lock at an alarming speed, but fortunately our favourite lock-keeper was waiting to catch our lines and make us fast.

Outside the lock we hoisted the reefed mainsail and small jib, and each of us steered in turn. Stephen, who had been grumbling that everything was upside-down in the home and you never knew who was in charge there nowadays, cheered up when it was his turn to take the helm. *Martha* was heeled far over with the water rushing along her lee deck and the wind singing an old sea-shanty in the rigging. Dagenham Reach was alive with shipping — freighters, tugs, coasters, the little ferry that crossed the river to Thamesmead — and the helmsman wore a happy grin as he manoeuvred the boat skilfully upriver and felt the tiller trembling under his firm grip.

'It's wicked out here!' he exclaimed, his face and hair glistening with spray. 'Wish we could stay here for ever, 'stead of goin' back to Norwich Road.'

Inspired by his success on the river, as soon as we had moored *Martha* at her pontoon in the marina Stephen asked if he could take *Water-Rat* out for a sail round the dock on his own — a bold plan as he had never before sailed a boat without someone else aboard.

He set off at an exhilarating speed, running before the wind towards the dock entrance while Ursula and I sprinted round the basin in case he had forgotten what to do at the other end. Unfortunately he had, and the mainsail did an unexpected gybe while the boom swung swiftly across and dealt him a stunning blow on the side of the head. We arrived just in time to grab the mast before *Water-Rat* set off on her travels again; and I quickly handed the sails while Ursula comforted Stephen, then we rowed sedately back to our pontoon for tea.

In June and July we had a few more outings in *Martha* on the river. Victor and Stephen came on the first Tuesday, having ridden all the way from Norwich Road on their new racing-bicycles; and Stephen generously allowed me to ride round the dock on his bicycle at the end of the afternoon! Then David came from Little Heath, on the last day of our favourite lock-keeper.

'I'm not looking forward to my retirement one little bit,' he told us. 'But Mr Cohen says it would cost too much to fit the old basin out with different lock-gates, see, so he's closing down next month and starting up some grand new place in Brighton, so they tell me. He's offered me early retirement and I don't s'pose anyone else would offer me a job at my age, so what can I do? But I tell you one thing — I shall miss your little gang of villains!'

'No good comin' rahnd Cyprus ter buy yer bits an' pieces arter next week, doll,' Madge said sombrely; ''cos they're goin' ter sweep us orff the face of the earf like autumn leaves, know what I mean?'

'Bleedin' shame I calls it,' observed Albert's big brother who had looked in to buy his fags. 'Even if they was ter turn it inter a millionaire's playgrahnd, it'll never be the same again.'

'I've also got to leave next month,' I told them; 'because Tony's closing down the marina and taking all his pontoons to Brighton.'

'Trust 'im!' The docker growled. 'S'prised 'e ain't takin' the effing lock gates as well.'

'I put a little somefink special in the bag fer you, doll, seein' as 'ow we might never see you agin,' Madge's sister whispered in my ear before I left the neighbourhood shop.

Back aboard *Martha*, I stared at the picture of a Scottish loch by moonlight on the lid of the box of liqueur chocolates; and the mountains around the loch gradually became bleary — like a Scotch mist creeping over the landscape when you least expect it.

July 11th was *Martha*'s last day at the London Marina with one of the Tuesday boys aboard. It was Stephen who came out with Ursula and me that afternoon — a Stephen oppressed by dark forebodings about his future.

'When me and Mark goes back to live with our dad, will I still be able to come sailin'? Even if the ole boat's gone to somewhere else?' he asked in an off-hand manner which did not deceive us.

'Yes, of course you will. Every other Tuesday for ever and ever,' I tried to reassure him.

The Edith Moorey Home was due to close down very soon, and all the remaining children were being sent back to their own homes, wherever possible, or to other Council homes till they reached school-leaving age.

'Seems like the whole world's comin' to an end,' Stephen grumbled, when I told him about the little shop in Cyprus.

There was a fresh north-east wind blowing that afternoon, and we sailed swiftly downriver to the entrance of Barking Creek where a string of barges were being chivvied through the tidal barrier by a very small tug. We tacked near Horse End and ran back up Gallion's Reach. But no one had their heart in sailing that day and Stephen continually wove the tiller from left to right while he asked countless unanswerable questions about his future.

'That tug doesn't know on which side you're planning to pass him,' Ursula took the boy to task. 'Listen! He's blowing a series of short blasts on his siren which means...?'

'He don't know what the hell I'm up to!' he grinned at last.

'Your intentions are unclear to me?' she corrected him in proper nautical parlance, a twinkle in her eye.

But Stephen had his moment of glory at the end of the day. *Martha* had passed through the lock and I was steering her back to her berth without paying much attention to what I was doing. Suddenly we all became aware of *Water-Rat* right ahead of us, moored across the head of our pen... and *Martha* advancing relentlessly towards her as if she wished to slice her little sister in half.

'Can't you make her go a little slower?' Ursula shouted anxiously from the bows.

I had already engaged the engine in full astern but it was not reacting fast enough to prevent the impending crash: until Stephen took a flying leap on to the pontoon grasping our stern line in one hand and, quick as lightning, took a turn round a cleat to arrest our forward surge.

'That was a fine bit of fast action. Well done, Stephen!' Ursula praised him.

'It wasn't anyfing much really, Hursula,' he mumbled, turning bright pink as he knelt down to make the stern line fast.

We ate our banana and apricot jam sandwiches in a hurry — it was such a sad occasion and no one wanted to linger there — then I took Stephen back to Norwich Road for the last time, and drove on to see how Philip and Victor were managing in their new home.

Victor had gone to visit his nan, but I found Philip with his mum high up in a tower block near the Stratford New Town freight terminal. He was standing on a chair trying to hang some curtains over the kitchen window while Margaret wandered around the room smoking, and offering him advice. He did not look exactly like someone riding on the crest of a wave, so I asked him if he was looking forward to going to the Sea Training College in ten days' time.

'Dunno,' he muttered, refusing to meet my eyes. ''Spect it'll all turn out O.K. in the end.'

★   ★   ★

Martha left the London Marina on a cold grey morning in August. A north wind blew across Gallion's Reach, churning the grey-green river into humpy white-capped waves.

The lock-keeper was a new man — a temporary stopgap till the marina had finally shed all its boats — and he surveyed *Martha* with indifferent eyes and let the water in so fast that we had a hard struggle to heave in on our lines before the boat was caught in the whirlpool.

Out on the river and safely clear of the lock gates, I looked back over my left shoulder. The dockmaster's office was like a blank face — not a glimmer of light nor hint of movement from within. One lone fisherman sat on the end of a derelict jetty near the road that led to nowhere, a line dangling from his patient hands and the butt-end of a cigarette screwed into a corner of his mouth. He did not look up nor show any signs of noticing our departure: but how could I expect him to grasp the heart-rending sadness of that particular moment, when the gates closed for ever behind *Martha*'s stern?

Martha *went to sea again...*

PART III
BEYOND THE FAR HORIZON

Chapter 20

Eleven years later...

A purple evening with a shiver of frost in the air and the ebb tide running fast. The slipway emerges, black and shiny, from the softly-singing river, and the *Cutty Sark* across the water is transformed into a dream-ship with her mainmast touching the first evening star. A curl of smoke rises from the shed behind me and, suddenly, an explosion of music, voices, laughter, a dog barking and the clang of a big steel gate.

It is Wednesday night at the clubhouse inside the Island Boatyard and the boys and girls are converging on the western end of Ferry Street, Isle of Dogs, some with a screech of tyres and others quietly, on foot. There is a driftwood fire spitting and crackling in the old black stove, and three girls sit in front of it roasting chestnuts and chatting about their babies. Jackie, the pretty round-faced girl on the far side of the stove, is Victor's wife; already

they have two sons, Adam and Carl, and Adam has just started going to school.

Victor is on leave from his ship, *The Pride of Bruges*, and just now he is engaged in a desperate battle with Nicky at table-tennis. Nicky, a sixteen-year-old with only one hand, is the champion player on the Isle of Dogs; he usually takes a handicap of ten points to give some of us a chance — after all, we taught him how to play the game not so long ago! But he still succeeds in winning most of the time.

Victor looks a happy man these days. He is working at the job he loves most of all, he earns a good wage and has married a splendid girl who brings up his children well and does her best to keep him on the straight and narrow! Mind you, it has not all been plain sailing...

About ten years ago, a week before Victor was due to go for his interview for the Merchant Navy, Dick suggested that it might help him to come round to our house for a mock-interview so that he would know what to expect. The Number 2 hair-cut era had passed, but our Victor had been front page news in the *Daily Express* recently — 'Gang of leather-clad youths from East London cause havoc on the sea-front at Southend... etcetera.'

Dick sat behind the kitchen table with a fierce expression on his face and ordered Victor to come in and close the door. He stomped into the room, glared at Dick and grunted 'Mornin' '.

Dick — 'Good morning, Sir! It doesn't matter how much you hate the sight of me, you stand to attention like a soldier and go on 'sirring' me every time I ask you a question, understand? Now, tell me, Victor, why you want to join the Merchant Navy?'

Victor — 'Dunno really. See the world I s'pose, and they say the pay's good?'

Dick — 'Tell me what your best subjects were at school, young man?'

Victor (after a long pause, with puce cheeks) — 'Well, I weren't bad at needlework... Sir.'

At that point Dick exploded: 'If you go to an interview wearing dirty old jeans like that, and giving those sorts of answers, you'll be out in the street in fifty seconds, you silly goat. You've got two or three extremely good certificates from Captain McLaren to show the interviewer, and you can tell him all about your experience on boats, how much you love the sea, how you long to go deep-sea, work among proper seafarers and broaden your outlook... build up a picture of yourself which will appeal to this man who holds your fate in his hands; and *never* mention pay, nor subjects like needlework! After all, you're not a young lady leaving a convent school! Square your shoulders and use your brains, boy.'

Victor had no one to take him to Prescott Street when the great day arrived, so we told him to come round to our house at 8 a.m. and I would drive him there. He arrived looking immaculate: shirt and trousers dazzlingly clean and well-ironed, face scrubbed, hair neatly trimmed and a certain look in his eyes which I failed to interpret at first. The traffic was light and we reached Aldgate far too early, so we went to a small café in a back street and I ordered tea and bacon sandwiches for two.

I remember that morning so clearly, as if it were yesterday. I was worried stiff — you might have supposed it was I who was going for the interview — while Victor chattered merrily, made silly jokes and took charge of the situation, even to getting up and paying the bill at ten minutes to nine.

I left him outside the Merchant Navy office five minutes later and he promised to phone me as soon as the interview was over, no matter how it had gone. I noticed a group of smartly-dressed youths heading towards those fatal doors as I drove away; and I felt a hollow sinking sensation in the pit of my stomach — like the prelude to a severe bout of seasickness.

An interminable two hours later the telephone rang and a chirpy voice on the other end of the line announced, 'I made it, Rozelle! Some of the uvvers never stood a chance 'cos they twisted 'em up proper on the nautical knowledge questions, but what wiv Dick's advice about what not to say an' me stifficates, they were right chuffed wiv me!'

Margaret, Victor's mum, and I drove him to Gravesend a few weeks later to start his course at the Sea Training College, A salt-laden wind blew across from the Tilbury Marshes, and the river was alive with sun-glitter and the churnings of big liners and tugs, and the music of ship's sirens way down Sea Reach. Victor had left us long before we said goodbye, his eyes gleaming with excitement and his spirit far away on some distant ocean.

Margaret looked anxious and sad, abandoning her little boy in such a huge impersonal place; but he strode through the iron gates like a conquering hero, secretly longing for us to hurry up and go home!

★   ★   ★

Victor passed out of the Sea Training College with excellent marks in January, 1981, and three months later he went to sea in his first ship, a P.& O. freighter called *Wild Grebe*. He had a lovely blonde girl-friend by then, and she often brought us news of him when she came out with me in *Martha* to help with a new group of small boys I was teaching at that time.

Victor began to write letters after he went to sea. Spending day after day plodding across the great oceans — he sailed half way round the world and back on that first voyage — he sometimes felt lonely and rather homesick, and his words reflected his moods in a poignant way. One of our first postcards came from New Zealand, with a picture of Mount Cook (the Cloud Piercer) on the front:

Dear Dick and Rozelle,
    Today I went skiing and had a lovely time. I'll send some photos when they are developed O.K. How's yourselves? I heard you bought a clubhouse or something. How's it coming along? I can't say much more. Some of the lads hired a car so we went touring New Zealand.

Love,
Vic ×

In September *Wild Grebe* reached the Red Sea where she had a long hot period of drifting to and fro, while her crew became increasingly bored and restless. Victor wrote us several letters telling us about his life aboard and his thoughts and hopes for the future. On June 28th he wrote:

Dear Dick and Rozelle,
    Hope you are well? The weather is hot today — 102° F. — and I've got a nice tan but it is still too hot for working in. We just left Shajah about an hour ago.
    I don't know if Lorraine told you but we're getting engaged on November 21st if I'm home and I'd like you to come to the party.
    What I'm really writing for is to thank you for what you done for me. You treated me like a son and I'm really grateful. I can't express myself but I'm having a great time.
    Now we're sailing for Kuwait, then on to Mina Quaboos and Durban and Cape Town, then back to Europe.
    I'm trying to save enough money to have a good party and buy a nice ring for Lol. I miss the sailing on *Martha* and *Roskilde*, and I'm just sitting here thinking what good times we had and I'm a bit homesick, but its parsing. It's a different experience going to different countrys and seeing how other people live. That's all for now but I'll write soon.

Lots of love,
Vic × × ×

He wrote again early in September telling us that he was in Aqaba, but they were going to drift for two or three weeks then go alongside to load up. It was not until the end of the month that he wrote to say;

I think we're going to stay here (in Aqaba) for another four weeks and I'm getting bored with this place.
    I've taken up training with one of the electricians — he's a boxer — and we run round

the ship 11 times a night (10,560 feet) which is 2 miles, then we do some exercises. I been doing it for 5 days and my legs still ake but I'm getting better.

I bought 2 tapes the other day. Guess what they were?? Wait for it: Beethoven (Classical Masterpieces) and Tchaikovsky (Sleeping Beauty). It may sound funny but I really like them. It's a strange thing what the sea does to ya! I must have some rare disease or something, cos me mates think I've gone mad.

I was sorry to hear about Ursula and hope she's better by the time you get this letter. If not, tell her Vic sends his love and hopes she's feeling better.

I should be coming home in about 4 to 6 weeks time.

Lots of love,
Vic ×

Keep smiling.

P.S. Write back soon.

P.P.S. Roses are red, violets are blue,
Look after yourselves as I care about you two.

Ursula was very ill in hospital with leukaemia at that time, and she died a few weeks later — a tragic loss to all of us and something which affected the boys very deeply.

Margaret and Victor at Tilbury at the end of his first voyage.

The *Wild Grebe* set off for the Cape of Good Hope in October, and our next letter from Victor was posted in Durban. He wrote a lyrical account of steering his ship across the Indian Ocean on black velvet nights studded with stars, and of phosphorescent bow-waves, like sweeps of emeralds, alive with leaping dolphins that kept pace with them all night long.

The ship docked at Tilbury in November, and Margaret and I were invited aboard to meet some of his mates before we drove Victor home. It was a nice ship that little freighter, with a happy atmosphere on the mess-deck and a leading-seaman in charge who had taken good care of Victor on his first voyage. He was given the choice of staying aboard *Wild Grebe* for a further six months and being promoted at the end of his next voyage, or taking his leave then waiting for whatever ship came along in two months' time.

It was a hard decision, but Victor had more than £4,000 in his pocket and a girl waiting to become engaged to him at home; and he was not yet eighteen and had felt very homesick at times during the past six months. So he decided to take his leave, never suspecting how much he would regret this choice in the months to come.

Victor came home a proud sailor, expecting a warm welcome and an attentive audience to listen to his tales of far-away places. But the reality was not like that at all: some of his relatives and those he had thought were his friends seemed jealous of his success, and more interested in his money than his broader outlook and the breath of pure salt air he brought into their midst.

The first meeting of the Martha McGilda Trust — L to R — Ursula, Emily, Dick, Marius Gray, Clare Gray. Opposite — Ian and Betty McLaren and David Weir.

'Make sure you open a bank account first thing tomorrow, and get some of that money put away before you spend it all!' I advised him on the way home.

'Good idea,' he mumbled, and gave me a big grin. But a few weeks later it had all gone: a new carpet for his mum, a fur coat for Lorraine as well as her ring, presents for all his family and friends and, finally, the party which was a splendid affair.

Victor came home with good marks in his Discharge Book and his love of the sea confirmed, but he had to wait for five or six months before he could get another ship. He often came to the Island Boatyard — the same place with a long slipway that David had pointed out to me from *Martha* some years before — to help with our new clubhouse and the heavy wooden dinghy we had acquired for the children to use on the river.

The boatyard itself was leased to a shipwright who soon filled it with boats of all sizes needing repairs, but we had reserved the shed on one side of the slipway for ourselves. It was gradually transformed into a small clubhouse for children, and the Trustees of the newly-formed Martha McGilda Trust held their first meeting there shortly before Ursula died.

Trevor Brooking signing a great many autographs after the opening of the clubhouse. 6th December 1982

The club was formally opened by the great West Ham footballer, Trevor Brooking, in December 1982. By that time, however, Victor had gone back to sea; a sadder and a wiser Victor, with no money in his pockets and no fiancée to await his return. They were both so young those two, each with quite different visions of what they wanted most in life.

Victor's new ship was the M.V. *Paludina*, running between Kuwait and the West Indies. His first postcards came from Curaçao, then Egypt; and some weeks later a letter arrived from Kuwait telling us of his troubles at home, and painting a rather gloomy picture of his life aboard and plans to spend his next leave in Australia.

In November Victor wrote during a gale in mid-Atlantic with the ship rolling badly. They had been compelled to stop in Malta for emergency repairs on their last passage through the Mediterranean, because a sea-water valve was about to collapse and the engine-room might have been flooded.

He told us he had some good mates on board and they had taken on a new radio officer in Curaçao. 'Now everyone goes up to the radio shack to get the football results as the Sparky is a *female* — and she's not bad-looking either!'

On her return voyage the *Paludina* sailed to Greece for extensive repairs, so Victor came home on leave in January; but on this occasion he was offered a job on a Shell tanker two months later. After the Red Sea and West Indies, life in winter off the Shetland Islands was tough and Victor found the crew were not inclined to welcome newcomers.

S.S.*Drupa*
10th March 1983

Dear Dick and Rozelle,

Hope your well. I'm fine. The ship is now at the Brent Oil Field in the North Sea and I'm on the 4–8 Watch. The weather forecast says it's going to blow Force 10, so I'll have to wrap up warm.

The crew are alright but they keep themselves to themselves. At the moment we are loading crude oil for Shellhaven, then up to Hounds Point, so hopefully I'll be able to get home for a few hours.

After this trip I'm thinking of going back to cargo ships. Well it's now 7.10, the weather has changed and we let go the mooring as it's too rough to carry on loading. There's three men in a Watch — one up for'ard, one on the maindeck and one having a cup of tea. Then we rotate as we have let go.

I'm going to get some sleep as I've got to be up at 4 o'clock in the morning, so I'll sign off now.

Love, from,
Vic

We received another letter in mid-April which held hints of a brighter future — a few sunbeams to illuminate the grim existence of a seaman working among the oil-rigs in the northern North Sea.

Dear Dick and Rozelle,

Hope your all well? I'm fine. I'm up off the Shetland Islands. We're going to Sullum Voe, then to Teesport. We go in tonight about eleven o'clock, for 24 hours, then two days back to Teesport. Then we go to anchor for about 10 days, then back to Sullum Voe to load for Shellhaven hopefully.

I'm going to Malta for three weeks in August with my girlfriend. The flight costs £185 and we're getting accommodation cheap as her uncle lives there.

I can't remember if you ever met Jackie, but you can take it from me she's no ordinary girl. She keeps me in my place and she makes sure I don't spend too much money while I'm at home.

Well, I'll have to sign off now as we've got a 3 hour stand-by.

Love,
Vic ×

Hope to see you soon.

★   ★   ★

Victor came home on leave early that summer, and he brought Jackie down to the club to meet us; then she came with him to help varnish *Martha*'s cockpit and, later on, for a weekend at St Margaret's Bay. In August they flew to Malta for their holiday and sent us a card telling us what a lovely time they were having out there.

Victor at home on leave.

Outside Dolphin's Leap...
Back row: Dick, me, Veronica and Emily.
Front row: Peter, George, David, Victor and Philip.

David inside Martha's *cabin, June 1986.*

A Thames sailing-barge stood out in stark relief.

Kally, Victor, Jackie and Mark in the Lagonda at St. Margarets' Bay.

Victor and Jackie at the Island Boatyard.

By October Victor was at sea again in a huge Shell tanker, S.S.*Opalia*, of 53,739 tons, bound across the Atlantic for Philadelphia, and later, Venezuela. He had always longed to visit America, but I suspect the dockside area of Philadelphia was rather an anti-climax, and *Opalia* was not a happy ship. One of her crew members continually threateaned to carve up some of the lads whose faces he did not care for — Victor's being one of them — and already he had stabbed another seaman in the kneecap after a bout of heavy drinking.

Shell Tanker S.S. Opalia *53,739 D.W. Tonnes.*

When the ship returned to Le Havre Victor asked if he could take his leave early rather than making another voyage aboard *Opalia*. The skipper released him with some reluctance, and I think he may have been given some bad marks in his Discharge Book because of this, for it was many months before he was offered a job on another ship; and then it was only a short voyage to fill in a gap on one of the Everard coasters.

Victor and Jackie were married at the Church of St Mary Magdalene, East Ham on a golden day in September. They had a white Rolls Royce to drive them to the reception, and a magnificent party for all their friends. A few days later Jackie's parents found their son-in-law a job as a milkman. The Merchant Navy was contracting, day by day, and it was becoming almost impossible for Victor to find a ship. The ship-owners' policy was to get rid of as many registered seamen as possible at that time, and they were offering voluntary redundancy to any men who had served for five years or more. Victor had not been at sea for long enough to qualify for this, but Jackie persuaded him to accept the £1,000 on offer, and to sever his ties with ships and the sea.

It was a comparatively small sum of money, but it was not long before the young couple's first baby was on the way and no further jobs at sea appeared to be forthcoming.

'It's a good idea to stay home and see your kids grow up,' advised his

Victor, Jackie and Philip in the church-yard.

family. But they had often been jealous of him in the past, and no one quite realized the effect it would have on our Victor.

Three bad years were to follow. He moved from job to job, but he had no particular interest in any of them and he seemed to be going rapidly downhill. He ate and drank too much, took very little exercise and must have been difficult to live with at home; and Jackie soon had two babies to look after, as well as a disgruntled husband. We hardly recognized him at Stephen's wedding, so heavy and down-hearted did he look. His job at that time was digging graves in the local cemetery.

The seamen's strike in Dover that summer was Victor's salvation. The P. & O. Company were only too anxious to find men who knew what they were doing aboard a ship; and many retired seamen came flocking south, avidly hunting for jobs in Dover and Folkestone.

Jack Dawson did all he could to help Victor, and Jackie encouraged him as well for she knew how unhappy he had been working on land. Arriving in Dover among the first of the ex-seafarers, P. & O. welcomed him with open arms and, despite the horrors that took place every day on the picket lines, Victor went joyfully back to sea on a cross-Channel ferry, *The Pride of Bruges*.

He spends every other week aboard, working on the Dover to Zeebrugge run, and alternate weeks at home, a life-style that suits him and his family ideally. He has plenty of time to spend with his boys while they are young and enough money to take all the family away on holiday twice a year.

One of the quartermasters on *The Pride of Bruges* was away ill some weeks ago, and Victor was put forward as his replacement. He has come a long way since those early days on *Martha*, showing off in front of Miss O'Brien and steering the old boat with a gleam of the future in his eyes!

Chapter 21

Lorraine is the blonde girl with the large blue eyes and sweet smile, sitting next to Jackie roasting chestnuts. She is a different Lorraine from Victor's first girl-friend. She and Philip also have two sons, Dean and Jay; children who seem to glow like Christmas candles among the thousands of boys and girls who live around them on a vast estate in Bow.

Philip has had a hard life compared with his younger brother. Some might say it was his own fault and others that he had a soft streak in his character which induced him to give in to others — the strong ones in his circle — for fear of hurting their feelings; so that his life has been a constant struggle to become master of his own fate.

He did not report to the Sea Training College at Gravesend on the day his course was due to start. No reasons were given, no excuses offered; but I suspect he was dissuaded by someone who did not wish to see him standing firmly on his own feet and even, perhaps, making a success of his life; someone who drew him a gloomy picture of the iron discipline and lack of freedom in the Merchant Navy, at the same time hinting that all his mates at home would soon forget him once he was away at sea. Whatever the reasons, he missed his first great opportunity to break away from his environment and see the world.

After leaving school Philip stayed on at home with his mum for a while, playing a lot of football and going to all the West Ham matches within his reach. At the same time he grew a shock of tightly permed blonde hair — very fashionable for boys that year!

Our friend, Jean, at St Margaret's Bay, found a job for Philip at a local farm before the harvest that summer. This turned out a great success as he liked working on the land and helping with the cows, and he got along well with the young farmer, Alastair, and his wife and small son. Jean would find some excuse to visit them once a week, then telephone us that evening: 'He's doing all right and Alastair says he works really hard on the farm,' she would tell us. 'Also he's made friends with their other lodger who works on one of the ferries. I've managed to get him interested in the village youth club and, would you believe it, he's helping to run the place now! Everyone loves him down here, so you need have no worries about one member of your gang.'

Just as we were beginning to say, 'How lucky Phil did not go to sea for he seems to have found the ideal life in the country,' he went home for the weekend to visit his mum and never came back. No telephone call nor letter reached Alastair and Janet to explain what had happened; one day he was there, working hard in the fields, eating huge meals with the family in the farm-house kitchen and making their little boy laugh, and the next day he had vanished. The child shed bitter tears when Phil did not return.

We soon discovered that he was leading quite a different style of life among his mates in Stratford and there was a girl, it was rumoured, somewhere in the offing. Jobs were not easy to find back in London so Philip worked for a few months with John Lewis, the shipwright who had taken the lease of our boatyard on the Isle of Dogs. During his spare time that autumn the boy chopped and stacked enough driftwood to keep us warm in the clubhouse all through the coming winter.

Philip was drinking in a pub near his home one night when he became involved in a brawl that was no concern of his nor his friends. A drunken lout brandishing the jagged edge of a broken glass mistook him for someone else and slashed his face without mercy, so that he needed a spell in hospital and many stitches in it afterwards. Poor Phil, only eighteen, his face carved up and no work, nor future prospects of it. But he had never suffered from self-pity, and there were certain aspects of his character that endeared him to all who knew him.

Philip got married that winter. We had a Christmas dance on a river-boat in December, and I noticed him staggering past me with an enormous black handbag suspended from one arm and a sheepish grin on his face.

'Wherever did you get that handbag?' I called after him in some alarm.

'It's me girl-friend's,' he laughed. 'She's got me where she wants me already, see, carryin' all her bits an' pieces for her!'

And that was how it worked out. They were married a month later and there was soon a baby on the way. The young couple were given a flat in a tower block in Canning Town and Philip moved from one job to another, trying to make ends meet: he became a fork-lift driver, a warehouseman, a van driver, a night-club attendant ... you name it. Whichever job paid the best, he would try it for a short while — sometimes two jobs at the same time.

We called to see Philip and his family one afternoon and found him trying to stop his two-year-old son from breaking up the furniture while he made our tea at the same time. He had just returned from work and looked worn out; and he was due to go on night-duty in four or five hours' time. His wife, meanwhile, sat around chain-smoking and telling us how hard it was to bring up kids in a tower block. She was expecting another baby that winter.

A short while after our visit she phoned us in great distress to say that Philip had been locked up because the Fuzz picked him up on some driving offence and they could not afford to pay the £100 fine. It was only a trivial affair — he had not caused an accident nor run over a pedestrian — and it seemed very unfair to us that he should go to prison when most people would have been able to pay the fine and soon forget all about it.

Dick and I drove up to Chelmsford that same night and parked outside the gaol. A warder opened the heavy wooden doors reinforced with metal bands and admitted us without pleasure, turning a huge key in the lock behind us with a grinding note of finality. Dick told the man why we had come, and the gaoler asked in a surly voice: 'How much money have you got on you?'

'It's none of your business,' Dick began to bristle; 'but I've brought enough to pay Philip's bail.'

The gaoler and my husband glared at one another like a pair of angry bull-frogs. We seemed to have reached a complete stalemate until a senior gaoler appeared on the scene and promised to produce Philip on receipt of X number of pound notes ('none of your cheques nor credit cards, thank-you very much!'). Because he had already been in prison for three days, his fine had been reduced by so much each day, we were informed.

We sat in a hot little room and waited for over an hour. We were locked in — Dick soon established this fact and it did nothing to soothe his frayed temper — and there was no means of escape nor ways of communicating with the outside world. At last a key turned in the lock and Philip was thrust into the waiting-room with a look of total bewilderment on his face. No one had told him what was happening, but a rough voice had suddenly ordered him out of the place where first offenders were 'banged up' for the night.

'Somebody loves you, kid,' the voice had informed him. 'Off you go!'

At last we escaped into the cold night air with that sinister building towering above us; but we were *outside* and not *inside* any longer, and Dick led the way towards a glow of red and gold lights where we celebrated all our releases!

A year or two later little Jeff came to visit his old friend, Philip, who had always been kind to him at Norwich Road.

We had almost lost sight of Jeff by then; except at Christmastime when he managed to get in touch with Emily, and always liked to come to our Christmas party. Jeff had not changed much over the years: he was by then a skinny lad of seventeen, very neat and well turned-out when he was invited to a party, but still the sad withdrawn child we had known for the past nine years. He revealed nothing of how he filled in the year between one

Christmas and the next — where he lived nor how he made ends meet.

'Poor little Jeff!' we said to each other after he had gone. 'I wonder how he manages all on his own?'

Then, without any warning, he turned up one evening at Philip's place, clearly in need of someone to comfort him. They shared their tea with him while he sat there, hour after hour; but Philip's wife had no intention of allowing the helpless waif to stay for the night, so at last he had to go.

A few days later we had an urgent telephone call from Peter Cobb: 'Had we heard the terrible news? Jeff had been murdered the previous night over Brixton way. It was some miserable kid like himself who had grown up in Care — they had been living rough together under the arches — and the other boy had rung up the police next morning and sobbed "I think I've hurt somebody very badly. You'd better come and get me!" '

Jeff's funeral was infinitely sad. His mother and youngest brother and sister were there, as well as Emily and Veronica and several of the boys. His mother announced with a harsh giggle that this was the second child she had buried, while his pale-faced brother and sister stood there in silence with tears pouring down their cheeks. Philip, Victor and Stephen looked almost as upset as the boy and girl standing near them.

It was a turning point in our lives, that tragic half hour in the churchyard, a moment when we all asked ourselves why we had failed to help another human being in desparate need. Were we, perhaps, too busy running our own all-important lives? It signalled a change in outlook among the Tuesday boys; barely perceptible at first, but a seed had been sown that grew and flourished as the months passed by.

I like to think that something good emerged from that heart-rending day: a small clear voice that spoke to the remaining seven boys: 'You all grew up together as brothers, sharing the same joys and sorrows, in the same home. Now you must go forward like brothers for the rest of your lives, keeping an eye on the other six and always ready to help if one of you should fall on hard times.'

After Jeff, there were longish intervals when we heard nothing of Philip. Then a rumour filtered through that he was living with his mum again. She had remarried and moved to East Ham, but the marriage only lasted for a few months. She kept a room free for Victor when he came home on leave, and for Philip, to come and go as he pleased.

The following Christmas he asked if he could bring a friend to the party in the clubhouse. Just as long as we had not already invited his wife and kids. And that was the beginning of Lorraine — the best thing that ever happened to our Philip.

Philip holding Jay, with Dean behind, on the beach at Brighton — August 1989.

*Lorraine with Kim (Steve's wife) and Jackie (Victor's wife) at St Margaret's Bay —
1989.*

She is an orphan who was brought up by loving foster-parents, and she has a strength and beauty of character that emerges like a brilliant sunrise from the dark shadows that often beset her.

Things have taken a distinct turn for the better in Philip's life this year. He has survived an operation for a gastric ulcer; he has a good job as a plumber's mate, with the hope of starting his own small business one day soon; he has become a steward at the West Ham football matches; and, above all else, he has a family and home to be proud of nowadays. The troubled years of his early youth seem to have faded away into the mists of long ago.

Peter went to Woodbridge in Suffolk soon after his sixteenth birthday, to begin his five year apprenticeship at Whisstock's famous boatbuilding yard.

There was one big problem to begin with — how to find him suitable

The young apprentice: Peter at Whisstock's Boatyard on the River Deben at Woodbridge. 1979

lodgings. Someone, however, in Newham Social Services Department knew of a nice young man who owned a house in Woodbridge, and he was persuaded to let Peter stay there for a small rental; also to provide him with breakfast and an evening meal. A short while after his departure for Suffolk, we received the following letter:

> Dear Rozelle — Dick,
>   I hope your both well and having happy sailing. I started work on Monday and it is O.K. The lads here are great and I get up at 6.30 each morning to start work at 8.00. and finish at about 10.00 at night, doing 5 hours overtime per day.
>   Anyway, by for now.
>   Lots of love, Peter × × × ×

Peter had always been a hard worker, and now he had an added incentive for doing so much overtime as he wanted to buy a motor-bicycle 'to come home on a Sunday and see me dad and all you lot!' as he put it.

Peter was happy working at Whisstock's that first year, and he had a good foreman who understood some of his problems — a Cockney in the heart of rural Suffolk who found it very hard to penetrate the enclosed, and often unwelcoming, society in which he now lived.

The digs, in the first place, were not a success. Peter's landlord was deeply religious, and he liked to say prayers and sing hymns at suppertime, and often held meetings in his house for like-minded people. Clearly he had hoped to capture a new stray sheep for his fold, but little Peter was made of sterner material than many of the local lads. One can only imagine what must have happened in that poor man's house...

Extra-loud pop music issuing from a giant wog-box in the lodger's bedroom, pitched to drown the earnest voices of those assembled for an evening of quiet contemplation in the sitting-room below; crude jokes to enliven the munching of the sparse food at mealtimes, and the odd swear word fouling the pure air like the buzzing of a bluebottle.

Peter, who was quite an experienced cook, did like a nice thick cut of rump steak to sink his teeth into at teatime — at least once or twice a week; but he soon discovered that this was not to be as his landlord was rather mean, and also very proud of the stringy vegetables which he grew in the back garden and served up in various guises.

'You jus' can't 'magine what it's like, Rozelle,' the boy's querulous voice informed me over the telepephone one evening. 'Nuffink but 'ymns an' Brussel sprouts to keep you fightin' fit after a 'ard day's work! The lads down the yard are O.K., but the social life's the pits.'

Peter Cobb organized a week's holiday for little Peter aboard one of the Ocean Youth Club's yachts the following summer, but he seemed reluctant to pay a third share of the holiday and it was about this time that we first suspected that he was running into debt. He had left his original lodgings by then , and gone to live in a friend's home for a few weeks before moving into a leaky old boat standing on the quay near Whisstock's Yard.

Each time Peter went home for the weekend, the question of money reared its dormant head like a sleepy cobra. He looked around him and perceived some of his mates, who earned good wages, throwing money around with expansive gestures and roaring about on 'wheels' with their girl-friends. No matter how hard he worked, for five long years the boy knew that he could not hope to earn much as an apprentice. And it seldom occurred to him to visualize himself as a qualified shipwright at the end of that period, in a far superior position to the rest of the gang.

Victor, home on leave, must have been the ultimate irritation. I do not know how Peter saw his own future at that time. Perhaps he did not look very far ahead, for suddenly he went on the rampage and *big* troubles loomed up on all sides of him. He was nearly half way through his apprenticeship when Whisstock's gave him the sack. They were very fair to him and overlooked the items that went missing from their yard for quite a long while; but, in the end, they had to call in the police.

Peter dyed his hair blond and went to live in the village of Shottisham, a few miles from Woodbridge. It was not long before he had found some building work to do in that neighbourhood. We had a letter from him soon afterwards:

2, Heath Drive,
Shottisham,
near Woodbridge,
SUFFOLK.

Dear Rozelle and Dick,

Thank you very much for your card. I was sorry I could not make it to your party but I work for myself and have been short of work and money. I'm glad you have got a Partnership in a Boatyard. It must be good fun.

I have just bought a new motor bike so I will be coming to London sometime in summer. But at the moment I have a lot of work thats just come in and I cannot really have a holiday. But will pop down one weekend to see you.

I have also bought my first car. It's only a Mini and I owe much to 'Martha McGilda' so I hope you don't mind me calling her Martha which I think suits her, don't you?

Oh! Did you know I am getting engaged? Her name is Billinder and we have been going together for nearly a year now. She is going to Belgium to be an opear girl for a year so we will get engaged in August. I know the wrightings bad thats because I have a cat leaning on my arm at the moment and she is getting heavy.

Anyhow good luck with the Boatyard. Say hello to Auntie Em for me and could you ask her to say hello to my dad for me. I send him a birthday card but he did not send me one. I must go and see Jim Spencer too if I do get time. Oh, Bob Marly's on the radio . . . hang on . . .

'MMMM' 3 mins later. Sorry about that but I do like Bob Marly. I also just looked out of the window and its still raining so I am not working today. I got to clean my bike anyway. By for now.

Lots of love,
Peter

We heard very little of Peter during the next few months. Emily drove up to Suffolk to visit him from time to time, but the reports she brought back were rather depressing. His attempts at running a one-man building firm were not very successful, and Billinder had faded out of the picture completely — perhaps she liked Belgium so much that she decided not to come home.

Peter Cobb arranged a dance at the Greenhill Centre for the Physically Handicapped in Newham the following winter. The plan was to make some money for the Martha McGilda Trust, to send a few of my second group of boys away on holiday with the East Coast Sail Trust or similar organizations. And all the original Tuesday boys were encouraged to join the party and bring their wives or girl-friends along with them.

Little Peter was back in London by that time, living with his dad and helping him in a market garden somewhere in the north-east suburbs. His hair had reverted to its normal colouring and he turned up at the party in high spirits and gave an impressive display of dancing with Emily as his partner. Stephen was there too, together with his first girl-friend and her parents. They were an intelligent and agreeable couple who observed us with discerning eyes. Their daughter, Beverley, was only sixteen at that time — a small blonde girl who blushed easily and gazed at Stephen with utter devotion when she thought no one else was looking.

A great sadness descended on all the Tuesday boys when someone asked if

Ursula was coming to the dance, and we were compelled to tell them that she had died in hospital the previous week. But the gloom which gripped our corner of the room was soon overshadowed by the arrival of Peter Cobb, a man aroused to the fury of a rampageous bull.

'Who let those bloody foreigners in?' he demanded angrily. 'Those bitches in mink coats with diamond-studded cigarette holders and men with great cigars stuck in their faces? They're sprinkling their filthy ash all over the buffet supper which the women who work here have spent all day preparing, and the men are throwing their weight around at the bar as if they owned the sodding place! Why don't we get together a few of the lads and chuck 'em out in the street?'

It transpired that they were members of Belgian high society, the guests of a girl who had bought ten tickets for the dance and thought her brother and his friends would be amused by an East End hop. Fortunately they sensed the hostile atmosphere before it was too late, and left the Greenhill Centre just as Big Peter was gathering together his forces.

Little Peter's partnership with his dad did not last for long. They had a monumental row and dad told him to get out, and never to darken his doors again. And that heralded the beginning of Peter's close association with the motor trade. He had always liked engines and been clever with mechanical things and, before his departure to Suffolk, he had often done a few hours' work on a Saturday with a car-dealer in Forest Gate.

For the next few years Peter immersed himself in hard work. He frequently laboured for eighteen hours a day to build up his own business, and to become independent by his middle twenties.

Every so often he would surface briefly to draw breath: once he turned up unexpectedly at Dolphin's Leap with his current girl-friend and her mother, who were on their way to France; another time he arrived in the middle of our Christmas party at the club — we had not invited him that year owing to a certain coolness. And, suddenly, there he was, advancing into the crowded room with a bottle of rum, like a dove of peace, held out towards us!

Peter and his girl-friend, Hazel, bought their own house two years ago, and he now runs a flourishing second-hand car business, attends auction sales each week, dresses smartly and knows how to look the part of a successful business man. But it is not all a piece of cake, as he often reminds us, and last year he had to sell the little motor-boat that he had so proudly purchased the previous summer. He is, nevertheless, the Boss in his own world; a boss who works endlessly to make a success of his business, and one who does not forget his old friends.

We often hear news of one or other of the boys who grew up with Peter at Norwich Road, finding a few days' work among his amazing collection of 'wheels', when they are on the dole; although I doubt whether any of them understand the meaning of a hard day's work in the same way that our Peter does.

★　★　★

Peter and Hazel aboard Roskilde *at Walton-on-Naze, summer 1988.*

Chapter 22

Rebecca is the name of the small dark girl roasting chestnuts with Lorraine and Jackie in front of the clubhouse stove. She is the bright star who began to shine in David's life two or three years ago; the first glow of light he had perceived for a very long time.

His early youth was filled with drama and violence: partly because his spirit sometimes demands the excitement and uncertainty of that way of living, and partly because he has had a rough deal right from the beginning — but most of all since he set fire to that house in Forest Gate.

We were able to visit David and take him out from time to time as long as he remained at Little Heath. After a few months, however, he was sent to H.M.S. *Formidable* at Bristol where he did a sea-training course, as well as learning a number of useful manual skills. I am not sure how he fared during those two years. We never saw him and he was not a letter-writer, so we imagined that he was studying hard to go to sea and told each other: 'What a good thing for our Dave. I hope he gets on as well as Victor when he joins the Merchant Navy.'

It had never occurred to us that this Bristol training-ship was like a floating Borstal where the régime was very tough and most of the boys were already hardened criminals. Book-work, mathematics and single-minded concentration had never been David's strong points; he was far better working with his hands under constant supervision — he admits this himself. And there is no doubt that he made some friends during his first two years in Bristol who were to alter the shape of his life when he returned there later on.

David longed to see his mum again during those endless months when he was virtually imprisoned aboard the training-ship; but she, needless to say, never attempted to visit him. He had been transferred to H.M.S. *Raleigh* on a short fire-fighting course when he received news that his stepfather had left her and she had had a heart-attack. He was allowed to go home at last to be with her; but it was not long after his return that his stepfather suddenly appeared on the scene again and told him to shift his gear pretty quickly or he'd kick him out of the house.

David found a room in a lodging-house in Canning Town, but it turned out to be full of very hostile black youths who made it quite clear that they did not care for the colour of David's skin. He was not the sort of boy to arouse bristly feelings in any stranger, no matter who they might be. He looks kind and gentle, has no strong racial prejudices and is usually the first person to help those in trouble. He had come home to London full of hopes and dreams, but these were soon shattered by the scum in that hostel who stole all his clothes as well as his pitifully few treasured possessions while he was out hunting for work. He found out that some of the staff helped the other boys filch his belongings when they had a few spare moments from doing more profitable burglaries round the neighbourhood.

Poor David had no good reports from school and no particular skills, and even Captain McLaren's certificate had been stolen from his holdall; so it was hardly surprising that he could not find a job.

We knew nothing of David's plight nor his whereabouts at that time — he tended to keep away from his friends during his patches of adversity. But a rumour filtered through that he was back in town, but had not wanted to come to our Christmas party because he had only a ragged old jersey and some oil-stained jeans to wear.

A few days later I succeeded in tracking him down and speaking to him on the telephone. He sounded very upset about the loss of his possessions, especially his seamanship certificate; so I promised I would ask Ian if he could make a copy of the original one. Also I said we would look around for any possible jobs that might suit him.

The following week David left Canning Town, and we did not hear from him again for several years. A petrol bomb had been chucked through his window by the National Front boys, who objected to the West Indian inmates of the hostel on principle; and this was the last straw for the unfortunate boy.

David hitched a lift back to Bristol, the only other place in England where he knew a few people and could count on some sympathy among his old friends. Two days later he was picked up by the police for TDA ('Taking and Driving Away' someone else's car), and he was locked up for a short while in a local Remand Home. He emerged briefly, then vanished completely: no address, no telephone number, no one, not even his sister, knew where to contact him.

'Well, I started drinkin' heavy,' David told me a few years later. 'Then I got into the drug scene an' got mixed up wiv the Bristol riots — that was wicked, that was! You should've seen the flames — shops, trees, rozzer-cars — everyfing went up that night!

'After that I was in *big* trouble. The fuzz got me along wiv some of the uvver lads an' we got sent to the nick for GBH, robbery wiv violence, possession of drugs, everyfing they could pin on to us.'

David spent the next two years in Portland Borstal, the worst spell in his whole life, he recalls. On his release he tried hard to go straight, and found temporary jobs working with pigs, fencing, driving a tractor and painting and decorating. It was during one of those brief intervals of employment that he met Paula, a girl who had been abandoned by her boy-friend and left with a little girl, Charlotte, to bring up. It was not long before David and Paula were married and their son, Nathan, was born. The marriage seemed to go well at first. He loved the baby and treated Charlotte as his own child, and he tried hard to settle down to a steady job and tranquil home life. But Paula's mother could never forgive David for having been to prison and, to make

Grown-up David aboard Martha McGilda *in the Wellington Dock in Dover.*
June 1986.

matters worse, the girl's previous boy-friend started prowling around their home on the excuse of visiting his daughter.

David, who was beginning to feel lonely and depressed, took to the bottle again to console himself. His wife, he suspected, was conspiring with her mother against him, and sometimes he would come home to find her with Charlotte's father in mother-in-law's house. Suddenly he decided to leave. Saying goodbye to the children caused him great sadness, but in other ways I think he was glad to spread his wings again and breathe the pure air away from that loathsome household.

David returned to London and found lodgings near his mother's home, then succeeded in getting a job as a lorry-driver's mate. He bought a new suit of clothes, tried hard to come to grips with his drink problem and seemed to be facing his future in a positive way. Occasionally he returned to Bristol to visit Charlotte and Nathan, but he seldom managed to see them as his mother-in-law, who now lived with Paula, invariably refused to let him into the house.

David came to stay with us at St Margaret's Bay that summer — a grown-up David with a small moustache whom we hardly recognized. He was wearing his new blue jersey and smart trousers when we came upon some ageing friends whose car had a puncture in its left rear tyre, and they were standing in the road looking rather forlorn and helpless. It was a muddy place and someone was needed to crawl underneath the chassis and fix the jack in position. David sprang into action before anyone else had uttered a word, and he soon had the flat tyre off and the spare one on. His clothes were covered with oil and mud by the time he had finished, but he did not complain. He was sailing about on gold-rimmed clouds that month, and the flaws in his character seemed insignificant compared with the shining virtues.

'All I want is to be able to see my kids whenever I can get the time off,' he told us that weekend; 'then I'd be O.K. and wouldn't feel like raisin' hell!'

'This is the Sergeant-in-Charge, Plymouth Police Station,' a gruff masculine voice on the other end of the line informed me. 'Ever heard of a lad called David S . . . , have you?'

'Yes, I've known him for years,' I admitted. 'What's he been up to now?'

'Well, he's the best boy we've got in the cells this week, as it happens.' The voice had become quite conversational. 'Really likeable character, know what I mean. He gave us your number, see. Tried his mum first but didn't get no joy, and he said you was an old friend and might be able to help him.'

I was allowed to speak to him on the telephone that evening, and the following story unfolded itself: David had attempted to see Charlotte and

Nathan again the previous week, but without success. He then became so enraged that he went out with some of his mates and got very drunk, and on their way home in a borrowed car — for which he was not insured to drive — he crashed into a bus full of people. Fortunately no one was injured but he was soon picked up by the police and, because of his past record, David was locked up without bail to await his trial. And Plymouth happened to be the nearest station with some room in their cells at the time. He had no money and no change of clothing, he told me, and was suffering from some skin complaint as well as a hacking cough because of the dirty and overcrowded conditions in which they were herded together.

We sent the boy a few pounds and had regular talks with the friendly sergeant who told us when he was being transferred to Brixton, and the date when his case was due to be heard. During those long days of hanging about in Plymouth, David made friends with another prisoner and dictated a letter which his mate wrote down in perfect copperplate handriting for him to send to us.

Hallo Dick and Rozelle,
   How are you? Well I am fine and putting on weight and trying to behave myself. Thanks very much for the money you sent me, and it came in quite handy for my soap, shampoo, toothpaste and tobacco.
   My oldest sister phoned the other day to let me know that she hasn't been able to contact my brief, as she does not know his name or address. My brief has not even got in touch with me. Do you think you could get me a good one on legal aid? My probation officer phoned me up and said that I was gonna get a prison sentence for this, so I think I will need all the help I can get.
   We should be leaving by next teusday, to return back to lambeth in South London. So could you phone me up then to see if we have left.
   They have two-ed me up now with a bloke named Alan Joseph. He is a very nice lad, but a bit nutty. I have been sharing my tobacco with him as he has no money and getting no visits. He is one of the best blokes in here. He is trying to teach me to read and write and I am trying to teach him to play chess.
   I have heard nothing from my parents as they have not been in contact, and also my girlfriend Janet has finished with me because her parents don't like the idea of her having a boyfriend in prison.
   Anyway me and my cell-mate are sitting here and will shortly write down some Cockney slang-words and their meanings for you. Take care, my cell-mate says hello, 'On the beach', which means see you later.

Dave S . . .

SLANG

Loaf of bread = Head	Barnet Fair = Hair
Mince pies = Eyes	I suppose = Nose
North and south = Mouth	Gregory Peck = Neck
Chalk farms = Arms	Elastic bands = hands
Scotch eggs = Legs	Kingdom come = Bum
Lilley and Skinner = Dinner	Battle cruiser = Boozer
Jennie Leys = Keys	Joanna = Piano

Highland fling = Ring
Bob Dylan = Villain
Currant bun = Sun
Bee's honey = Money
Bees-wax = Tax
Porkpie = Lie
Lee Marvin = Starving
Mars Bar = Scar
Wobble = To go mad.

Noah's Ark = Dark or park
John Hopper = Copper (police)
Fisherman's daughter = Water
Cape of Good Hope = Soap
Jack and Jill = Till
Haystack = Back
Sherbet Dab = Stab
Burnt cinder = Window

After his transfer to Brixton, we were unable to speak to David again until his case came up in the Court in Stratford. He had a very good lawyer who pleaded skilfully on his behalf; and suddenly I found myself standing in front of the magistrate, knees trembling, being asked a number of searching questions about the boy's character and his past history.

I do not remember what I replied. I was far too alarmed to pick my words with care and strict adherence to the truth, the whole truth, etcetera. But I remember the magistrate thanking me with a charming smile for having taken the trouble to attend the Court. And, five minutes later, there we both were outside on the pavement with David — a *free* David with only a ban on driving, a further period on probation and a fine of a hundred or so pounds to be paid during the next few months.

We brought him home for lunch and Dick gave him some money to buy clothes and a few essentials. Then the sun came out from behind a bank of dark clouds, and David's life began to change.

David and Becky sitting on the running-board of Dick's old Bentley.

He went to live with his elder sister in a flat in Shadwell, and his brother-in-law found him a temporary job as a painter and decorator. He paid off his fine in a matter of weeks and he met Becky, the little dark-haired girl who lived at the far end of the corridor and was a friend of his sister's family.

Becky, or Rebecca as she signs her letters when she is feeling formal, was a tremendously hard worker and also rather lonely at the time she first met David. Well, they soon fell in love, and when his job came to an end she worked six days a week and several evenings as well to support them both. This inspired David to find another job, no matter what it was, a soon as possible; and the next time we saw him he was an attendant and chucker-out in an amusement arcade — work that required a great deal of strength and courage.

A few months later he appeared at the clubhouse one evening wearing a very smart uniform and the broadest grin we had ever seen spread across his face; David had just been made a guard for a well-known security firm! His employers, who turned out to be a bunch of crooks, exploited him to the full, knowing how hard it was for the boy to find work (he has always believed in telling the truth about his past life, and never hiding any of the facts in order to get a better job).

During his first week they sent David alone to guard a notorious super-market in Ealing. It was raided by a gang of ex-convicts regularly once or twice a week and he received constant threats from their leader, but he soon proved that he was quite fearless and well able to deal with such scum. Lonely building sites were often his night-duty pitches, and if they happened to include a telephone in his little hut he sometimes 'gave us a bell' about one o'clock in the morning:

'Hello, Dicky!' a chirpy voice would address my sleep-drenched husband; 'how's everyfing down your way tonight? Bet you'll never guess what's just occurred right under me nose? I caught a burglar in the act of breakin' an' enterin'. What d'you fink of that for a lark!'

Becky had a baby a few months ago — a boy called James Richard William. James is David's own second name, William is after David's father who did his best to help when the couple were going through a very lean time; and his middle name is after my Dick!

Today they are a complete happy family, and although David had a terrible bout of asthma recently which caused him to lose his job, he has plenty to live for nowadays and a bright future within his reach. One can only hope that he will stretch out and grasp it with all his might.

Chapter 23

'I just couldn't've got anywhere in life if I'd stayed on at Norwich Road,' John tried to explain. 'I felt trapped there, like a fly caught in a spider's web, know what I mean? I had to get away some place else before I could begin to stand on my own feet.'

John had left the Edith Moorey Home before the fight between Peter and Victor, to go to Violet Ayres Lodge at Buckhurst Hill. His foster-father had become increasingly vindictive and his real father had vanished like thistle-down on the wings of the wind, so there was no point in his staying on at Newham nourishing forlorn hopes.

Violet Ayres Lodge was a large mixed home in the eastern suburbs, and John seemed to settle down there very happily at first. We only saw him once during that period — at Emily's Christmas party the following winter. He had brought a girl-friend with him from his new home, and they spent the entire evening gazing into each other's eyes or wrapped around each other on the dance floor. Not long afterwards we heard that she was expecting a baby and they were going to be married.

Five years or more were to pass before we saw John again, while only the occasional rumour reached us in the meantime. Peter Cobb told us that he had heard the marriage was running into difficulties; and, later on, that John had joined the army and been sent to Germany for a year. On his release he went to live in Wellingborough to be near his family; but another long period of silence ensued before he came back into our lives again, bringing with him his little daughter, Nina. He had a good job and a home of his own in Wellingborough by that time, but his marriage had virtually come to an end.

The girl was, perhaps, typical of some of the children who grow up in Care. She had no strong family of her own to support her — her short life history had been one of intense tragedy — and although, like so many young girls, she had a glowing mental picture of herself as a married woman running her own home and pushing babies around in prams, the reality turned out to be more than she could face. Before very long she refused to leave the house and gave up all pretence of looking after Nina, doing housework and trying to run a comfortable home for her family, so that all these chores fell on John's shoulders, as well as his long hours at work to make ends meet.

One summer's day the following year Emily rang up to say that she had John and a friend of his staying with her, and she would like to bring them over to see me. And that was the first time I met Louise.

'How do these boys manage it?' I asked myself, as I have done several times before and since. 'They prowl around in their jungles for a few years, then suddenly they appear with a quite exceptional girl on their arm — as if they could be plucked like ripe cherries from the trees in June!'

Louise has a beautiful peaceful face, unlimited patience and a hidden strength of character that can cope with the toughest contingencies. It is not really surprising because she comes of a family of barge people who spent their lives on the canals and rivers where no softly-nurtured city child would survive for long. They were strong simple folk whose life-style and philosophy flourished under the broad skies, the sun, the rain and the stars.

Louise was already sharing the responsibility of bringing up Nina, the child to whom John was devoted, although she had a secretarial job in Wellingborough which kept her very busy all the week.

John brought Louise and Nina to Victor and Jackie's wedding that autumn, and confided to us that he was trying to get a divorce so that he and Louise could soon be married.

'And I've got another bit of exciting news to tell you!' he whispered, with a gleam in his eyes; 'but don't let on to anyone else yet, till I'm quite sure. It's about my dad; I got in touch with this place that says they can trace missing persons for you, and they think they've tracked him down to somewhere in New Zealand! There's some bishop out there they told me to write to, as he knows all the people who've settled in his neck of the woods.'

Poor John, still in search of his father; and the excitement mounted as he got closer and closer to that mythical man in New Zealand, until his intermediary had promised an actual telephone number with which he would be able to speak to Dad personally — to hold a real conversation with him!

He rang us up to tell us the thrilling news and to share with us his plans for the future: 'I'm doing lots of overtime and saving up to take Louise out there to meet my dad after we're married,' he said; 'but the only big worry is Nina, in case the Court won't let us take her out of the country.'

John's divorce had gone through by that time, and we had received an invitation to his marriage to Louise in Wellingborough on the 4th of October, 1986. Dick had promised to drive the bride and her father to the church in his old Lagonda, and the married couple from the church to the reception afterwards.

The Norwich Road gang: Hazel, Peter, Jackie, Philip, Victor, Lorraine and David.

It turned out to be a golden autumn day as we rumbled up the M1 with 'Mansel' on a trailer behind us and David sleeping peacefully on the back seat. The Norwich Road gang had arrived in force that day: Emily and Veronica with Philip, Peter, Victor, Lorraine, Hazel and Jackie, and they soon helped us unhitch the Lagonda from its trailer and decorate it with white ribbons and red flowers.

Dick had brought his straw boater to wear for the wedding, and a thunderous cheer arose from the crowd outside the United Reform Church as he drove up in great style with Louise and her father in the back. The best man had kept a prime position clear for 'Mansel' to occupy during the service, and as soon as the bride and bridegroom emerged, covered with confetti, their chauffeur drove them away into the autumn sunset while they waved to the populace lining either side of the High Street.

'Look just like royalty perched up in that old car!' I heard someone say as Emily and I made our way towards the Tithe Barn, a charming old building set in a large garden where the reception was to take place.

We were soon joined by all the boys and girls from London, and we waited and waited...but still no bride and bridegroom. Louise's family and the wedding guests were rapidly becoming impatient, stamping their feet and craning their necks down the drive when a loud 'poop-pooping' noise on a brass horn announced the arrival of the Lagonda.

'Where the hell've you been?' the best man demanded peevishly.

'Round and round the town!' replied the happy couple, with big grins and shining eyes.

The bride and bridegroom — after the service.

Dick told us later that he had suggested driving them to the Tithe Barn by a roundabout route, but they were enjoying themselves so much that he was compelled to circle the town three times before they were satisfied.

It was a lovely reception. After photographs in the twilit garden there was a splendid banquet for the hungry wedding guests, followed by music and dancing. The strangers from London were given a warm welcome by Louise's family and friends and John's work-mates. The bride, in her elegant lace wedding-dress, kept a constant eye on Nina and whirled her around on the dance-floor whenever she was beginning to look droopy-mouthed.

Dick and I left when the party was in full swing as we had a long way to drive home, unlike the Norwich Road gang who were planning to spend the whole weekend in Wellingborough. David and Victor came out to help us hitch 'Mansel' securely on to the trailer again; and I remember standing in the car-park with them under the starry sky, listening to the distant music and the wind sighing in the upper branches of the trees.

'It's been a special sort o' weddin', come to think of it,' Victor observed, voicing my own thoughts at that moment. He was going through his 'fish on dry land' period just then, before he returned to the Merchant Navy.

'Let's wish them all the luck in the world', we said, 'for they certainly deserve it.'

John's never-ending search for his dad was rewarded by some sort of contact at last; a disembodied voice from the other side of the world announced that he had married again and was living in a remote part of the country, and his health was none too good — he suffered from this and that . . .

No great surge of warmth and love came across the wires; perhaps that was too much to expect after all those years, but John was not deterred from making his plans to visit New Zealand. I do not know what Louise felt about this obsession of his; she was rather a silent girl, and supremely tactful. Perhaps she thought as we did, that a man who abandoned his own son when he was a small child was unlikely to welcome him with open arms twenty years later.

When it became clear to the man in New Zealand that John and his bride would soon be heading that way, he phoned up in a state of panic and announced that he was not John's father after all. No one really knows the truth of the matter now; perhaps he is or perhaps he is not? It was a bitter blow for poor John to receive — but it was, perhaps, the best thing that could have happened in the end.

John and Louise have been able to buy their own house in Wellingborough, he runs a mini-cab business and they now have a family of three: Nina, who stayed on with her dad and new mum, and another little girl, Layla; and this winter, a baby boy as well.

The last time we heard from them was a postcard from Umag in Jugoslavia which said:

To Dick and Rozelle,
   Decided to leave the kids at home and come away for a fortnight. Weather fantastic, having a wonderfull time. Going to Venice in a couple of days.
   Some very nice villages and old Roman ruins here.
                    Buy for now,
                    John and Louise

Chapter 24

'Excuse me, Madam!' I looked up from my book to find the angry red face of a British Rail dining-car attendant hovering above me. 'D'you happen to know a young scallywag — fair hair, 'bout fifteen years of age — who's just ordered a double whisky in my bar?'

'Eh, I'm not sure . . . I might do,' I mumbled unhappily as I followed him along the swaying corridor to find Stephen cosily ensconced in a corner of the bar, the last few drops of some yellowish-gold liquid quivering in the bottom of his glass.

'So that's where you've got to, you little scumbag!' I exploded. He raised both hands in front of his face and giggled convulsively behind them.

'Follow me!' I commanded, trying desperately to put some authority into my voice. 'And find Mark on the way back, will you?'

It had been one of those nightmare excursions to Walton-on-Naze. Ever since *Martha* left the London Marina I had been taking parties of children to Essex once a fortnight to sail among the little islands and winding channels of the Walton Backwaters; certainly an idyllic sailing ground in fine weather, but a long and tedious journey there and back. Dave Morton, the ex-Salvation Army house-father from Norwich Road, had brought a new boy and a group of girls on one occasion and we had spent a most enjoyable afternoon afloat. There were, however, two boys left of the original Tuesday boys — Stephen and Mark; and although they were now living with their dad, they showed no signs of wishing to forgo their Tuesday outings.

The first time I took them to sail in *Martha* at Walton was during their half-term holiday. Victor was back home from the Nautical College at Gravesend that week, so the four of us set off for the seaside in high spirits. I had taken the precaution of bringing a pack of cards and a navigational quiz to keep the boys occupied during the journeys, and the outward bound one passed peacefully enough with Mark winning at beggar-my-neighbour and Victor providing some useful hints on how to cheat at poker.

The afternoon at Walton was a disaster. The weatherman had been warning about a deep Atlantic low approaching the British Isles for the past few

days, but I had chosen to ignore him; so there we were, battling along the
Walton Channel against a rising gale with pelting rain, trying to reach the
Island Point Buoy which is, after all, only two miles from the marina.

Victor and Stephen wisely retreated inside the cabin and partially closed
the doors. Mark, who was made of sterner stuff, kept me company in the
cockpit but admitted that it was the pits out there as he shook a dollop of sea-
water out of one ear and *Martha* plunged up and down in the short breaking
seas.

'Shall we just sail round the buoy, then straight back home?' I suggested.

'Best idea you've 'ad today!' Mark grinned briefly before another big wave
pounded on the Pye Sand and caught us beam on in the narrow channel.
Maddening giggles, meanwhile, issued from the warm dry passengers inside
the cabin.

It rained and blew harder than ever, and a sodden and rather silent group
caught the late afternoon train back to London. I was sitting alone with my
thoughts in a corner of our compartment somewhere between Colchester and
Chelmsford, when suddenly I became aware of several very peculiar objects
flying past the window: first an electric light bulb, followed by a roll of pink
lavatory paper which streamed out in the wind like a child's kite; then a
white lacy bundle that bore a striking resemblance to an antimacassar...

I leapt to my feet and raced along the corridor into First Class; and there
sat my crew, lounging comfortably in one of the enclosed compartments,
wearing those innocent-baby expressions that told me everything; also I
observed a telltale space above Stephen's head, in contrast to the other five
seat-backs which were adorned with white lace antimacassars.

'Out of here!' I roared — only just in time as the ticket-collector appeared
two minutes later; but we were all four deeply absorbed in a game of rummy
back in our own compartment by then.

Our next outing to Walton took place in July, at the beginning of the
school holidays. Victor had gone to sea in May so there were only the three
of us on that occasion, and I had been watching the barograph for several
days to make sure that we could expect fine weather for a change.

Stephen had just left school as his sixteenth birthday was in three weeks'
time. He tended to throw his weight around in front of Mark, I noticed,
standing in the corridor smoking rather ostentatiously and refusing to take
part in any card games or light conversation. On the last lap of the journey
Mark ventured persuasively: 'Why don't we take a look down the pier,
Rozelle? Jus' for a few minutes like, to see what's buzzin' down there?'

'We've come up here to go sailing today,' I replied decisively. 'It's a
perfect day — not a bit like last time — and we're going out to sea. You'd like
that, wouldn't you, Mark?'

An hour or so later we motored out of the marina and I picked up a

mooring buoy in the Twizzle while I hoisted the mainsail, as neither of the boys showed any inclination to steer. After a hectic few minutes we were under way with both sails pulling nicely, the sun blazing out of a sapphire-blue sky and *Martha* singing a beautiful song as she sped down the Walton Channel and out to sea. But Stephen and Mark were stretched out on the bunks inside the cabin, fast asleep!

I sailed out to the Pye End Buoy, and on the way back I noticed the tall mainmast of a Thames sailing-barge soaring above Stone Point. It turned out to be *Sir Alan Herbert* anchored near the sandy spit, with Jim and Caroline Spencer waving to me from the foredeck and asking us all aboard for tea. I moored *Martha* alongside the barge, then woke the boys and told them about our invitation but they refused to budge; so I climbed aboard the other vessel and spent a happy half hour in her cabin talking to our old friends.

It was that same afternoon, later on, that the dining-car attendant came to fetch me because of the scallywag who had ordered whisky in his bar. After Stephen had found his brother, both boys sauntered in with conciliatory smirks on their faces — clearly they had been rehearsing how best to handle me before they appeared.

'That's the very last time we go sailing,' I announced, before they had a chance to open their mouths. 'I've started with a new group from our local school in Limehouse now, and they really love spending a few hours out on the boat. So that's it. I'm not going to waste any more of my time on you two.'

The remainder of the journey passed in a sepulchral silence.

Back in London that night, I had a telephone call from a man with a deep gruff voice: 'I'm Steve and Mark's dad,' he declared; 'and I want to know the truth about what happened this afternoon. When you told the kids you weren't going to take them out sailing again, did you mean you're never going to see them any more?'

There was a longish pause and I had a sudden and very powerful premonition that this man, whom I had only glimpsed once before in my life, was all prepared to come round to our house and sort me out if I said 'Yes, I never want to see them again.'

Fortunately, I did not really feel that way at all; only rather angry that they had wasted such a lovely day and been such a menace on the train. I explained this to him, then added: 'No, I'd like to go on seeing them for the rest of my life as I've grown very fond of them strangely enough, however poisonous their behaviour is at times!'

There was a deep sigh at the other end of the line. 'You've taken a big weight off my mind,' the gruff voice informed me; 'I won't need to come round your place after all!'

★   ★   ★

Mark's life took on a regular pattern after he left the Edith Moorey Home. He played truant from school almost every day, he developed quite a taste for snooker and other people's cars and he had violent eruptions with his dad from time to time. These usually ended in a visit to his grandmother's as she had always taken his side and nursed a special affection for him.

After his sixteenth birthday there was no need to play truant any longer, so Mark decided to try out one or two jobs — just to prove that he was a mature working man. His first one was on a fruit farm at Winchelsea in Sussex, and a week after he arrived there we received the following letter:

To Dick and Rozelle,
   I am relley in joyoyoing the work, its quite easy to pick up then expected. Dont relley know what to say right now because its be a long day, its 1.00 pm as I right this letter and I must be up at 6.30 so I will say good by now and write you later.
                              hope to see you later
                                    Love
                              Mark × × ×

'Fancy Mark working really hard on a farm!' I said to Emily. 'He must have turned over a new leaf since he left school.'

'I wouldn't be too sure,' she chuckled. 'Let's just wait and see.'

He was back in London a week later, explaining to all his friends that it was only seasonal work he had been doing — just to get his hand in for a serious job.

Walking into Calais — Mark, Victor Stephen, their girl-friends and I, with Emily behind us.

Sunday evening at Dolphin's Leap. Jackie, Me, Victor, Dick, Kally and Mark.

Then Kally came along. I am not sure exactly when or how Mark first met her as we did not often see him in those days. But he had been invited to spend a day in France with us one Sunday in July, and he rang up a few days beforehand to tell us about his girl-friend and to ask if she could come too.

'Yes, of course, bring her along,' I told him. 'We'll be delighted to meet her.'

Nine of us crossed to Calais on *The Spirit of Free Enterprise* that Sunday. Victor and Stephen and their girl-friends were staying with us for the weekend, and Emily brought Mark and Kally down in her car. We had a splendid day in France and came home full of hope for Mark and his future.

Kally was a lovely girl: big and strong, and rather fierce till you knew her well; but she was an enthusiast who believed in living her life to the full, and she had set her mind on teaching Mark how to do the same. She was not strong enough, however, to keep him at work for very long, nor to change his way of life beyond a certain point.

He was picked up by the police for some driving offence the following spring, and locked up for three months in an open prison because he was a first offender.

> H.M. Detention Centre,
> Hollesley Bay Colony,
> Woodbridge, SUFFOLK.
> 'Bosmere Unit'
> 5 September 1983

Dear Dick, Rossel,

Thank you for your letter. I am sorry Ive not replied for a while but Ive only been able to afford a couple of letters for Kally. I will like to think about your jobs you have afford me but its not the right place to think about things where I am. but if possible when I get out on the 30th September if you could find the time maybe we could sit down and have a chat. Ive only got 27 days left and that should go quite farst.

Ive lost some waite but I am much fitter because of the P.E. Steve came up to visit last week and I was plessed to here that Jeff had a nice funnaral.

I am a bit sick I am in here for my 18 birthday but my dad says hes going to get me a nice birthday present. And give me a party. I hope you both felling well and the dog is well. he must be very big now. Emeliy did not give me my photo album back but I would like it if possible. Still sorry its such a short letter and will write anouther one as soon as possible.

> All my love
> Mark × × × ×

P.S. Hope to here from you soon.

Kally was not discouraged by Mark going to prison, and she was there to greet him with open arms when he came home. They were still together the following summer when we had planned to have a camping weekend for four of the children at St Margaret's Bay. Victor had borrowed some 'wheels' to bring the party down from London, and I knew it was going to be a happy weekend as soon as Mark's girl stepped out of the car.

'Kally kept rabbitin' on last evenin' she was so 'xcited!' Mark told me as I peeled the potatoes. 'She pulled all 'er cloves out of the cupboard an' kept tryin' fings on. "Which do I look nicest in, this dress or that?" she kept askin' me. "They won't mind what you wear," I keeps tellin' 'er, but she jus' wouldn't listen to me!'

Victor had brought Jackie with him — they were due to be married in two months' time — and we did all the old familiar things; but everything was new to Kally who brought a touch of magic to each hour of the day. Dick took the four children for a ride in his Lagonda in the rain and I can picture them now: Mark in the front and Kally laughing her head off as she held a rainbow-coloured umbrella over Victor and Jackie on the back seat.

It was still raining when Jack and Miriam Dawson arrived for our barbecue supper on Saturday night so the boys built a fire inside the old lighthouse instead; and there we all sat, grilling our sausages with smoke tears pouring down our cheeks and laughter echoing up and down the spiral staircase. The rain stopped around midnight and presently the moon came out from behind a bank of dark clouds. When we had cleared away the remains of the barbecue we left Mark and Kally standing on the edge of the cliff gazing at the lights of France on the far side of the Dover Straits — two silhouettes in the moonlight, trying so hard to hold on to their beautiful transient dreams.

On Sunday evening we went to the Granville Hotel for dinner — a dressing-up occasion before the boys and their girls drove back to London. Kally appeared in a marvellous white dress speckled with little red and green figures and the word 'Voila!' inscribed in red and green at various salient points!

Just before they left that evening the children gave us a present which has been greatly treasured ever since: a silver-plated sailing-boat (very like *Martha*) set in a green agate sea.

Mark and Kally split up the following winter. I do not know why it happened — perhaps she was too bossy for his taste, or perhaps she could not face spending the rest of her life with him? Whatever the reason, it was a sad day for Mark and although he put a brave face on the matter I often felt that he missed her bitterly.

He came to St Margaret's again in the late summer, bringing with him a dark pale-faced girl called Sue who was clearly pregnant. It was one of those nightmare weekends when nothing goes right; the food appears to stick in people's throats, the entertainments provided make them yawn and one counts the hours till Sunday evening! Mark was the one person, however, who retained his sense of humour, tried to help in the house and made us smile when we had begun to grind our teeth.

He told Jean that he had no intention of getting married in the near future;
but he had supposed that he was master of his own fate at that time. A
hurried registry office wedding was fixed up just before the baby was due,
and the bride's brother came with a hatchet to make sure there was no
change of heart at the last moment!

We saw very little of Mark in the years to follow. He appeared at the club
on one occasion, however, to let us know that he had just been made a
Security guard. He was very pleased with himself that night, but sadly it did
not last for long. Then there was a brief spell with British Rail, but Mark
had always found it hard to waste a fine day at work when he might be
playing golf instead.

He and Sue and their two children live at the top of a tower block in
Barking, and I believe that his life has reverted to a regular pattern again:
doing roofing jobs with Dad if they are on speaking terms; doing whatever
else comes along when they are not, interspersed with longish periods of
relaxation in between!

★   ★   ★

Mark and Sue's wedding. Mark sitting between his dad and Sue.

Stephen was the boy who announced that he would never be Mr Average, but he was planning to be someone really *big* one day soon. That has been his theme song ever since he left school, and I really believe him at times. It would not surprise me if he became the Chairman of British Coal or the Governor of the Bank of England at some future date!

The transition from being in Care to living at home was no simple matter. At the Edith Moorey Home, whatever its disadvantages, everything material had been provided: regular nourishing meals, new clothes at frequent intervals, excursions, holidays, pocket money, etcetera. And suddenly the two boys were thrown on to their own resources, often without money to buy food or clothes, and when they did have a little cash they were usually responsible for their own cooking, cleaning and laundry. It was not surprising that many of the children who came out of Care took the easy option and turned to crime.

Stephen started his working life immediately after our final sailing expedition in *Martha*. Queen's Market at Upton Park was just round the corner from his dad's home, and he soon found a job working at a fruit and vegetable stall in the market. I paid him an unexpected visit there one day, and was pleased to see how cheeful he looked chatting up the customers and proving that he could hold down a responsible job and bring in the cash as well as any quick-witted salesman with a gift of the gab. The stall was a

family affair, and after Stephen had worked there for a few months the boss would often leave him in charge for a whole day on his own.

Later that year, however, Dad moved to a house in Dagenham and the boys went with him. Stephen had a yearning to go into the building trade and a friend of ours at St Margaret's Bay managed to arrange an interview for him with G. P. Trentham, the well-known building firm at Rainham in Essex.

The interview went rather well — the boss discussed sailing and fast cars with the boy, it appears, and ignored his building skills, or possible lack of them — and he was offered a job as a labourer on three months' trial. I took him out to lunch during those early days and it was clear that he was having a tough time.

'It's bleedin' hard work there,' he confessed; 'shovellin' dirty great loads of muck all day long. An' one of the other labourers throws a wobbler every time he sees me — calls me the Governor's pet, he does! I'd lay him out flat if he wasn't such a big bastard!'

Despite the teething problems, Stephen was offered a permanent job at Trentham's at the end of his three months' trial, and he soon became a fully-fledged member of a building team with beefy arms and a healthy glow to his skin.

He was only seventeen when he met Beverley at a club in Dagenham which he used to visit with his grandad and grandma. Beverley, just out of school, had already found a good job with a silversmith in Hatton Garden, and she was the same little blonde girl who came to the dance at the Green-hill Centre with her parents to chaperone her.

There was no doubt that she worshipped the ground that Stephen trod on. And he himself changed out of all recognition during the early months of their acquaintance, becoming more responsible and unselfish, painting pictures for his girl and doing odd jobs for her parents at the weekends, and no longer hiding his face behind his hands to snigger in private. A gradual transformation into manhood was taking place, and for a short while he lived inside a magic cocoon, being greatly loved and fancying that the way to the stars was all quite simple.

A year later the inevitable happened. Beverley, who was born under the sign of Aries, had a forceful character and did not care to hang about; once she had made up her mind on a subject she wanted action — swift conclusive action. Stephen had not yet proposed marriage, so she decided to do so herself.

This was, of course, a fatal psychological error as the boy immediately began to feel cornered — like a rabbit in a cul-de-sac with a weazel blocking the entrance. It occurred to him that his weekends were not always as amusing as those described by some of his mates, and he began to yearn for

Stephen and Beverley on the river wall at Greenwich.

some exciting 'wheels' of his own — preferably a Ferrari or a Porsche Targa, like the one in which Dick used to buzz around Forest Gate when Stephen was a little boy. All these things cost money, and there were other considerations as well: some new clothes (he had always been a smart dresser), a set of golf clubs to show Mark he was not the only one who could ponce about on the golf course and a gigantic music machine, like the one Victor had brought home from sea.

None of these requirements had much to do with saving up to get married, so the beautiful friendship of Stephen and Beverley came to a sudden and dramatic end. She was not one to compromise nor wait around patiently for several years; but for a long while after their break poor Stephen seemed like a lost soul, obsessed with his own tragic thoughts and lonely situation.

By that time he had moved into the office at Trentham's as the labouring job had not proved a total success. Shortly afterwards his first great chance in life occurred: he was offered an apprenticeship as a draughtsman in civil engineering. But, like Peter before him, I think he realized that he would never stay the course: it would entail living on a pittance for three years till he passed his exams, and studying hard for several hours each evening if he were to continue earning his keep in the daytime. This would mean forgoing most of the pleasures he craved, so reluctantly he turned down the offer.

After three years at Trentham's Stephen felt it was time to move on. He did not much care for office work, so he found a job as a kitchen porter with a catering firm off Fleet Street. This turned out to be a very different kind of life. He travelled to work on a crowded suburban train each morning, worked for long hours in a steaming kitchen, then back to Dagenham with the strap-hanging commuters whom he rapidly grew to hate.

'Sometimes I long for the muddy buildin' sites an' the fresh air again,' he would tell us. 'They're like a load of silly sheep, those City turds: tight collars that nearly frottle 'em, fancy ties, lah-di-dah voices an' all pushin' an' shovin' to get to work, as if they was doin' somefing really important, know what I mean!'

Stephen stayed on at the canteen for nearly two years, being promoted to head porter before he left to work with his dad in the roofing business. He was hoping to earn much more money and he certainly learnt a few things about how to mend a leaking roof during the next few months, but in every other way the job was an overwhelming failure. Neither Stephen nor Mark have ever been able to work with their dad for long without some volcanic eruption disturbing the tranquil family relationship one might have hoped for once the boys were grown-up.

On the home front, however, a new element had entered Stephen's life which was to prove quite irresistible. His stepmother turned out to have a very beautiful niece who lived in Ilford, a girl called Kim who looked like a film-star and worked in a health food shop not far from Dagenham.

Stephen and Kim were on holiday at Walton-on-Naze when I was first introduced to her. He had wanted to bring her down to the marina to go for a sail in *Martha*, so I arranged to meet them in the car-park. My first impression was quite startling: Kim was certainly very attractive and had the most charming smile which illuminated her whole face; but when I first saw her she was scowling peevishly — clearly she had no desire to go sailing in some strange female's boat. And as soon as she consented to step out of the car I noticed that she was wearing flimsy pink shoes with razor-sharp stiletto heels! Immediately my thoughts turned to *Martha*, my beloved boat, and rather rudely I left them standing in the car-park while I ran along the pontoons to fetch a spare pair of sailing-shoes for the girl to wear.

It was an unfortunate beginning, but Kim began to enjoy herself as the day wore on and I grew to like her very much when I knew her better. She soon

Stephen wearing Dick's driving helmet and goggles.

inspired Stephen to look for another job, and to go on a month's course with a view to starting his own small business. He was put in charge of telephone sales in his next job at Passmore's, an old-established firm of builders' merchants who had recently moved into Docklands. It was a responsible position and he looked all set to move up the ladder of promotion to managerial heights at last.

Stephen and Kim came down to visit us at St Margaret's Bay that summer, and they brought David (just out of Portland Borstal) along with them. *Martha* was moored in Dover at the time, so the boys were able to have a nostalgic sail around the harbour in her; and Kim, wearing brand-new sailing-shoes she had just purchased, steered the boat for the first time.

Stephen would have liked to become engaged that winter — after he and Kim had been on holiday to Corfu together — but she seemed reluctant to commit herself at first and said she wanted more time to think it over before

Outside St John's Church, Ilford — Mark, Kim and Stephen.

making such a big decision; but in the end he persuaded her to say 'Yes'.

They were married on March 28th, 1987, a day of gale-force winds and brilliant shafts of sunlight. Dick drove the bride and her father to St John's Church, Ilford in 'Chandos', his 1924 Bentley, and there were squeals of protest from the bride as her enormous skirt was bundled into the back of the car amid roars of applause from the onlookers. Dick was wearing his Edwardian chauffeur's uniform that day and, after the service, 'Chandos' made a splendid picture with Stephen and Kim in the back, driving slowly along the streets of Ilford to the reception.

A week later we had a postcard from the Isle of Wight:

To Dick and Rozelle,
  Having a beautiful honeymoon its wonderful down here everyone's really friendly we went to tropical Birdland today bring some photos home to show you Weather is quite nice least it hasn't rained yet going to play golf tomorrow found a great golf course there's lots to see and do and beautiful scenery see you when we get back
Love   Stephen and Kim

★   ★   ★

Stephen changed his job again that summer, to become a salesman for a mass-produced clothing firm — stressful work which often entailed driving round trying to extract debts owing to the firm from resentful Asiatic shop-keepers. The young couple were living in a single room in Ilford at the time, and this put a great strain on the marriage until the Housing Department gave them a very nice council house at Chadwell Heath. Poor Kim, unfortuntely, had had a miscarriage and lost her first baby before they escaped from the room in Ilford.

They came to stay with us at St Margaret's Bay soon after the move to their new home, and Stephen helped Dick to build a brick wall in our garden.

'I've never been so happy in me whole life before,' he confided to me as he smeared fresh cement on his trowel. 'Kim's going to have another baby soon and everything's great since we got our own place. All I need now is the right kind of job so I can get on in the world like I told you I would!'

Stephen and Kim made a lovely home for themselves in Chadwell Heath, and they were floating around among the stars last April when she gave birth to a baby son whom they called Scott. The fact that Stephen had lost his salesman's job — he did have this foolish habit of hinting to his employers that he desired rapid promotion as he was really made of boss material himself — seemed of small importance. He had easily found work in the past, ever since he left school, and he would certainly land on his feet again in a few weeks' time; possibly a job that was more to his taste, with a discerning Governor who would immediately perceive the amazing potential of his new employee.

These optimistic dreams did not, however, materialize. Stephen found plenty of occasional work: little Peter often had a few days' employment to offer one of his mates, and Dad provided some roofing jobs from time to time; but a week later he would be sitting around at home again, filling in application forms and going for gruelling interviews. One day a marvellous under-manager's roofing job dropped out of the sky: £500 a week and several men at his beck and call who did much of the hard work. Stephen 'gave us a bell' a few days later — he sounded far away, like the first man to step on the moon — to tell us that he and Kim were thinking of moving to a very select two-bedroomed house in Barkingside in a few months' time.

Some extra men were required for an urgent roofing job the following week, and Stephen made the fatal mistake of offering employment to his dad and Mark who were both on the dole. They let him down with a resounding bang, and by Friday evening he had lost his job; the foolish optimist back in the valley of despair.

Kim, meanwhile, had gone back to work herself for two days a week, and was paying a friend to mind the baby. But suddenly, it seems, she had had enough. The words in the Marriage Service about taking a partner for better or for worse had slipped her memory, and she was no longer prepared to weather the 'worse' side of the picture. On Christmas Eve Stephen discovered that she had another man in tow, and the bottom dropped out of his world.

Victor came home on leave just then and took charge of his mate, inviting him to stay for a few days and taking him out to get drunk in the evenings. The worst was over by the time he came to visit us on New Year's Day, but he was still moving around in a state of stunned bewilderment with no idea of how to defend himself against all the horrors that were in store for him.

Two months later: Stephen has at last found a lawyer to help him fight the divorce action that Kim is intent on bringing against him; and he now has a good job with a concrete-treating firm. He works for ten hours a day and knows that he will get the sack if he does not arrrive on the site exactly at 0730 each morning. As soon as he had proved himself to the Governor he managed to persuade the man to employ David (who had been out of work since his asthma attack last summer) in his team as well.

Thus we pause to draw a curtain over the ever-changing lives of the Tuesday boys...Brushing aside grim reality, we advance into the magic country beyond the far horizon, softly singing the words of a much-loved verse:

> The moon is up, the stars are bright
> The wind is fresh and free;
> We're out to seek for gold tonight
> Across the silver sea!

★ ★ ★

Footnote: *Three of the Tuesday Boys, John, Stephen & Victor, have volunteered to join the Forces in Saudi Arabia — two in the Army & Victor in the Merchant Navy.*   *January 1991*

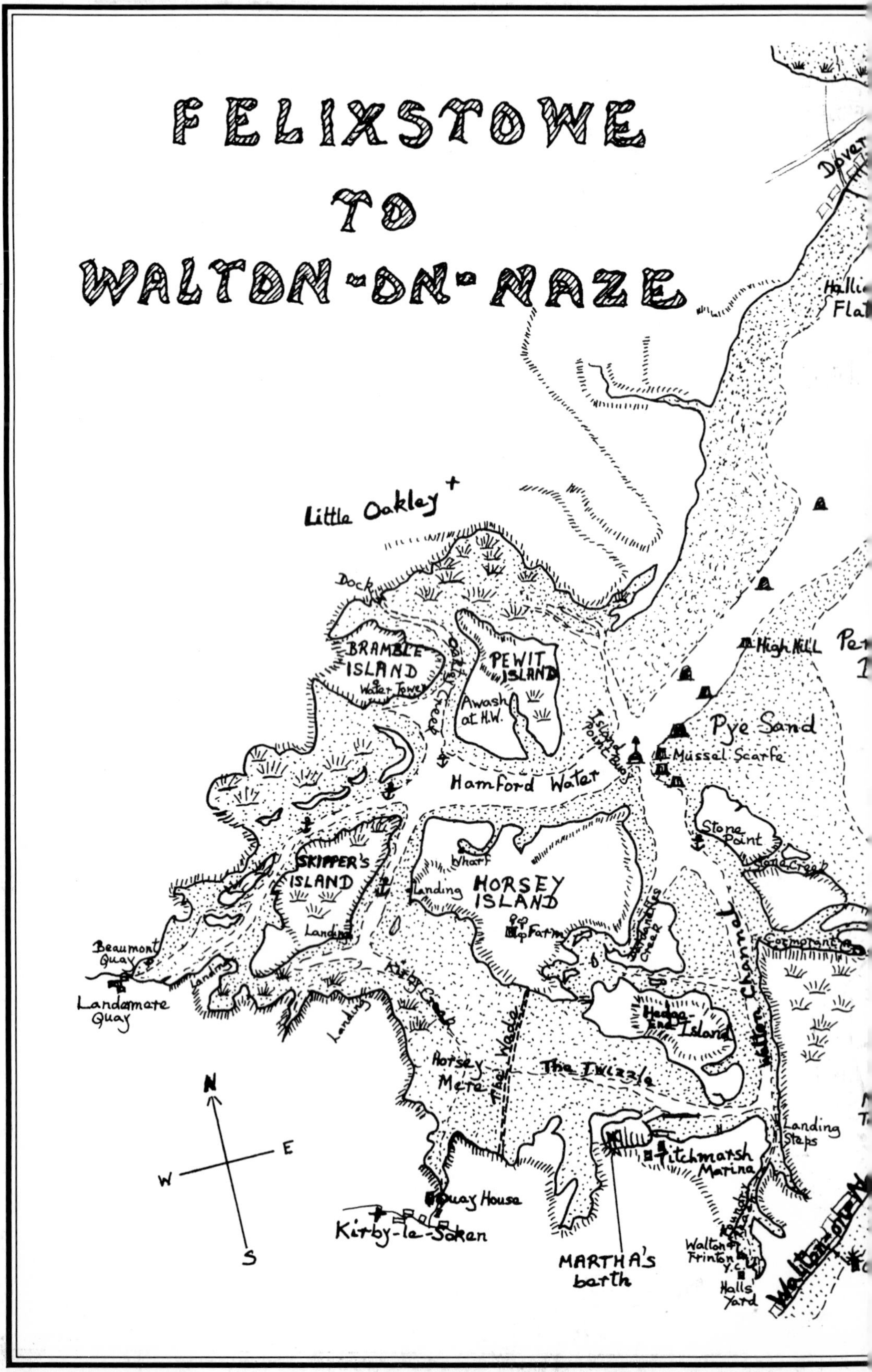

FELIXSTOWE
TO
WALTON-ON-NAZE

Dover

Halli
Flat

Little Oakley +

Dock

BRAMBLE
ISLAND
Water Tower

PEWIT
ISLAND

Awash
at H.W.

High Hill

Pe
I

Pye Sand

Mussel Scarfe

Hamford Water

Stone
Point

Stone Creek

SKIPPER'S
ISLAND

Wharf

Landing

HORSEY
ISLAND

Farm

Cormorant

Landing

Beaumont
Quay

Landing

Kirby Creek

Honey
Island

Landamate
Quay

Land

Horse
Mere

The Twizzle

Landing
Steps

N

E

W

S

Titchmarsh
Marina

Quay House

Kirby-le-Soken

MARTHA's
barth

Walton
Frinton Y.C.

Halls
Yard

Walton-on-Naze